OUTER RING (SADOVOYE)

INNER RING (B

D1049436

TVERSKAYA
SQ

MYASNITSKAYA ST

7

5

4 LYUBYANSKAYA SQ.

TEATRALNAYA
SQ **6**

MAROSEIKA ST

REVOLUTION
SQ

NIKOLSKAYA

NEW SQ

LYUBYANSKY PROEZD

MANEZH
SQ

ILYINKA

OLD SQ

SLAVYANSKAYA
SQ

ALEXANDER GARDEN

3

RED SQ

1

2

VARVARKA

KREMLIN

8

MOSKVORETSKY

MOSCOW RIVER

BRIDGE

10

— GORKI PARK

RUSSIAN

AT A GLANCE

PHRASE BOOK & DICTIONARY FOR TRAVELERS

BY THOMAS R. BEYER, JR.
Chair and Professor of Russian
Middlebury College
Middlebury, Vermont

Second Edition

BARRON'S

All inquiries should be addressed to:
Barron's Educational Series, Inc.
250 Wireless Boulevard
Hauppauge, New York 11788
http://www.barronseduc.com

International Standard Book No. 0-7641-1251-1

Library of Congress Catalog Card No. 00-131722

Illustrations: Juan Suarez

PRINTED IN HONG KONG
9 8 7

CONTENTS

PREFACE

So you're taking a trip to one of the most fascinating countries in the world. That's exciting! In more ways than one, this new phrase book will prove an invaluable companion that will make your stay far more interesting and truly unforgettable.

This phrase book is part of a series published by Barron's Educational Series, Inc. In these books we present the phrases and words that a traveler most often needs for a brief visit to a foreign country, where the customs and language are often different. Each of these phrase books highlights the terms particular to that country, in situations that the tourist is most likely to encounter. With a specially developed key to pronunciation, this book will enable you to communicate quickly and confidently in colloquial terms. It is intended not only for beginners with no knowledge of the language, but also for those who have studied Russian and have some familiarity with it.

Some of the unique features and highlights of the Barron's series are:

- Easy to follow *pronunciation keys* and complete phonetic transcriptions of all words and phrases in the book.
- Compact dictionary of commonly used words and phrases—built right into the phrase book so there's no need to carry a separate dictionary.
- Useful phrases for the *tourist*, grouped together by subject matter in a logical way so that the appropriate phrase is easy to locate when you need it.
- Special phrases for the *business traveler*, including banking terms.
- Comprehensive section on *food and drink*, with food terms you will find on menus; these terms are often difficult or impossible to locate in dictionaries.
- *Emergency phrases* and terms we hope you won't need: medical problems, theft or loss of valuables, replacement or repair of watches, cameras, and the like.
- *Sightseeing itineraries*, shopping tips, practical travel tips to help you get off the beaten path and into the countryside, to the small towns and cities, and to neighboring areas.
- A *reference section* providing important signs, conversion tables, holidays, time phrases, days of the week, and months of the year.
- A brief *grammar section*, with the basic elements of the language briefly explained.

Enjoy your vacation and travel with confidence. You have a friend by your side.

ACKNOWLEDGMENTS

I would like to thank the following individuals and organizations for their assistance on this project:

Elena Kochneva of the Pushkin Russian Language Institute, Aeroflot, and Intourist. Mostly I am grateful to the dozens of friendly and courteous Russians in Moscow and St. Petersburg, including the "key ladies," my shoe shine man, the hairdressers at the St. Petersburg Hotel, the attendants at the Krasnopresnensky Baths, the lovely woman at the watch repair shop on Pushkin Street, the taxi drivers, and all who ensured that words and phrases in the book reflect the current state of the Russian language.

Travel Tips   Your longest wait in Russia may be for your suitcases to come off the plane. You can save yourself considerable time and irritation by packing any belongings in a carry-on bag. If you travel light you can easily fit in a week's clothing and personal goods. Remember that bags must be able to fit under the airplane seat, even though many major airlines now have spacious overhead bins. If in doubt, check with the airline concerning the dimensions for carry-ons.

For the security of your belongings and safety of mind, it is wise not to pack any valuables in your checked baggage. It is also possible, at some airports, to have your entire suitcase enclosed in plastic wrapping to prevent opening or tampering before your destination. This is an inexpensive little extra precaution that you may wish to consider.

INTRODUCTION TO THE RUSSIAN LANGUAGE

Russian is the official language of the Russian Federation (**Российская Федерация**). There are some 150 million ethnic Russians. Until the fall of the Soviet Union in 1991, Russian was also used in all the republics and the study of the language was mandatory in Soviet schools. Russian was frequently used as the language of communication between Russians and citizens of Eastern European countries, where Russian was a required language in most schools. There are probably as many as 250 to 300 million people who understand and can speak Russian, but for many of them it will be a second language. This is particularly true for those born before 1980.

Even as the use and knowledge of English grows, Russian still can serve as a means of communication beyond the borders of the Russian Federation. It is important, however, that you recognize and respect the difference between Russia and those independent states created when the Soviet Union dissolved. People will appreciate your awareness that not everyone in their country is Russian. Especially when traveling to the other countries, I have found it useful to learn a few courtesy phrases, such as *Hello*, *Thank you*, *Please*, and *You're welcome* in the local language.

Russian is a Slavic language, closest to Ukrainian and White Russian, but also related to Polish, Czech, Slovak, Slovenian, Croatian, Serbian, Macedonian, and Bulgarian. Its alphabet dates to the ninth century, when the monks Cyril and Methodius developed a written language for the Slavs. The Cyrillic alphabet, as it is called, has much in common with the Greek alphabet. With a little work you will be able to read the signs and texts that make most of Russia still a mystery for many Westerners. Most Russians are delighted and flattered by foreigners who attempt to speak their language. Your efforts will be greatly rewarded.

QUICK PRONUNCIATION GUIDE

The Cyrillic alphabet has thirty-three letters. Many of them will be familiar to you from English, and several others resemble Greek letters. As in English, each letter is only an approximation of how a sound is pronounced. The guide below should get you started in speaking Russian.

STRESS

Each Russian word has only one syllable that is stressed or under accent. Russians know where the stress is and do not write the accent marks. We will indicate the stressed syllable with capital letters in our transcription as an aid for your pronunciation.

VOWELS

Russian has five vowel sounds, but ten vowel letters. Five of the letters are "hard" and five are "soft." The one vowel sound in each word that is stressed receives special emphasis. As you speak Russian try, in the beginning, to exaggerate your pronunciation.

HARD VOWELS

RUSSIAN LETTER	RUSSIAN SOUND	ENGLISH SYMBOL	EXAMPLE
а	**a** as in **A**men	*A**	да *DA*
э	**e** as in **e**cho	*E*	схо *Ekho*
ы	**y** as in hair**y**	*Y*	мы *MY*
о	**o** as in hell**o**	*O*	но *NO*
у	**u** as in r**u**le	*U*	ну *NU*

* Any English symbol may appear either capitalized (*A*) indicating that it is stressed, or lower case (*a*) indicating that it is not stressed.

SOFT VOWELS

RUSSIAN LETTER	RUSSIAN SOUND	ENGLISH SYMBOL	EXAMPLE
я	**ya** as in **ya**hoo	YA	я *YA*
е	**ye** as in **ye**s	YE	нет *NYET*
и	**ee** as in b**ee**	I	ива *Iva*
ё	**yo** as in **yo**-yo	YO	полёт *paLYOT*
ю	**u** as in **u**nion	YU	юмор *YUmar*

CONSONANT LETTERS

RUSSIAN LETTER	RUSSIAN SOUND	ENGLISH SYMBOL	EXAMPLE
б	**b** as in **b**at	B	банк *BANK*
в	**v** as in **v**ote	V	вот *VOT*
г	**g** as in **g**o	G	гол *GOL*
д	**d** as in **d**og	D	да *DA*
ж	**zh** as in a**z**ure	ZH	жена *zhiNA*
з	**z** as in **z**oo	Z	за *ZA*
й	**y** as in bo**y**	Y	мой *MOY*
к	**k** as in **k**ayak	K	касса *KAsa*
л	**l** as in **l**ot	L	лампа *LAMpa*
м	**m** as in **m**all	M	муж *MUSH*
н	**n** as in **n**ote	N	нос *NOS*
п	**p** as in **p**apa	P	парк *PARK*
р	**r** as in **r**abbit	R	рот *ROT*
с	**s** as in **s**un	S	суп *SUP*
т	**t** as in **t**oe	T	такси *taKSI*
ф	**f** as in **f**und	F	фунт *FUNT*
х	**ch** as in Ba**ch**, lo**ch**	KH	ах *AKH*
ц	**ts** as in **ts**ar	TS	царь *TSAR'*
ч	**ch** as in **ch**eap	CH	читает *chiTAyit*
ш	**sh** as in **sh**ow	SH	шапка *SHAPka*
щ	**sh** as in **sh**eep	SH	щи *SHI*
ъ	hard sign		not pronounced
ь	soft sign		not pronounced

THREE RULES OF PRONUNCIATION

1. Russians pronounce the **o** sound (as in hell**o**) only when it is stressed. When some other vowel is stressed in a word, the letter **o** is pronounced as an **a**. For example, **кот** (*KOT*), but **котá** (*kaTA*). When the letters **е, я,** and sometimes **а** are not stressed, they are pronounced **i** as in the English word **it**.

2. Consonants can be hard **ну** (*NU*) or soft **нет** (*NYET*). The soft **n** is like the sound in the word o**n**ion. A consonant is hard unless it is followed by a soft vowel letter **я, е, и, ё, ю** or the soft sign **ь**.

3. At the end of a word, or before voiced consonants, **б, в, г, д, ж,** and **з** become their voiceless counterparts, **б → п, в → ф, г → к, д → т, ж → ш, з → с**. Examples: **ход** *KHOT*, **баб** *BAP*, **ног** *NOK*, **автомат** *aftaMAT*, **водка** *VOTka*.

All these changes happen automatically for the native speaker. But if you carefully repeat the examples on the cassette along with the audioscript, you too can sound like a Russian!

Travel Tips If you have had to change your plans and cannot use your airline ticket, you can apply for a complete refund. Treat your ticket as if it were cash, and return it to your travel agent or to the airline for your money back. Note, however, that some charter tickets are nonrefundable. If you do not use the ticket, you have lost the money, but if you take out special flight insurance, you can collect your refund for that charter ticket from the insuring company.

THE BASICS FOR GETTING BY

MOST FREQUENTLY USED EXPRESSIONS

The expressions in this section are the ones you'll use again and again—fundamental building blocks of conversation, ways to express your wants or needs, and some simple interrogative forms that you can use to construct all sorts of questions. It's a good idea to practice these phrases until you know them by heart.

Hello.	**Здравствуйте.**	*ZDRASTvuytye*
Yes.	**Да.**	*DA*
No.	**Нет.**	*NYET*
Maybe.	**Может быть.**	*MOzhit BYT'*
Please.	**Пожалуйста.**	*paZHAlusta*
Thank you.	**Спасибо.**	*spaSIba*
Thank you very much.	**Большое спасибо.**	*bal'SHOye spaSIba*
Excuse me!	**Извините!**	*izviNItye*
Pardon me!	**Простите!**	*praSTItye*
Make way!	**Дорогу!**	*daROgu*
Watch out! Careful!	**Осторожно!**	*astaROZHna*
Just a minute!	**Минуточку!**	*miNUtachku*
That's all right.	**Хорошо.**	*kharaSHO*

It doesn't matter.	**Ничего.** *nichiVO*
Good morning.	**Доброе утро.** *DObraye Utra*
Good afternoon.	**Добрый день.** *DObry DYEN'*
Good evening.	**Добрый вечер.** *DObry VYEchir*
Good night.	**Спокойной ночи.** *spaKOYnay NOchi*
Comrade	**Товарищ** *taVArish*
Mister	**Господин** *gaspaDIN*
Miss, Mrs.	**Госпожа** *gaspaZHA*
Good-bye.	**До свидания.** *da sviDAniya*
Until tomorrow.	**До завтра.** *da ZAFtra*
See you later.	**Пока.** *paKA*
Do you speak English?	**Вы говорите по-английски?** *VY gavaRItye pa-anGLIYski*
I speak a little Russian.	**Я говорю немного по-русски.** *YA gavaRYU niMNOga pa-RUski*
Do you understand?	**Вы понимаете?** *VY paniMAyitye*
I understand.	**Я понимаю.** *YA paniMAyu*
I don't understand.	**Я не понимаю.** *YA NYE paniMAyu*
I'm listening.	**Я слушаю.** *YA SLUshayu*
Speak up!	**Говорите!** *gavaRItye*
What?	**Что?** *SHTO*
What did you say?	**Что вы сказали?** *SHTO VY skaZAl*

How do you say _____	Как _____	*KAK*
in Russian?	по-русски?	*pa-RUski*
What does that mean?	Что это значит?	*SHTO Eta ZNAchit*
Please repeat.	Повторите, пожалуйста. *paftaRItye paZHAlusta*	
I'm an American (*m*)	Я американец.	*YA ameriKAnits*
I'm an American (*f*)	Я американка.	*YA ameriKANka*
I'm British. (*m*)	Я англичанин.	*YA angliCHAnin*
I'm British. (*f*)	Я англичанка.	*YA angliCHANka*

Russian often has distinctive forms for men and women. We will use the abbreviation (*m*) to indicate masculine and (*f*) to indicate feminine.

I'm Canadian. (*m*)	**Я канадец.** *YA kaNAdits*
I'm Canadian. (*f*)	**Я канадка.** *YA kaNATka*
My name is _____.	**Меня зовут _____.** *miNYA zaVUT*
What's your name?	**Как вас зовут?** *KAK VAS zaVUT*
How are you?	**Как поживаете?** *KAK pazhiVAyitye*
Fine.	**Хорошо.** *kharaSHO*
And you?	**А вы?** *A VY*
Where is _____?	**Где _____?** *GDYE*
the bathroom	**туалет** *tuaLYET*
the entrance	**вход** *FKHOT*
the exit	**выход** *VYkhat*
the telephone	**телефон** *tiliFON*
a taxi	**такси** *taKSI*
our bus	**наш автобус** *NASH aFTObus*
Which way did they go?	**Куда они пошли?** *kuDA aNI paSHLI*
to the right	**направо** *naPRAva*
to the left	**налево** *naLYEva*
straight ahead	**прямо** *PRYAma*
How much does it cost?	**Сколько стоит?** *SKOL'ka STOit*
I'd like _____.	**Мне хочется _____.** *MNYE KHOchitsa*
Please bring me _____.	**Принесите мне, пожалуйста _____.** *priniSItye MNYE paZHAlusta*

Please show me _____.	**Покажите мне, пожалуйста _____.** *pakaZHYtye MNYE paZHAlusta*
I'm hungry. (*m*)	**Я голоден.** *YA GOladin*
I'm hungry. (*f*)	**Я голодна.** *YA galaDNA*
I'm thirsty.	**Мне хочется пить.** *MNYE KHOchitsa PIT'*
I'm tired. (*m*)	**Я устал.** *YA uSTAL*
I'm tired. (*f*)	**Я устала.** *YA uSTAla*
What's that?	**Что это?** *SHTO Eta*
What's up?	**В чём дело?** *F CHOM DYEla*
What's new?	**Что нового?** *SHTO NOvava*
I (don't) know.	**Я (не) знаю.** *YA (NYE) ZNAyu*

QUESTIONS

Who?	**Кто?** *KTO*
What?	**Что?** *SHTO*
Where?	**Где?** *GDYE*
Where to?	**Куда?** *kuDA*
When?	**Когда?** *kagDA*
Why?	**Почему?** *pachiMU*
How?	**Как?** *KAK*
How much?	**Сколько?** *SKOL'ka*

EXCLAMATIONS

Ouch!	**Ой!**	*OY*
That hurts.	**Больно.**	*BOL'na*
You're super!	**Молодец!**	*malaDYETS*
Darn it!	**Чёрт возьми!**	*CHORT vaz'MI*
Well!	**Ну!**	*NU*
How beautiful!	**Как красиво!**	*KAK kraSIva*
Ugh!	**Фу!**	*FU*
That's awful!	**Ужасно!**	*uZHASna*
Great! Wonderful!	**Замечательно!**	*zamiCHAtil'na*
That's the one!	**Вот это!**	*VOT Eta*
My goodness!	**Боже мой!**	*BOzhe MOY*
Cheers!	**На здоровье!**	*na zdaROvye*
Quiet!	**Тише!**	*TIshe*
Shut up!	**Молчите!**	*malCHItye*
That's enough!	**Хватит!**	*KHVAtit*
Never mind!	**Ничего!**	*nichiVO*
Of course!	**Конечно!**	*kaNYESHna*
With pleasure!	**С удовольствием!** *s udaVOL'stviyim*	
Let's go!	**Пошли!**	*paSHLI*
What a shame!	**Как жаль!**	*KAK ZHAL'*

Nonsense!	**Ерунда!** *yirunDA*	
Are you crazy?	**Вы с ума сошли?** *VY s uMA saSHLI*	
What a fool!	**Какой дурак!** *kaKOY duRAK*	
Good luck!	**Всего хорошего!** *fsiVO khaROshiva*	

PROBLEMS, PROBLEMS, PROBLEMS (EMERGENCIES)

Hurry up!	**Спешите!** *spiSHYtye*
Look!	**Смотрите!** *smaTRItye*
Watch out! Be careful!	**Осторожно!** *astaROZHna*
Listen!	**Слушайте!** *SLUshaytye*
Wait!	**Подождите!** *padaZHDItye*
Fire!	**Пожар!** *paZHAR*
I have lost _____.(m)	**Я потерял _____.** *YA patiRYAL*
I have lost _____.(f)	**Я потеряла _____.** *YA patiRYAla*
my suitcase	**мой чемодан** *MOY chimaDAN*
my purse	**мою сумку** *maYU SUMku*
my briefcase	**мой портфель** *MOY partFYEL'*
I am lost! (m)	**Я потерялся!** *YA patiRYALsya*
I am lost! (f)	**Я потерялась!** *YA patiRYAlas'*
We're lost.	**Мы потерялись.** *MY patiRYAlis'*
What's the matter with you?	**Что с вами?** *SHTO s VAmi*

What (the devil) do you want?	**Что вам нужно?**	*SHTO VAM NUZHna*
Leave me alone!	**Оставьте меня в покое!**	*aSTAF"tye miNYA f paKOye*
Go away!	**Пошёл вон!**	*paSHOL VON*
Help!	**Помогите**	*pamaGItye*
I'm going to call a cop!	**Я позову милиционера!**	*YA pazaVU militsiaNYEra*
Get out!	**Вон!**	*VON*
Stop him!	**Задержите его!**	*zadirZHYtye yiVO*
He's stolen _____.	**Он украл _____.**	*ON uKRAL*
She's stolen _____.	**Она украла _____.**	*aNA uKRAla*
■ my passport	**мой паспорт**	*MOY PASpart*
■ my ring	**моё кольцо**	*maYO kal'TSO*

my wallet	**мой бумажник**	*MOY buMAZHnik*
my watch	**мои часы**	*maI chiSY*

Does anyone speak English?	**Кто-нибудь говорит но-английски?**	*KTO-nibut' gavaRIT pa-anGLIYski*

I want to telephone _____.	**Я хочу позвонить _____.**	*YA khaCHU pazvaNIT'*
the American Embassy	**в американское посольство**	*v amiriKANskaye paSOL'stva*
the British Embassy	**в английское посольство**	*v anGLIYskaye paSOL'stva*
the Canadian Embassy	**в канадское посольство**	*v kaNADskaye paSOL'stva*

NUMBERS

If you really want to get around in Russia you will need to know the numbers in Russian. This knowledge is essential for shopping, arranging meetings, ordering tickets, and so on. In a word, knowing the numbers is an essential part of daily communication. The following list contains the cardinal and ordinal numbers along with some other useful quantities.

CARDINAL NUMBERS

0	**нуль**	*NUL'*
1	**один**	*aDIN*
2	**два**	*DVA*
3	**три**	*TRI*
4	**четыре**	*chiTYrye*
5	**пять**	*PYAT'*
6	**шесть**	*SHEST'*

7	семь	*SYEM'*
8	восемь	*VOsim'*
9	девять	*DYEvit'*
10	десять	*DYEsit'*
11	одиннадцать	*aDInatsat'*
12	двенадцать	*dviNAtsat'*
13	тринадцать	*triNAtsat'*
14	четырнадцать	*chiTYRnatsat'*
15	пятнадцать	*pitNAtsat'*
16	шестнадцать	*shistNAtsat'*
17	семнадцать	*simNAtsat'*
18	восемнадцать	*vasimNAtsat'*
19	девятнадцать	*divitNAtsat'*
20	двадцать	*DVAtsat'*
21	двадцать один	*DVAtsat' aDIN*
22	двадцать два	*DVAtsat' DVA*
23	двадцать три	*DVAtsat' TRI*
24	двадцать четыре	*DVAtsat' chiTYrye*
25	двадцать пять	*DVAtsat' PYAT'*
26	двадцать шесть	*DVAtsat' SHEST'*
27	двадцать семь	*DVAtsat' SYEM'*
28	двадцать восемь	*DVAtsat' VOsim'*
29	двадцать девять	*DVAtsat' DYEvit'*
30	тридцать	*TRItsat'*
31	тридцать один	*TRItsat' aDIN*

40	сорок	*SOrak*
41	сорок один	*SOrak aDIN*
50	пятьдесят	*pidiSYAT*
60	шестьдесят	*shizdiSYAT*
70	семьдесят	*SYEM'disit*
80	восемьдесят	*VOsim'disit*
90	девяносто	*diviNOSta*
100	сто	*STO*
101	сто один	*STO aDIN*
110	сто десять	*STO DYEsit'*
200	двести	*DVYESti*
300	триста	*TRISta*
400	четыреста	*chiTYrista*
500	пятьсот	*pit'SOT*
600	шестьсот	*shist'SOT*
700	семьсот	*sim'SOT*
800	восемьсот	*vasim'SOT*
900	девятьсот	*divit'SOT*
1000	тысяча	*TYsicha*
2000	две тысячи	*DVYE TYsichi*
5000	пять тысяч	*PYAT' TYsich*
1,000,000	миллион	*miliON*
2,000,000	два миллиона	*DVA miliOna*
5,000,000	пять миллионов	*PYAT' miliOnaf*
1,000,000,000	миллиард	*miliART*

ORDINAL NUMBERS

first	**первый**	*PYERvy*
second	**второй**	*ftaROY*
third	**третий**	*TRYEti*
fourth	**четвёртый**	*chitVYORty*
fifth	**пятый**	*PYAty*
sixth	**шестой**	*shiSTOY*
seventh	**седьмой**	*sid'MOY*
eighth	**восьмой**	*vas'MOY*
ninth	**девятый**	*diVYAty*
tenth	**десятый**	*diSYAty*

USEFUL QUANTITIES

a half	**половина**	*palaVIna*
a quarter	**четверть**	*CHETvirt'*
ten of a kind	**десяток**	*diSYAtak*
100 grams	**сто грамм**	*STO GRAM*
a little bit	**немного**	*niMNOga*
too little	**слишком мало**	*SLISHkam MAla*
a little less	**поменьше**	*paMYEN'she*
a lot	**много**	*MNOga*
too much	**слишком много**	*SLISHkam MNOga*
a little more	**побольше**	*paBOL'she*
a pair	**пара**	*PAra*
once	**один раз**	*aDIN RAS*

twice	**два раза**	*DVA RAza*
many times	**много раз**	*MNOga RAS*
one more time	**ещё раз**	*yiSHO RAS*

Travel Tips Russian law demands that all purchases and transactions be done in rubles. How and where can you get Russian money? Traveler's checks, once the preferred method, are not accepted by all local banks or exchange points. They will want cash, and some accept only new currency and almost-flawless bills. You can also use your ATM card or credit card to obtain Russian cash at a number of banking machines, especially in the large cities. Be sure to check on what charges will apply before leaving home.

WHEN YOU ARRIVE

PASSPORT CONTROL

When you arrive in Russia you will first proceed to the Passport Control Desk (**Паспортный контроль** *PASpartny kanTROL'*). There your passport and visa will be examined, and after stamping your visa the border guard will return both passport and visa to you. You must then claim your bags on the baggage carousel and pass through customs. There are two lanes. If you have nothing to declare you may proceed through the Green Line (**Зелёный коридор** *ziLYOny kariDOR*). If you have more than $500 (U.S. dollars) in foreign currency or traveler's checks you must proceed to the Red Line (**Красный коридор** *KRASny kariDOR*). Here you will hand over your customs declaration form, which contains a list of valuables (jewelry, cameras, etc.) and of currencies and traveler's checks in your possession. **Note that you may not bring Russian rubles into the country.** The customs official may ask to examine your luggage and then will initial and stamp your declaration form and return it to you. Please keep it with you. You will need it to exchange money at authorized bank outlets and you must hand it in upon departure.

Here is my passport.	**Вот мой паспорт.**	*VOT MOY PASpart*
Here is my visa.	**Вот моя виза.**	*VOT maYA VIza*
I'm a tourist.	**Я турист.**	*YA tuRIST*
I'm a businessman.	**Я бизнесмен.**	*YA bisnisMYEN*
I'm on a business trip.	**Я по бизнесу.**	*YA pa BISnisu*

T-6
Англ.

Keep for the duration of your
stay in the RF or abroad.
Not renewable in case of loss.

Persons giving false information in the Customs
Declaration, or to Customs officers shall render
themselves liable under laws of the RF.

CUSTOMS DECLARATION

Full name _____

Citizenship _____

Arriving from _____

Country of destination _____

Purpose of visit _____
(business, tourism, private, etc.)

My luggage (including hand luggage) submitted for Customs inspection consists of
_____ pieces.

With me and in my luggage I have:

I. Weapons of all descriptions and ammunition _____

II. Narcotics and appliances for the use thereof _____

III. Antiques and objects of art (paintings, drawings, icons, sculptures, etc.)_____

IV. Russian rubles, Russian State Loan bonds, Russian lottery tickets _____

V. Currency other than Russian rubles (bank notes, exchequer bills, coins), payment voucher
(cheques, bills, letters of credit, etc.), securities (shares, bonds, etc.) in foreign currencies,
precious metals (gold, silver, platinum, metals of platinum group) in any form or condition,
crude and processed natural precious stones (diamonds, brilliants, rubies, emeralds, sap-
phires and pearls), jewelry and other articles made of precious metals and precious stones,
and scrap thereof, as well as property papers:

| Description | Amount/quantity | | For official use |
	in figures	in words	
US Dollars			
Pounds Sterling			
French Francs			
Deutschemarks			

VI. Russian rubles, other currency, payment vouchers, valuables and any objects belonging
to other persons _____

    I am aware that, in addition to the objects listed in the Customs Declaration, I must
submit for inspection: printed matter, manuscripts, films, video- and sound recordings,
postage stamps, pictorial matter, endangered species of wild fauna and flora, wildlife parts,
etc., as well as items not for personal use.

I also declare that my luggage sent separately consists of _____ pieces.

(Date) _____ 2000   Owner of luggage _____
(signed)

I'll be here for _____.	**Я здесь буду _____.**	*YA ZDYES' BUdu*
a few days	**несколько дней**	*NYEskal'ka DNYEY*
a few weeks	**несколько недель**	*NYEskal'ka niDYEL'*
a month	**один месяц**	*aDIN MYEsits*
I'm alone. (*m*)	**Я один.**	*YA aDIN*
I'm alone. (*f*)	**Я одна.**	*YA aDNA*
I'm with my wife.	**Я с женой.**	*YA z zhiNOY*
I'm with my husband.	**Я с мужем.**	*YA s MUzhim*
I'm with my family.	**Я с семьёй.**	*YA s siM'YOY*

CUSTOMS

Here is my declaration.	**Вот моя декларация.** *VOT maYA diklaRAtsiya*
I have nothing to declare.	**Мне нечего декларировать.** *MNYE NYEchiva diklaRIravat'*
These are my suitcases.	**Вот мои чемоданы.** *VOT maI chimaDAny*
These are souvenirs.	**Это сувениры.** *Eta suviNIry*
They are for my personal use.	**Это мои личные вещи.** *Eta maI LICHniye VYEshi*
Do I have to pay duty?	**Мне нужно платить пошлину?** *MNYE NUZHna plaTIT' POSHlinu*
May I close my bag?	**Можно закрыть чемодан?** *MOZHna zaKRYT' chimaDAN*

BAGGAGE AND PORTERS

Baggage carts can be rented inside the luggage area. If you need a porter be sure he has the appropriate identification badge. When you have cleared customs you will enter the main hall of the airport. If you are with a tourist group or have been invited by a Russian organization, your hosts will probably be waiting for you at the Meeting Point (**Место встречи** *MYESta VSTRYEchi*). If you are traveling alone you might have already prepaid for some services, such as transfer to your hotel, etc. In any case, there will be an information desk (**Информация** *infarMAtsiya*) where someone can help you arrange transportation.

Where can I find a cart?	**Где можно взять тележку?** *GDYE MOZHna VZYAT' tiLYEZHku*
Porter, please!	**Носильщик, пожалуйста!** *naSIL'shik paZHAlusta*
These are our (my) bags.	**Вот наши (мои) вещи.** *VOT NAshi (maI) VYEshi*

Be careful with this one.	**Осторожно с этим.** *astaROZHna s Etim*
I'll carry this one.	**Этот я сам понесу.** *Etat YA SAM paniSU*
Put them down here.	**Положите их сюда, пожалуйста.** *palaZHYtye IKH syuDA paZHAlusta*
Thank you very much.	**Спасибо большое.** *spaSIba bal'SHOye*
This is for you.	**Вот вам.** *VOT VAM*

AIRPORT TRANSPORTATION

If you are with a group or have been met, transportation to your hotel will be provided. If you are completely on your own, you will probably want to take an official taxi or go with one of the private cars offering livery service. As in most countries, it is not advisable to take a private car. Be sure to take an official taxi with a meter, or to agree on a price beforehand. If you already know your way around Moscow, there is an inexpensive bus to the River Station (**Речной вокзал** *richNOY vagZAL*) of the metro. The trip is not that much longer, and the adventure plus your savings make it worthwhile.

Where is our bus?	**Где наш автобус?** *GDYE NASH aFTObus*
Does this bus go downtown?	**Этот автобус идёт в центр?** *Etat aFTObus iDYOT f TSENTR*
I want to go to the hotel _____.	**Я хочу ехать в гостиницу _____.** *YA khaCHU YEkhat' v gaSTInitsu*
Cosmos	**Космос** *KOSmas*
Petersburg	**Петербург** *pitirBURK*
Savoy	**Савой** *saVOY*

How much is the fare?	**Сколько стоит?** *SKOL'ka STOit*
That's too expensive!	**Это слишком дорого!** *Eta SLISHkam DOraga*
That's fine. Let's go.	**Хорошо. Поехали.** *kharaSHO paYEkhali*

Travel Tips For a special souvenir, you might visit the shop at Bolshaya Dmitrovka 9 in Moscow. The store offers for sale proof sets of coins from the Bank of Russia's Mint (**Монетный двор** *maNYETny DVOR*). They also sell commemorative rubles and bank notes from the Soviet and even pre-revolutionary periods.

BANKING AND MONEY MATTERS

It is illegal to bring Russian currency into the Russian Federation, yet you must pay for goods and services in Russian rubles. Consequently, you will have to exchange your own "hard" currency at an official currency exchange outlet (**Обмен валюты** *abMYEN vaLYUty*). In major cities you may obtain Russian rubles from an ATM (**банкомат** *bankaMAT*) with your bank card or credit card. Traveler's checks are not accepted everywhere.

Since you cannot take unspent rubles with you, experienced travelers avoid accumulating too many rubles toward the end of their stay. As with many things in Russia, the rules of the game change constantly—so inquire at your own bank and credit card offices before you leave, and ask your Russian hosts for the latest information when you arrive.

EXCHANGING CURRENCY

I want to exchange _____.	**Я хочу обменять _____.** *YA khaCHU abmiNYAT'*
▧ American dollars	**американские доллары** *amiriKANskiye DOlary*
▧ British pounds	**английские фунты** *anGLIYskiye FUNty*
▧ Canadian dollars	**канадские доллары** *kaNADskiye DOlary*
▧ traveler's checks	**дорожные чеки** *daROZHniye CHEki*
Here is my customs declaration.	**Вот моя декларация** *VOT maYA diklaRAtsiya*

What is the exchange rate?	**Какой обменный курс?** *kaKOY abMYEny KURS*
Where must I sign?	**Где мне расписаться?** *GDYE MNYE raspiSAtsa*
Large bills, if possible.	**Если можно, крупными купюрами.** *YEsli MOZHna KRUPnymi kuPYUrami*
Small bills, if possible.	**Если можно, мелькими купюрами.** *YEsli MOZHna MYEL' kimi kuPYUrami*
Please give me change for this.	**Разменяйте, пожалуйста.** *razmiNYAYtye paZHAlusta*
Give me a receipt, please.	**Дайте мне квитанцию, позалуйста.** *DAYtye MNYE kviTANtsiyu paZHAlusta*

The exchange rate and charges vary from place to place. Your hotel might not have the most advantageous rate—but be careful not to exchange large amounts of currency in public view. You must present your passport and your declaration form. To change rubles back into a foreign currency upon departure you will need your original exchange receipt. To keep track of your expenses, you may want to convert the following amounts of rubles to the equivalents in your own currency.

RUSSIAN RUBLES	MY CURRENCY
10	
25	
50	
100	
1000	

RUSSIAN MONEY

The basic format of Russian currency, kopecks and rubles, has remained stable for hundreds of years. There are one hundred kopecks in a ruble. But the value of that ruble has fluctuated enormously, and often reevaluations mean that what was once 1000 rubles is now only 1 ruble! As of the year 2000, the following coins and bills were in circulation. (Look for coins and bills dated 1997 or later.) Silver-colored 1- and 5-kopeck pieces. Bronze-colored 10- and 50-kopeck pieces. Silver-colored 1-, 2-, and 5-ruble coins. Ruble notes are issued in denominations of 5-, 10-, 50-, 100-, 500-ruble bills.

TIP: kopeck (**копейка** *kaPEIka*) coins have the image of Saint George slaying the dragon; ruble (**рубль** *RUBL'*) coins have the Russian coat of arms: the two-headed eagle.

CREDIT CARDS

Most American and European major credit cards are accepted at hotels and in hotel restaurants, clubs, and bars. This is often a convenient and safe way to pay for purchases. The charges in rubles will be automatically converted by your credit card company or bank into dollars or your local currency. But be sure to keep your receipts for all these transactions.

Do you accept credit cards?	**Вы принимаете кредитные карточки?** *VY priniMAyitye kriDITniye KARtachki*
I have only this credit card.	**У меня только такая кредитная карточка.** *U miNYA TOL'ka taKAya kriDITnaya KARtachka*
Must I pay in hard currency?	**Надо платить валютой?** *NAda plaTIT' vaLYUtay*
May I pay cash?	**Можно платить наличными?** *MOZHna plaTIT' naLICHnymi*

BANKING

Currently, foreign organizations and individuals may have an account with an ever increasing number of banks.

I would like to open an account.	**Я хочу открыт счёт.** *YA khaCHU atKRYT' SHOT*
I want to make a deposit.	**Я хочу выдать вклад.** *YA khaCHU VYdat' FKLAT*
I want to make a withdrawal.	**Я хочу принять вклад.** *YA khaCHU priNYAT' FKLAT*
I need a deposit slip.	**Мне нужен приходный ордер.** *MNYE NUzhin priKHODny ORdir*
I need a withdrawal slip.	**Мне нужен расходный ордер.** *MNYE NUzhin rasKHODny ORdir*

TIPPING

Russians, particularly in the major cities, expect tips similar to those in Berlin, London, New York, Paris, Rome, and Tokyo. Check your restaurant bill and other establishments for a service charge already included. Otherwise 10–20% is the expectation—especially if you are pleased with the service. Porters expect the equivalent of at least one dollar per bag. For small courtesies the equivalent of a dollar will be warmly appreciated.

AT THE HOTEL

If you are traveling with a group, your hotel arrangements will have already been made through one of the many travel organizations. Individuals who have confirmed hotel reservations will have a prepaid voucher from their travel agent. If you are being met by an official organization, it will have arranged accommodations. When you arrive at the airport, go directly to the Information Desk or meet your hosts.

GETTING TO YOUR HOTEL

Here is my voucher.	**Вот мой ваучер.**	*VOT MOY VAUchir*
At which hotel will I be staying?	**В кокой гостинице я буду?**	*F kaKOY gaSTInitse YA BUdu*
I want to go to the hotel ____.	**Я хочу поехать в гостиницу ____.**	*YA khaCHU paYEkhat' v gaSTInitsu*
▪ Cosmos	**Космос**	*KOSmas*
▪ International	**Международная**	*mizhdunaRODnaya*
▪ Intourist	**Интурист**	*intuRIST*
▪ Petersburg	**Петербург**	*pitirBURK*
▪ Metropole	**Метрополь**	*mitraPOL'*
▪ National	**Националь**	*natsiaNAL'*
▪ Baltic	**Прибалтийская**	*pribalTIYskaya*
▪ Rossiya	**Россия**	*raSIya*
Is it far?	**Она далеко?**	*aNA daliKO*
Is it near?	**Она близко?**	*aNA BLISka*

What's the number of my bus?	**Какой номер моего автобуса?** *kaKOY NOmir mayiVO aFTObusa*
What's the number of my car?	**Какой номер моей машины?** *kaKOY NOmir maYEY maSHYny*

CHECKING IN

When you arrive at the hotel, you must present your passport, which will be registered. Be sure to ask for its return. You may need your passport for identification, to exchange money, and to gain entry into many offices, including your embassy. At many hotels, you will obtain and return your key at the front desk or with a floor attendant. You will be issued a Guest Card (**Карта гостя** *KARta gaSTYA*) as identification for security personnel at the hotel entrance. Carry it with you.

I reserved a single room.	**Я забронировал номер на одного.** *YA zabraNIraval NOmir na adnaVO*
We need a double room.	**Нам нужен номер на двоих.** *NAM NUzhin NOmir na dvaIKH*
I reserved a deluxe room.	**Я забронировал номер люкс.** *YA zabraNIraval NOmir LYUKS*
Where can I get the key?	**Где мне взять ключ?** *GDYE MNYE VZYAT' KLYUCH*
When can I pick up my passport?	**Когда можно получить паспорт?** *kagDA MOZHna paluCHIT' PASpart*
On what floor is my room?	**На каком этаже мой номер?** *na kaKOM etaZHE MOY NOmir*
Where is the elevator?	**Где лифт?** *GDYE LIFT*

Where is the service bureau?	**Где бюро обслуживания?** *GDYE byuRO apSLUzhivaniya*
When is the restaurant open?	**Когда ресторан открыт?** *kagDA ristaRAN atKRYT*
Is there a snack bar on the floor?	**Есть буфет на этаже?** *YEST" buFYET na etaZHE*
Do I need a ticket for breakfast?	**Мне нужен талон на завтрак?** *MNYE NUzhin taLON na ZAFtrak*

ON YOUR FLOOR

You may have a "key lady" (**дежурная** *diZHURnaya*) who sits at a desk on your floor and can provide you with a key. She will also bring you tea, wake you up, arrange for minor repairs, and provide extra soap, towels, and the like. In brief, she can do many things to make your life easier.

Hello! My name is _____.	**Здравствуйте! Меня зовут _____.** *ZDRASTvuytye miNYA zaVUT*
My key, please.	**Мой ключ, пожалуйста.** *MOY KLYUCH paZHAlusta*
Room No. 5.	**Номер пять.** *NOmir PYAT'*
Room No. 16.	**Номер шестнадцать.** *NOmir shistNAtsat'*

You need not say the entire number for your room, such as 1420, 719, 633. Instead, you can use the last two digits of the room number on that floor.

Please bring me _____.	**Принесите мне, пожалуйста _____.** *priniSItye MNYE paZHAlusta*
an ashtray	**пепельницу** *PYEpil'nitsu*
a bar of soap	**кусок мыла** *kuSOK MYla*
a blanket	**одеяло** *adiYAla*
some boiling water	**кипяток** *kipiTOK*
a bottle of mineral water	**бутылку минеральной воды** *buTYLku miniRAL'nay vaDY*
a cot	**раскладушку** *rasklaDUSHku*
some envelopes	**конверты** *kanVYERty*
a glass of tea	**стакан чая** *staKAN CHAya*
another pillow	**ещё подушку** *yiSHO paDUSHku*
some postcards	**открытки** *atKRYTki*
another towel	**ещё полотенце** *yiSHO palaTYENtse*
more hangers	**ещё вешалки** *yiSHO VYEshalki*

| some toilet paper | туалетную бумажку *tuaLYETnuyu buMAZHku* |
| writing paper | бумагу для писем *buMAgu dlya PIsim* |

| Just a minute! | Минуточку! *miNUtachku* |

| Come in! | Входите! *fkhaDItye* |

| Please place it there. | Положите, пожалуйста, туда. *palaZHYtye paZHAlusta tuDA* |

| Please wake me at _____. | Разбудите меня _____. *razbuDItye miNYA* |

| 6:00 AM | в шесть часов *f SHEST' chiSOF* |

| 6:30 AM | в половине седьмого *f palaVInye sid'MOva* |

| 7:00 AM | в семь часов *f SYEM' chiSOF* |

| 7:30 AM | в половине восьмого *f palaVInye vas'MOva* |

| Where can I press _____? | Где можно гладить _____? *GDYE MOZHna GLAdit'* |

| Can you repair _____? | Вы можете чинить _____? *VY MOzhitye chiNIT'* |

| Can you wash _____? | Вы можете стирать _____? *VY MOzhitye stiRAT'* |

| my dress | моё платье *maYO PLAt'ye* |

| my jacket | мой пиджак *MOY pidZHAK* |

| my shirts | мои рубашки *maI ruBASHki* |

| my slacks | мои штаны *maI shtaNY* |

| my socks | мои носки *maI naSKI* |

| my suit | мой костюм *MOY kaSTYUM* |

COMPLAINTS

There is no ____.	Нет ____. *NYET*
cold water	холодной воды *khaLODnay vaDY*
hot water	горячей воды *gaRYAchey vaDY*

____ doesn't work.	____ не работает. *NYE raBOtayit*
The faucet	Смеситель *smiSItil'*
The lamp	Лампа *LAMpa*
The plug	Розетка *raZYETka*
The radio	Радио *RAdio*
The refrigerator	Холодильник *khalaDIL'nik*
The sink	Умывальник *umyVAL'nik*
The shower	Душ *DUSH*
The switch	Выключатель *vyklyuCHAtil'*
The telephone	Телефон *tiliFON*
The television	Телевизор *tiliVIzar*
The toilet	Унитаз *uniTAS*

It's too cold in my room.	**В номере слишком холодно.** *v NOmirye SLISHkam KHOladna*
It's too hot in my room.	**В номере слишком жарко.** *v NOmirye SLISHkam ZHARka*
The window doesn't open.	**Окно не открывается.** *akNO NYE atkryVAyitsa*
The window doesn't close.	**Окно не закрывается.** *akNO NYE zakryVAyitsa*
The room hasn't been cleaned.	**Номер не убран.** *NOmir NYE Ubran*

HOTEL SERVICES AND SIGNS

You will probably see some of the following signs in your hotel.

Administrator	**АДМИНИСТРАТОР** *adminiSTRAtar*
Bank	**БАНК** *BANK*
Bar	**БАР** *BAR*
Barber Shop/ Beauty Salon	**ПАРИКМАХЕРСКАЯ** *parikMAkhirskaya*
Cafe	**КАФЕ** *kaFYEY*
Cashier	**КАССА** *KAsa*
Checkroom	**КАМЕРА ХРАНЕНИЯ** *KAmira khraNYEniya*
Coatroom	**ГАРДЕРОБ** *gardiROP*
Currency Exchange	**ОБМЕННЫЙ ПУНКТ** *abMYEny PUNKT*
Emergency Exit	**ЗАПАСНЫЙ ВЫХОД** *zaPASny VYkhat*
Information	**ИНФОРМАЦИЯ** *infarMAtsiya*
Lunch Break	**ПЕРЕРЫВ** *piriRYF*
Newspaper Stand	**ГАЗЕТНЫЙ КИОСК** *gaZYETny kiOSK*
Nightclub	**НОЧНОЙ БАР** *nachNOY BAR*
No Vacancy	**МЕСТ НЕТ** *MYEST NYET*

Passport Desk	**ПАСПОРТНЫЙ СТОЛ** *PASpartny STOL*
Post Office	**ПОЧТА** *POCHta*
Reception Room	**ПРИЁМНАЯ** *priYOMnaya*
Restaurant	**РЕСТОРАН** *ristaRAN*
Restroom (men's)	**МУЖСКОЙ ТУАЛЕТ** *mushSKOY tuaLYET*
(ladies')	**ЖЕНСКИЙ ТУАЛЕТ** *ZHENsky tuaLYET*
Sauna	**САУНА** *SAUna*
Service Bureau	**БЮРО ОБСЛУЖИВАНИЯ** *byuRO apSLUzhivaniya*
Snack Bar	**БУФЕТ** *buFYET*
Souvenirs	**СУВЕНИРЫ** *suviNIry*
Swimming Pool	**БАССЕЙН** *baSYEYN*
Theater Desk	**ТЕАТРАЛЬНЫЙ СТОЛ** *tiaTRAL'ny STOL*

CHECKING OUT

I'm departing today.	**Я сегодня уезжаю.** *YA siVODnya uyiZHAyu*
When is checkout time?	**Когда расчётный час?** *kagDA rasSHOTny CHAS*

Please order a taxi for me.	**Закажите мне такси, пожалуйста.** *zakaZHYtye MNYE taKSI paZHAlusta*
How will you be paying?	**Как вы будете платить?** *KAK VY BUditye plaTIT'*
I'll pay with a credit card.	**Я плачу кредитной карточкой.** *YA plaCHU kriDITnay KARtachkay*
I left my suitcase in the room.	**Я оставил чемодан в номере.** *YA aSTAvil chimaDAN v NOmirye*
Let the bellboy bring it down.	**Пусть швейцар принесёт.** *PUST' shviyTSAR priniSYOT*

Travel Tips Touring on the cheap? You can save on many daily expenses by avoiding the convenient tourist outlets where high prices seem to be the rule. Frequently, tickets for theater events can be obtained at outdoor kiosks for prices that average Russians can afford and are willing to pay. A meal in a place catering to locals may cost you a fraction of what they charge in the hotel restaurants. Be adventuresome—when in Moscow do as the Muscovites do. Simply observe the local customs, use some of your newly learned Russian phrases, and smile.

A final tip to save money: use the subway for transportation around the city. You avoid the traffic, save money, and treat yourself to an excursion through the magnificent underground architecture of many subway stations.

GETTING AROUND TOWN

If you really want to explore the country, get out and about on your own. You'll certainly want to walk along some of the busier streets, and you should also be familiar with the excellent systems of public transportation in most major cities.

THE METRO

In Moscow, St. Petersburg, and other large cities you absolutely must try out the subway (**метро** *miTRO*). The system is clean and very inexpensive, and many of the stations themselves are architectural masterpieces. You can find the metro by the big red capital **M**. The trains run from 6:00 AM until approximately 1:00 AM, but you will want to get on your last train around midnight. The trains run with very short intervals, sometimes as little as thirty seconds during rush hour. Moscow has the most extensive system, based on a circular main line (**Кольцевая линия** *kal'tsiVAya LIniya*). Several lines intersect the circle and meet at various places near the middle of the city. Each station has a large map, and you can find a map inside each subway car. On the wall you will see a complete listing of the stations on your particular line. To enter the metro you must purchase at the cashier's booth (**Касса** *KAsa*) either an electronic ticket (**электронный билет** *elikTROni biLYET*) or a token (**жетон** *zhiTON*) and insert it into one of the automatic gates. If you will be riding frequently, why not purchase a ticket for several trips (**проезд** *praYEST*) at once.

Where is the nearest _____?	**Где ближайшая _____?**	*GDYE bliZHAYshaya*
subway station	**станция метро**	*STANtsiya miTRO*

МОСКОВСКИЙ МЕТРОПОЛИТЕН

ИСПОЛЬЗОВАТЬ ДО	СТОИМОСТЬ (РУБ)	№ БИЛЕТА
— /	4	0007119056

Билет для проезда в метрополитене на одну поездку.

Подделка проездных документов преследуется по закону.

How can I get to _____?	**Как проехать _____?** *KAK praYEkhat'*
downtown	**в центр** *f TSENTR*
Red Square	**на Красную площадь** *na KRASnuyu PLOshat'*
Moscow University	**в МГУ** *v EM GA U*
the Hotel Rossiya	**в гостиницу Россия** *v gaSTInitsu raSIya*
How many more stops?	**Сколько ещё остановок?** *SKOL'ka yiSHO astaNOvak*
Where should I get off?	**Где мне выйти?** *GDYE MNYE VYti*
Do I have to transfer?	**Мне надо пересесть?** *MNYE NAda piriSYEST"*
Please tell me when to get off.	**Скажите, пожалуйста, когда мне выйти.** *skaZHYtye paZHAlusta kagDA MNYE VYti*

Careful, the doors are closing.	**Осторожно, двери закрываются.** *astaROZHna DVYEri zakryVAyutsa*

You will see several signs inside the metro. You should know what they mean.

Don't lean against the doors.	**Не прислоняться** *NYE prislaNYAtsa*
Entrance	**Вход** *FKHOT*
Exit to the city	**Выход в город** *VYkhat v GOrat*
No entrance	**Нет входа** *NYET FKHOda*
Reserved for	**Место для** *MYESta dlya*
the handicapped	**инвалидов** *invaLIdaf*
the elderly	**лиц пожилого возраста** *LITS pazhyLOva VOZrasta*
and passengers with children	**и пассажиров с детьми** *i pasaZHYraf z dit' MI*
Transfer	**Переход** *piriKHOT*

TRAMS, TROLLEYBUSES, BUSES

You are likely to encounter trams or trolley cars that run on tracks (**трамвай** *tramVAY*), trolleybuses that have tires but are connected overhead to electric cables (**троллейбус** *traLYEYbus*), and regular buses (**автобус** *aFTObus*). You can use a monthly pass or purchase a book of tickets (**проездные билеты** *prayizNYye biLYEty*) at most street corner kiosks. In many cities the honor system is in effect, and you must stamp your ticket in a ticket punch (**компостер** *kamPOStir*) or put your coins in the cash box and tear off a ticket. Spot checks are made, and if you do not have a valid ticket you will be subject to a fine and a brief lecture on

social responsibility. If you lack the correct change, you
might ask your fellow passengers to help. All trams,
trolleybuses, and buses are identified by a number.

Where is the nearest _____ stop?	**Где ближайшая остановка _____?** *GDYE bliZHAYshaya astaNOFka*
■ tram	**трамвая** *tramVAya*
■ trolleybus	**троллейбуса** *traLYEYbusa*
■ bus	**автобуса** *aFTObusa*

How much is the fare?	**Сколько стоит проезд?** *SKOL'ka STOit praYEST*

What is the next stop?	**Какая следующая остановка?** *kaKAya SLYEduyushaya astaNOFka*

Does this bus go to _____?	**Этот автобус идёт до _____?** *Etat aFTObus iDYOT da*
■ the Bolshoi Theater	**Большого театра** *bal'SHOva tiAtra*
■ the Hermitage	**Эрмитажа** *ermiTAzha*

How many stops?	**Сколько ещё остановок?** *SKOL'ka yiSHO astaNOvak*

Are you getting off?	**Вы выходите?** *VY vyKHOditye*

A book of tickets, please.	**Абонементную книжку, пожалуйста.** *abaniMYENTnuyu KNISHku paZHAlusta*

Punch my ticket, please.	**Пробейте, пожалуйста.** *praBYEYtye paZHAlusta*

Can you give me change?	**Не разменяйте?** *NYE razmiNYAYtye*

TAXIS

Metered taxis can also transport you at very reasonable prices, but it is not always easy to find a free one. A little green lamp in the windshield indicates that the taxi is free. You may hail a taxi on the street or seek out the nearest cab stand, marked by a capital T on a checkered background. In addition to metered taxis, many private car operators (**частники** *CHASniki*) are willing to take you to your destination for a few rubles. You will see that Russians readily make use of these private entrepreneurs, but you are advised to use caution. Never enter a car with other passengers, always agree on the price before setting off for your destination, and if you are the least bit uncomfortable, send this one on his way.

Is there a taxi stand near by?	**Есть поблизости стоянка такси?** *YEST' paBLIzasti staYANka taKSI*
Are you free?	**Вы свободны?** *VY svaBODny*
I want to go _____.	**Я хочу поехать _____.** *YA khaCHU paYEkhat'*
to the airport	**в аэропорт** *v aeraPORT*
to this address	**в этот адрес** *v Etat Adris*
to the hotel	**в гостиницу** *v gaSTInitsu*
to Kiev Station	**на Киевский вокзал** *NA KIyivski vagZAL*
to the Kremlin	**в Кремль** *F KRYEML'*
How much does it cost?	**Сколко стоит?** *SKOL'ka STOit*
Faster. I'm late.	**Быстрее. Я опаздываю.** *bySTRYEye YA aPAZdyvayu*

A little slower, please.	**Помедленее, пожалуйста.** *paMYEdliniye paZHAlusta*
Stop here.	**Остановитесь здесь.** *astanaVItyes' ZDYES'*
Go straight.	**Прямо.** *PRYAma*
To the right.	**Направо.** *naPRAva*
To the left.	**Налево.** *naLYEva*
Is it still far?	**Ещё далеко?** *yiSHO daliKO*
Please wait for me.	**Подождите меня, пожалуйста.** *padaZHDItye miNYA paZHAlusta*
How much do I owe?	**Сколько с меня?** *SKOL'ka s miNYA*
This is for you.	**Это для вас.** *Eta dlya VAS*

SIGHTSEEING

Where is the service bureau?	**Где бюро обслуживания?** *GDYE byuRO apSLUzhivaniya*
Where is the excursion office?	**Где экскурсионное бюро?** *GDYE ekskursiOnaye byuRO*
I need an interpreter.	**Мне нужен переводчик.** *MNYE NUzhin piriVOTchik*
How much does it cost _____?	**Сколько стоит _____?** *SKOL'ka STOit*
▪ for an hour	**за час** *za CHAS*
▪ for a day	**за день** *za DYEN'*
There are two (three, four) of us.	**Нас двое (трое, четверо).** *NAS DVOye (TROye, CHETvira)*
Where can I buy _____?	**Где мне купить _____?** *GDYE MNYE kuPIT'*
▪ a guide book	**путеводитель** *putivaDItil'*
▪ a map of the city	**план города** *PLAN GOrada*
▪ a phrase book	**разговорник** *razgaVORnik*
Is there a city tour?	**Есть экскурсия по городу?** *YEST' ekSKURsiya pa GOradu*
What are the main attractions?	**Какие главные достопримечательности?** *kaKIye GLAVniye dastaprimiCHAtil'nasti*
Where does it leave from?	**Откуда отправляется?** *atKUda atpravLYAyitsa*

We would like to see _____.	**Мы бы хотели смотреть _____.** *MY BY khaTYEli smaTRYET'*
the Bolshoi Theater	**Большой театр** *bal'SHOY tiATR*
Red Square	**Красную площадь** *KRASnuyu PLOshat'*
the Kremlin	**Кремль** *KRYEML'*
Moscow University	**МГУ** *EM GA U*
GUM (the department store)	**ГУМ** *GUM*
Children's World	**Детский Мир** *DYETski MIR*
the Aurora	**Аврору** *avROru*
the Winter Palace	**Зимний дворец** *ZIMni dvaRYETS*
the Armory	**Оружейную палату** *aruZHEYnuyu paLAtu*
a market	**рынок** *RYnak*
the cathedral	**собор** *saBOR*
the cemetery	**кладбище** *KLADbishe*
the city hall	**городской совет** *garatSKOY saVYET*
a church	**церковь** *TSERkaf'*
the concert hall	**концертный зал** *kanTSERTny ZAL*
the gardens	**сады** *saDY*
the institute	**институт** *instiTUT*
the library	**библиотеку** *bibliaTYEku*
the monastery	**монастырь** *manaSTYR'*
the monument	**памятник** *PAmitnik*
the museum	**музей** *muZYEY*

▧ the river	**реку**	*RYEku*
▧ the stadium	**стадион**	*stadiON*
▧ the tower	**башню**	*BASHnyu*
▧ the zoo	**зоопарк**	*zaaPARK*

Is it open?	**Открыто?** *atKRYta*
Is it closed?	**Закрыто?** *zaKRYta*
What is the admission price?	**Сколько стоит билет?** *SKOL'ka STOit biLYET*
May I take photos?	**Можно фотографировать?** *MOZHna fatagraFIravat'*

A SIGHTSEEING ITINERARY

Russia has a rich history and culture. In addition to the major cities of Russia, Moscow and St. Petersburg, there are dozens of other cities and villages with a splendid architectural tradition. You also should not miss the opportunity to sample the great variety of cultures and cuisines of the individual republics, each of which has its own distinctive character. What follows is merely a sketch—a broad overview of some places in Moscow and St. Petersburg that you might want to see if they are not included in your tour, or if you are traveling on your own and designing your own sightseeing schedule.

MOSCOW

Begin your visit to Moscow with an excursion around the city (**экскурсия по городу** *ekSKURsiya pa GOradu*), now the capital of the Russian Federation. Here the old mixes with the new, and nowhere is the combination more apparent than on Red Square (**Красная площадь** *KRASnaya PLOshat'*) and in the Kremlin (**Кремль** *KRYEML'*). Once the stronghold of the Russian tsars and highlighted by magnificent cathedrals, including the landmark St. Basil's, the square was the center of world attention for the parades on May Day (May 1) and the Anniversary of the Revolution (November 7). Here is the famous Lenin Mausoleum (**Мавзолей Ленина** *mavzaLYEY LYEnina*). Inside the Kremlin walls is the seat of the Russian government, along with the famous Palace of Congresses (**Дворец съездов** *dvaRYETS SYEZdaf*), often open to the public for ballet and opera performances. Here too is the famous Armory (**Оружейная палата** *aruZHEYnaya paLAta*), now a museum celebrating Russia's regal past. There is also an opportunity to see the diamond collection, the Russian Crown Jewels (**Алмазный Фонд** *alMAZny FONT*). Turning to modern Moscow, the most famous museums here are the Tretyakov Gallery (**Третьяковская галерея** *trit'yaKOF'skaya galiRYEya*) and the Pushkin Museum, with excellent collections of Western art. You can visit the Television Tower at Ostankino for an unparalleled view of the city. Another favorite spot for photos is near Moscow University, overlooking the Moscow River. Often you will see newlyweds who come here for a picture-taking session.

Should you wish to get out into the countryside, a day trip can bring you to the estate of Leo Tolstoy at Yasnaya Polyana. Another worthwhile destination is the town of Sergiev Posad, where the Russian Orthodox Church keeps alive century-old traditions. Here you'll find an Orthodox seminary and working cathedrals, along with the final resting place of Boris Godunov. For a change of pace you might want to visit the home of the Russian cosmonauts (**космонавты** *kasmaNAFty*) at Star City (**Звёздны** *(ZVYOZny)*).

ST. PETERSBURG

Created as a "window to Europe" by Peter the Great in the first part of the eighteenth century, St. Petersburg—then Leningrad as it was named—quickly became the capital and the architectural showplace of the Russian empire. No expense was spared on the palaces, ministries, and churches that adorn the center of the city. Crisscrossed by numerous canals, it is a true "Venice of the North." The city has a wealth of attractions: the Palace Square, site of the storming of the

Winter Palace (**Зимний дворец** *ZIMni dvaRYETS*), the Peter and Paul Fortress (**Петропавловская крепость** *pitraPAVlafskaya KRYEpast'*), the Russian Mint, and the Peter and Paul Cathedral, which became the resting place of the Romanov emperors. The dark side of Russian history can be seen in the fortress cells where Dostoevsky and other leading intellectuals were once imprisoned. Here at the Smolny Institute, the first school for women in Russia, Lenin planned the revolution that changed the face of the Russian Empire in the twentieth century. Do not miss the Hermitage (**Эрмитаж** *ermiTASH*), second only to the Louvre in Paris for its collection of art. You might also visit some of the other residences of the tsarist family, Peter the Great's country palace with its magnificent fountains (**Петродворец** *pitradvaRYETS*), or the stately homes at Pushkino (**Пушкино**) and Pavlovsk (**Павловск**).

To see Old Russia, you might plan a trip to Suzdal (**Суздаль**), a city preserved as a museum of Russian architecture. Here you will be treated to Russian meals baked and served in clay pots, along with a taste of Russian mead (**медовуха** *midaVUkha*).

RELIGIOUS SERVICES

Churches and cathedrals are everywhere! The Russian Orthodox churches are far more than architectural monuments. If you wish to attend services please be advised that women are expected to have something covering their heads (a kerchief will do). Many monasteries follow a strict dress code, and jeans or casual slacks may not be tolerated. Religious services of other denominations are held regularly. Inquire at your hotel or contact your embassy for up-to-date information on times and places.

Is there _____ nearby?	**Есть поблизости _____?** *YEST' paBLIzasti*
■ a Catholic church	**католический костёл** *kataLIchiski kaSTYOL*

a Protestant church	протестантская церковь *pratiSTANTskaya TSERkaf'*
an Orthodox church	православная церковь *pravaSLAVnaya TSERkaf'*
a mosque	мечеть *miCHET'*
a synagogue	синагога *sinaGOga*

At what time is the service? **Когда служба?** *kagDA SLUZHba*

I would like to speak with _____. **Я хотел бы поговорить _____.** *YA khaTYEL BY pagavaRIT'*

a priest	со священником *sa sviSHEnikam*
a minister	с пастором *s PAStaram*
a rabbi	с раввином *s raVInam*

Travel Tips Many Russians still carry a net bag (**сеточка** *SYEtachka*) or a plastic bag when they go out for the day: they call it an **авоська** *aVOS'ka*, meaning "just in case." Many Russian items are not packaged, and you still may not receive free bags in many stores.

PLANNING A TRIP

During your stay you may want to plan a trip to additional places of interest. You can travel throughout Russia by plane, train, ship, bus, or car.

Travel Tips Travelers with physical challenges are advised to plan carefully for a trip to Russia. In planning your trip, be sure to contact travel agencies and organizations that have had recent experience with issues of access. You might want to check the internet for up-to-date information and practical tips. Keep in mind that Russia lags significantly behind Canada, the United States, and countries in Western Europe in providing access to basic services, from attractions to lodging and transportation. While the infrastructure is lacking, you will find many sympathetic individuals willing to try to accommodate your needs. But your expectations should be realistic and sensitive to the limitations and realities of Russian life.

AIR TRAVEL

Where is the check-in counter?	**Где регистрация?** *GDYE rigiSTRAtsiya*
When is there a flight to _____?	**Когда полёт в _____?** *kagDA paLYOT v*
■ St. Petersburg	**Санкт Петербург** *SANKT pitirBURK*
■ Riga	**Ригу** *RIgu*
■ Tashkent	**Ташкент** *tashKYENT*
■ Tbilisi	**Тбилиси** *tbiLIsi*

A one-way ticket to _____.	**Один билет до _____.** *aDIN biLYET da*
Irkutsk	**Иркутска** *irKUTska*
Kiev	**Киева** *KIyiva*
A round-trip ticket.	**Туда и обратно.** *tuDA I aBRATna*
A seat _____.	**Место _____.** *MYESta*
next to the window	**у окна** *u akNA*
on the aisle	**у прохода** *u praKHOda*
in the smoking section	**в салоне для курящих** *f saLOnye dlya kuRYAshikh*
in the non-smoking section	**в салоне для некурящих** *f saLOnye dlya nikuRYAshikh*
in first class	**в первом классе** *f PYERvam KLAsye*
in business class	**в бизнес классе** *v BIZnis KLAsye*
in economy (tourist) class	**в туристическом классе** *f turiSTIchiskam KLAsye*
What does the ticket cost?	**Сколько стоит билет?** *SKOL'ka STOit biLYET*
Will a meal be served?	**Кормить будут?** *karMIT' BUdut*
When does the aircraft depart?	**Когда вылетает самолёт?** *kagDA VYlitayit samaLYOT*
When does it arrive?	**Когда прибывает?** *kagDA pribyVAyit*
How long is the flight?	**Сколько времени длится полёт?** *SKOL'ka VRYEmini DLItsa palYOT*
I'll check this suitcase.	**Этот чемодан я сдаю в багаж.** *Etat chimaDAN YA ZDAyu v baGASH*

What is our flight number?	**Какой номер нашего рейса?** *kaKOY NOmir NAshiva RYEYsa*
This is your boarding pass.	**Вот посадочный талон.** *VOT paSAdachny taLON*
This is your baggage claim check.	**Вот багажная бирка.** *VOT baGAZHnaya BIRka*
Please confirm my reservation.	**Потвердите моё бронирование.** *patvirDItye maYO braNIravaniya*
We are now boarding.	**Объявляется посадка.** *abyavLYAyitsa paSATka*
Please check these _____.	**Проверьте, пожалуйста, эти _____.** *praVYER'tye paZHAlusta Eti*
▇ films	**плёнки** *PLYONki*
▇ computer disks	**компьютерные диски** *kamPYUtirniye DISki*
Please do not x-ray them.	**Не просветьте, пожалуйста.** *NYE praSVYET'tye paZHAlusta*

NOTE: Airport security X-ray machines have become increasingly sensitive, and most will not damage your film. To be on the safe side, you might have computer disks and valuable photographic memories checked by hand. You can always ask politely. If the attendant refuses, bow to his wishes.

SHIPBOARD TRAVEL

Where is the dock?	**Где пристань?** *GDYE PRIstan'*
When does the next boat leave for _____?	**Когда следующий теплоход до _____?** *kagDA SLYEduyushi tiplaKHOT da*

How long does the trip take?	**Сколько времени в пути?** *SKOL'ka VRYEmini f puTI*
When do we land?	**Когда мы приплываем?** *kagDA MY priplyVAyim*
When do we sail?	**Когда мы отплываем?** *kagDA MY atplyVAyim*
A first-class ticket.	**Билет первого класса.** *biLYET PYERvava KLAsa*
A tourist-class ticket.	**Билет туристического класса.** *biLYET turiSTIchiskava KLAsa*
I would like a cabin.	**Я хотел бы каюту.** *YA khaTYEL BY kaYUtu*
I don't feel well.	**Мне плохо.** *MNYE PLOkha*
Do you have anything for sea-sickness?	**Есть у вас что-нибудь от морской болезни?** *YEST" u VAS SHTO-nibut' at marSKOY baLYEZni*

TRAIN SERVICE

Traveling by train can be a pleasant way to go between cities. The overnight trains between Moscow and St. Petersburg or other cities offer an opportunity to make acquaintances, avoid weather delays at airports, and get a good night's sleep. Moscow has several train stations, which serve different destinations. Be sure to ask from which station your train departs.

I want to get to _____.	Мне на _____.	*MNYE na*
Kazan Station	Казанский вокзал	*kaZANski vagZAL*
Kiev Station	Киевский вокзал	*KIyifski vagZAL*
Leningrad Station	Ленинградский вокзал	*lininGRATski vagZAL*
Riga Station	Рижский вокзал	*RISHki vagZAL*
Yaroslav Station	Ярославский вокзал	*yaraSLAFski vagZAL*
A first-class ticket.	Билет в мягком вагоне.	*biLYET v MYAkam vaGOnye*
A second-class ticket.	Билет в купейном вагоне.	*biLYET v kuPYEYnam vaGOnye*
A round-trip ticket please.	Обратный билет, пожалуйста.	*aBRATny biLYET paZHAlusta*
A non-smoking compartment.	Купе для некурящих.	*kuPE dlya nikuRYAshikh*
When does the train leave?	Когда отправляется поезд?	*kagDA atpravLYAyitsa POyist*
From what platform?	С какой платформы?	*s kaKOY platFORmy*

Where is Car # ____?	**Где вагон номер ____?** *GDYE vaGON NOmir*
Where is my seat/berth?	**Где моё место?** *GDYE maYO MYESta*
Is there a dining car?	**Есть вагон-ресторан?** *YEST' vaGON ristaRAN*
Bring us some tea, please.	**Принесите нам чаю, пожалуйста.** *priniSItye NAM CHAyu paZHAlusta*
Where are we now?	**Где мы сейчас?** *GDYE MY siCHAS*
Will we arrive on schedule?	**Мы прибываем по расписанию?** *MY pribiVAyim pa raspiSAniyu*
Are we late?	**Мы опаздываем?** *MY aPAZdyvayim*

Travel Tips If you are traveling on your own, finding a restaurant and ordering a meal can be time consuming. You can probably get a cup of coffee, juice, and rolls or pastries for breakfast at your hotel buffet. For a delicious lunch without a wait, try the smorgasbord (**Шведский стол** *SHVETski STOL*) available for a few dollars at one of the hotels for foreigners. If the hotel fare is a bit pricey you can certainly visit any of the fast food outlets or kiosks that can be found wherever visitors gather. In the evening you might do as Russians do and eat at the theater buffet. You should go early (at least forty-five minutes before the performance) to avoid the rush and the lines. It might result in a new acquaintance and a conversation.

DRIVING A CAR

You may rent a car in Russia or drive your own car into the country. Be sure to ask about insurance and whether mileage and gas are included in the quoted rate. You should be familiar with European rules of the road and international road signs. Most major highways have signs in the Latin alphabet as well as Cyrillic, so you should have no trouble getting around. In major cities you generally are not permitted to make a left turn from major roadways unless there is a special left-turn lane. Instead, drive through the intersection, and after approximately fifty meters you can make a U-turn, after which you can turn right onto the desired street. This is called the **разворот** *razvaROT*. Russians drive with their parking lights on in cities and use the headlights only outside city limits or on unlit stretches of road.

ROAD SIGNS

Russia uses the international system of traffic signs. You should familiarize yourself with the important ones.

CAUTION SIGNS

Опасность	Caution
Скользкая дорога	Slippery Road
Пешеходный переход	Pedestrian Crossing
Опасный поворот	Dangerous Curve
Железнодорожный переезд	Railroad Crossing

REGULATION SIGNS

Главная дорога	Main Road
Уступите дорогу	Yield

Стоп	Stop
Преимущество встречного движения	Oncoming Traffic Has Right of Way
Въезд запрещён	No Entry
Движение запрещено	No Traffic
Разворот запрещён	No U-turn
Обгон запрещён	No Passing
Остановка запрещена	No Stopping
Стоянка запрещена	No Parking
Максимальная скорость	Maximum Speed
Конец ограничения	End of Restriction

PRESCRIPTIVE SIGNS

Минимальная скорость	Minimum Speed
Лёгковые автомобили	Cars Only
Пешеходная дорожка	Pedestrian Path

INFORMATION SIGNS

Место стоянки	Parking
Место для разворота	U-turn Permitted
Стоянка такси	Taxi Stand
Остановка трамвая	Trolley Stop
Объезд	Detour
Тупик	Dead End
Пост ГАИ	Traffic Police

Caution

No U-turn

Yield

Slippery Road

No Passing

Stop

Pedestrian Crossing

No Stopping

Oncoming Traffic Has
Right of Way

Dangerous Curve

No Parking

No Entry

Railroad Crossing

Maximum Speed

No Traffic

End of Restriction

Traffic Police

Parking

Minimum Speed

U-turn Permitted

Main Road

Cars Only

Dead End

Taxi Stand

Pedestrian Path

Trolley Stop

Detour

PARKING

Parking has become a major issue. There are lots of private parking lots and metered systems. Be sure you know what the rules are before you earn a pricey ticket for failing to comply. And watch for the NO PARKING signs (blue sign with a single red diagonal line), or NO STOPPING (blue with crossed red lines).

CAR RENTALS

You might want to reserve a rental car in advance through a travel agent or over the internet. You will also be able to rent a car once inside Russia. Rates can vary considerably, so be sure to compare the different rates and options. You will need a valid driver's license and may need to have a credit card or leave a sizeable deposit.

I would like to rent _____.	**Я хотел бы взять на прокат _____.** *YA khaTYEL BY VZYAT' na praKAT*
▥ a car	**машину** *maSHYnu*
▥ a van	**микроавтобус** *mikraaFTObus*
▥ with a driver	**с водителем** *s vaDItilim*
▥ without a driver	**без водителя** *byez vaDItilya*
What kinds of cars do you have?	**Какие у вас машины?** *kaKIye u VAS maSHYny*
I prefer _____.	**Я предпочитаю _____.** *YA pritpachiTAyu*
▥ a small car	**маленькую машину** *MAlin'kuyu maSHYnu*
▥ a large car	**большую машину** *bal'SHUyu maSHYnu*
▥ automatic transmission	**автоматическое переключение скоростей** *aftamaTIchiskaye piriklyuCHYEniye skaraSTYEY*

How much does it cost _____?	**Сколько она стоит _____?** *SKOL'ka aNA STOit*
▦ per hour	**за час** *za CHAS*
▦ per day	**за день** *za DYEN'*
▦ per week	**за неделю** *za niDYElyu*
▦ per month	**за месяц** *za MYEsits*
▦ per kilometer	**за километр** *za kilaMYETR*
How much is the insurance?	**Сколько стоит страхование?** *SKOL'ka STOit strakhaVANiye*
Is gas included?	**Бензин входит в стоимость?** *binZIN FKHOdit f STOimast'*
Do you accept credit cards?	**Вы принимаете кредитные карточки?** *VY priniMAyitye kriDITniye KARtachki*
▦ which?	**какие?** *kaKIye*
Here is my driver's license.	**Вот мои водительские права.** *VOT maYI vaDItil'skiye praVA*
Must I leave a deposit?	**Мне нужно оставить залог?** *MNYE NUZHna aSTAvit' zaLOK*
What kind of gas does it take?	**На каком бензине она работает?** *na kaKOM binZInye aNA raBOtayit*

ON THE ROAD

Excuse me!	**Извините!** *izviNItye*
Can you tell me?	**Вы не скажете?** *VY NYE SKAzhitye*
Where's the road to _____?	**Где дорога в _____?** *GDYE daROga v*

Is this the road to _____?	**Эта дорога в _____?** *Eta daROga v*
Where does this road go?	**Куда идёт эта дорога?** *kuDA iDYOT Eta daROga*
How do I get to _____?	**Как мне проехать в _____?** *KAK MNYE praYEkhat' v*
How many kilometers to _____?	**Сколько километров до _____?** *SKOL'ka kilaMYEtraf da*
Do you have a road map?	**У вас есть автодорожная карта?** *u VAS YEST' aftadaROZHnaya KARta*
Can you show me on the map?	**Вы можете мне показать на карте?** *VY MOzhitye MNYE pakaZAT' na KARtye*
In which direction should I go?	**В какое направление мне ехать?** *f kaKOye napravLYEniye MNYE YEkhat'*

AT THE SERVICE STATION

LIQUID MEASUREMENTS (APPROXIMATE)		
LITERS	U.S. GALLONS	IMPERIAL GALLONS
30	8	6½
40	10½	8¾
50	13¼	11
60	15¾	13
70	18½	15½
80	21	17½

DISTANCE MEASURES (APPROXIMATE)	
KILOMETERS	MILES
1	0.62
5	3
10	6
20	12
50	31
100	62

I'm running out of gas.	**Бензин у меня кончается.** *binZIN u miNYA kanCHAyitsa*
Where is the nearest service station?	**Где ближайшая бензоколонка?** *GDYE bliZHAYshaya binzakaLONka*
Twenty liters, please _____.	**Двадцать литров, пожалуйста _____.** *DVAtsat' LItraf paZHAlusta*
of regular (93 octane)	**девяносто третьего** *diviNOSta TRYEt'iva*
of super (95 octane)	**девяносто пятого** *diviNOSta PYAtava*
Please check _____.	**Проверьте, пожалуйста _____.** *praVYER'tye paZHAlusta*
the battery	**аккумулятор** *akumuLYAtar*
the brakes	**тормоза** *tarmaZA*
the carburetor	**карбюратор** *karbyuRAtar*
the ignition system	**зажигание** *zazhiGAniye*
the lights	**фары** *FAry*
the oil	**масло** *MAsla*
the spark plugs	**свечи** *SVYEchi*
the tires	**шины** *SHYny*
the water	**воду** *VOdu*
Can you _____?	**Вы можете _____?** *VY MOzhitye*
charge the battery	**зарядить аккумулятор** *zariDIT' akumuLYAtar*
change the oil	**сменить масло** *smiNIT' MAsla*
grease the car	**смазать машину** *SMAzat' maSHYnu*
change the tire	**сменить колесо** *smiNIT' kaliSO*
Where are the rest rooms?	**Где туалеты?** *GDYE tuaLYEty*

ACCIDENTS, REPAIRS

It overheats.	**Она перегревается.** *aNA pirigriVAyitsa*
It doesn't start.	**Она не заводится.** *aNA NYE zaVOditsa*
It doesn't go.	**Она не идёт.** *aNA NYE iDYOT*
I have a flat tire.	**У меня спустила шина.** *u miNYA spuSTIla SHYna*
The radiator is leaking.	**Радиатор протекает.** *radiAtar pratiKAyit*
The battery is dead.	**Аккумулятор сел.** *akumuLYAtar SYEL*
The keys are locked in the car.	**Ключи остались в машине.** *klyuCHI aSTAlis' v maSHYnye*
Is there a repair shop nearby?	**Поблизости есть автосервис?** *paBLIzasti YEST' aftaSYERvis*
Can you help me?	**Вы можете мне помочь?** *VY MOzhitye MNYE paMOCH*
Can you lend me _____?	**Можете одолжить _____?** *MOzhitye adalZHYT'*
a flashlight	**фонарь** *faNAR'*
a hammer	**молоток** *malaTOK*
a jack	**домкрат** *damKRAT*
pliers	**плоскогубцы** *plaskaGUPtsy*
a screwdriver	**отвёртку** *atVYORTku*
a wrench	**гаечный ключ** *GAyichny KLYUCH*
Do you have _____?	**У вас есть _____?** *u VAS YEST'*
a bolt	**болт** *BOLT*

■ a bulb	**лампочка**	*LAMpachka*
■ a filter	**фильтер**	*FIL'tir*
■ a nut	**гайка**	*GAYka*

Can you fix the car? — **Можете машину починить?** *MOzhitye maSHYnu pachiNIT'*

Do you have this spare part? — **У вас есть эта запчасть?** *u VAS YEST' Eta zapCHAST'*

There's something wrong with ____. — **Что-то не в порядке с ____.** *SHTO-ta NYE f paRYATkye s*

■ the directional signal	**сигнальным огнём**	*sigNAL'nym agNYOM*
■ the door handle	**ручкой**	*RUCHkay*
■ the electrical system	**электрической системой**	*elikTRIchiskay siSTYEmay*
■ the fan	**вентилятором**	*vintiLYAtaram*
■ the fan belt	**ремнём вентилятора**	*rimNYOM vintiLYAtara*
■ the fuel pump	**бензонасосом**	*binzanaSOsam*
■ the gears	**скоростями**	*skaraSTYAmi*
■ the gear shift	**сцеплением**	*tsiPLYEniyim*
■ the headlight	**фарой**	*FAray*
■ the horn	**гудком**	*gutKOM*
■ the ignition	**зажиганием**	*zazhiGAniyim*
■ the radio	**радио**	*RAdio*
■ the starter	**стартером**	*STARtiram*
■ the steering wheel	**рулём**	*ruLYOM*
■ the taillight	**задней фарой**	*ZADnyey FAray*
■ the transmission	**переключением скоростей**	*piriklyuCHEniyim skaraSTYEY*
■ the water pump	**водяным насосам**	*vadiNYM naSOsam*
■ the windshield	**ветровым стеклом**	*vitraVYM stiKLOM*

карбюратор
CARBURETOR

радиатор
RADIATOR

аккумулятор
BATTERY

фара
HEADLIGHT

шасси
CHASSIS

шина
TIRE

дверная ручка
DOOR HANDLE

капот
HOOD

стеклоочиститель
WINDSHIELD WIPER

багажник
TRUNK

задняя фара
TAILLIGHT

бампер
BUMPER

гудок HORN
рулевое колесо STEERING WHEEL
рычаг переключения GEAR SHIFT
сигналные огни DIRECTIONAL SIGNAL
радио RADIO
ручной тормоз HAND BRAKE
сцепление CLUTCH PEDAL
тормоз BRAKE PEDAL
газ GAS PEDAL

Please look at _____.	**Посмотрите, пожалуйста _____.** *pasmaTRItye paZHAlusta*
the brakes	**тормоза** *tarmaZA*
the bumper	**бампер** *BAMpir*
the exhaust	**выхлопную трубку** *vykhlapNUyu TRUPku*
the fender	**решётку** *riSHYOTku*
the gas tank	**бензобак** *binzaBAK*
the hood	**капот** *kaPOT*
the trunk	**багажник** *baGAZHnik*

What's the matter?	**В чём дело?** *F CHOM DYEla*
Can you do it today?	**Можете сделать это сегодня?** *MOzhitye ZDYElat' Eta siVODnya*
How long (will it take)?	**Как долго?** *KAK DOLga*
Is everything O.K.?	**Всё в порядке?** *FSYO f paRYATkye*
How much do I owe you?	**Сколько с меня?** *SKOL'ka s miNYA*

ENTERTAINMENT AND DIVERSIONS

BALLET, CONCERTS, MOVIES, OPERA

No trip to Russia is complete without a visit to the theater. If you are with a group, a theater visit is probably included in your schedule. If you are on your own, you can order tickets through the theater desk in your hotel. You may also find a ticket at one of the many theater kiosks throughout the city. If you suddenly find that your evening is free, you might try to purchase a cancellation ticket by going to the theater about an hour before the performance. The most famous of Moscow's theaters is, of course, the Bolshoi (**Большой театр** *bal'SHOY tiATR*)—home to an opera and a ballet company. The Bolshoi Ballet often performs in the Palace of Congresses (**Дворец съездов** *dvaRYETS SYEZdaf*) in the Kremlin. You can also see opera and ballet in Moscow at the Stanislavsky Musical Theater (**Музыкальный театр имени Станиславского** *muzyKAL'ny tiATR Imini staniSLAFskava*). An opportunity overlooked by some tourists is the Operetta Theater (**Театр оперетты** *tiATR apiRYEty*), which performs Russian and foreign musicals and is one of the loveliest theaters in Moscow. Music lovers will not want to miss the Chaykovsky Concert Hall (**Концертный зал имени Чайковского** *kanTSERTny ZAL Imini chayKOFskava*). Visitors to St. Petersburg will surely want to see a performance at the Kirov Theater (**Театр имени Кирова** *tiATR Imini KIrava*) or the Maly Theater (**Малый театр** *MAly tiATR*).

Other special events in Moscow are the world famous Circus (**Цирк** *TSYRK*), sporting events, including spectacular hockey and soccer matches, the Russian version of the ice-capades (**Балет на льду** *baLYET na L'DU*), and song-and-dance ensembles, including the Red Army Chorus, Beriozka, the Pyatnitsky Choir, and individual artists. Ask your friends, hosts, and hotel personnel for their recommendations.

I would like to see ____.	**Я хотел бы смотреть ____.** *YA khaTYEL BY smaTRYET'*
■ a ballet	**балет** *baLYET*
■ the circus	**цирк** *TSYRK*
■ a concert	**концерт** *kanTSERT*
■ a hockey match	**хоккей** *khaKYEY*
■ a movie	**фильм** *FIL'M*
■ an opera	**оперу** *Opiru*
■ a soccer match	**футбол** *fudBOL*

What is playing?	**Что идёт?** *SHTO iDYOT*
Who is playing?	**Кто играет?** *KTO iGRAyit*
Is it an opera or a ballet?	**Это опера или балет?** *Eta Opira Ili baLYET*
I like ____.	**Я люблю ____.** *YA lyuBLYU*
■ classical music	**классическую музыку** *klaSIchiskuyu MUzyku*

▪ modern music	**современную музыку** *savriMYEnuyu MUzyku*
▪ folk music	**народную музыку** *naRODnuyu MUzyku*
What kind of film is it?	**Что ето за фильм?** *SHTO Eta za FIL'M*
A comedy?	**Комедия?** *kaMYEdiya*
A drama?	**Трагедия?** *traGYEdiya*
A love story?	**Любовная история?** *lyuBOVnaya iSTOriya*
A musical?	**Музыкальный фильм?** *muzyKAL'ny FIL'M*
A mystery film?	**Детектив?** *ditikTIF*
A science fiction film?	**Научно-популярный фильм?** *naUCHna-papuLYARny FIL'M*
A war film?	**Фильм о войне?** *FIL'M a vayNYE*
Are there seats for tonight's performance?	**Есть билеты на сегодня вечером?** *YEST' biLYEty na siVODnya VYEchiram*
What kind of seats do you have?	**Какие у вас места?** *kaKIye u VAS miSTA*
One orchestra seat, please.	**Один в партере, пожалуйста.** *aDIN f parTYErye paZHAlusta*
Two balcony seats.	**Два в балконе.** *DVA v balKOnye*
Three in the first ring.	**Три в первом ярусе.** *TRI f PYERvam YArusye*
What are the least expensive seats?	**Какие самые дешёвые места?** *kaKIye SAmiye diSHOviye miSTA*

When does the performance begin?	**Когда спектакль начинается?** *kagDA spikTAKL' nachiNAyitsa*
When is the performance over?	**Когда спектакль кончается?** *kagDA spikTAKL' kanCHAyitsa*
Who has an extra ticket?	**У кого лишний билет?** *u kaVOLISHny biLYET*
Are they letting people in?	**Уже пускают?** *uZHE pusKAyut*
Please go in.	**Проходите, пожалуйста.** *prakhaDItye paZHAlusta*

When you arrive at the theater you should show your ticket, then proceed to the coat check racks (**Гардероб** *gardiROP*). You must leave your coat and hat, and you may leave your briefcase or packages. Many women change from boots into more comfortable and attractive shoes. There is no charge for cloakroom service, but a modest fee is charged for rental of opera glasses. The few rubles that the attendants earn this way substitute for tips. In addition, custom permits those returning opera glasses to go to the head of the line after the performance.

Opera glasses, please.	**Бинокль, пожалуйста.** *biNOKL' paZHAlusta*
I'll take a program.	**Я возьму программку.** *YA vaz'MU praGRAMku*
Where are our seats?	**Где наши места?** *GDYE NAshi miSTA*
Who is the conductor?	**Кто дирижёр?** *KTO diriZHOR*
Who's singing?	**Кто поёт?** *KTO paYOT*
Who's dancing?	**Кто танцует?** *KTO tanTSUyit*
Will there be an intermission?	**Будет антракт?** *BUdit anTRAKT*

YOUR TICKET

Your theater ticket will contain much valuable information. Examine it carefully. On the front will be printed the name and symbol of your theater, the starting time of the performance, the location of your seats, including row and seat number, and the date of the performance. The back of the ticket will give the title of the performance and may provide information on public transportation to the theater.

The theater	Большой Театр *Bolshoi*
	Кремлёвский Дворец съездов *Palace of Congresses*
	Малый Театр *Maly*
	Музыкальный Театр *Stanislavsky Musical*
Starting time	Начало в 12 часов *Noon*
	Начало в 19 часов *7:00 PM*
	Начало в 20 часов *8:00 PM*
Location	Партер *Orchestra*
	Амфитеатр *Rear Orchestra*

Бельэтаж	*Mezzanine*
Балкон	*Balcony*
Ложа	*Box*
1 Ярус	*First Ring*
Правая сторона	*Right*
Левая сторона	*Left*
Середина	*Center*
Ряд	*Row*
Место	*Seat*
Цена	*Price*

NIGHT LIFE

For late evening entertainment there are more than ample opportunities, from nightclubs (**ночной клуб** *nachNOY KLUP*) to casinos (**казино** *kaziNO*). A note of caution: Many of these establishments are expensive in the extreme. If you are on a budget, check the price list. A sure sign of high prices is that they are listed in U.S. dollars or **y.e.** (conventional units, i.e. the ruble equivalent of 1 U.S. dollar).

Let's go to a nightclub.	**Пойдём в ночной бар.** *payDYOM nachNOY BAR*
Are reservations necessary?	**Надо заказать заранее?** *NAda zakaZAT' zaRAniye*
I feel like dancing.	**Мне хочется танцевать.** *MNYE KHOchitsa tantsiVAT'*
Is there a discotheque here?	**Здесь есть дискотека?** *ZDYES' YEST' diskaTYEka*

What is the cover charge?	**Сколько стоит входной билет?** *SKOL'ka STOit fkhadNOY biLYET*
A table close to the stage.	**Столик поближе к сцене.** *STOlik paBLIzhe k TSE'nye*
When does the show begin?	**Когда варьете начинается?** *kagDA var'yiTYE nachiNAyitsa*

QUIET RELAXATION: CARDS, CHESS

Do you have a deck of cards?	**Нет ли у вас колода карт?** *NYET LI u VAS kaLOda KART*
Would you like to play cards?	**Не хотите играть в карты?** *NYE khaTItye iGRAT' f KARty*
Do you want to shuffle?	**Перетасуете?** *piriTAsuyitye*
Cut the deck!	**Снимите!** *sniMItye*
hearts, diamonds, clubs, spades	**черви, бубны, трефы, пики** *CHERvi, BUBny, TRYEfy, PIki*
ace, king, queen, jack	**туз, король, дама, валет** *TUS, kaROL', DAma, vaLYET*
Whose turn is it?	**Кому ходить?** *kaMU khaDIT'*
It's your deal.	**Вам сдавать.** *VAM zdaVAT'*
What's the score?	**Какой счёт?** *kaKOY SHOT*
You win.	**Вы выиграли.** *VY VYigrali*
I lose.	**Я проиграл.** *YA praiGRAL*

Do you want to play _____?	**Хотите играть _____?**	*khaTItye iGRAT'*
checkers	**в шашки**	*f SHASHki*
chess	**в шахматы**	*f SHAKHmaty*
We need a board.	**Нам нужна доска.**	*NAM nuzhNA daSKA*
We need the pieces.	**Нам нужны фигуры.**	*NAM nuzhNY fiGUry*
the king	**король**	*kaROL'*
the queen	**королева**	*karaLYEva*
the rook	**ладья**	*laD'YA*
the bishop	**слон**	*SLON*
the knight	**офицер**	*ofiTSER*
the pawn	**пешка**	*PYESHka*
Check.	**Шах.**	*SHAKH*
Checkmate.	**Мат.**	*MAT*

SPORTS

In addition to watching the popular spectator sports, Russians love to spend time outdoors. You might spend the afternoon in one of the major parks or go swimming in one of the outdoor pools open all year. Winter sports include skating, sledding, and cross country skiing near Lenin Hills. You can also play tennis, and a golf course recently opened near Moscow.

BEACH OR POOL

Oh! It's hot!	**Ой! Как жарко!**	*OY KAK ZHARka*
Let's go swimming.	**Пойдём купаться.**	*payDYOM kuPAtsa*

Let's go to the beach.	**Пойдём на пляж.** *payDYOM na PLYASH*
Let's go to the pool.	**Пойдём в бассейн.** *payDYOM v baSYEYN*
How do you get there?	**Как туда проехать?** *KAK tuDA praYEkhat'*
What's the admission charge?	**Сколько стоит билет?** *SKOL'ka STOit biLYET*
What's the water temperature?	**Сколько градусов воды?** *SKOL'ka GRAdusaf vaDY*
I (don't) know how to swim.	**Я (не) умею плавать.** *YA (NYE) uMYEyu PLAvat'*
Is there a lifeguard?	**Есть спасатель?** *YEST spaSAtil'*
Where is the locker room?	**Где камера хранения?** *GDYE KAmira khraNYEniya*
Can I rent _____?	**Можно взять на прокат _____?** *MOZHna VZYAT" na praKAT*
◾ an air mattress	**надувной матрац** *naduvNOY maTRATS*
◾ a beach ball	**мяч** *MYACH*
◾ a boat	**лодку** *LOTku*
◾ a chaise longue	**шезлонг** *shizLONG*
◾ a beach towel	**полотенце** *palaTYENtse*
◾ an umbrella	**зонт** *ZONT*
◾ water skis	**водные лыжи** *vadNIye LYzhi*
I need to buy _____.	**Мне надо купить _____.** *MNYE NAda kuPIT"*
◾ a bathing cap	**шапочку** *SHApachku*

■ a bathing suit	**купальник**	*kuPAL'nik*
■ bathing trunks	**плавки**	*PLAFki*
■ sunglasses	**солнечные очки**	*SOL'nichniye achKI*
■ suntan lotion	**крем от загара**	*KRYEM at zaGAra*

WINTER SPORTS

I want to go ____.	**Я хочу кататься ____.**	*YA khaCHU kaTAtsa*
■ ice skating	**на коньках**	*na kan'KAKH*
■ skiing	**на лыжах**	*na LYzhakh*
■ sledding	**на санках**	*na SANkakh*

Where can I buy _____?	**Где купить _____?** *GDYE kuPIT'*
■ bindings	**крепления** *kriPLYEniya*
■ boots	**ботинки/сапоги** *baTINki/sapaGI*
■ cross country skis	**беговые лыжи** *bigaVIye LYzhi*
■ downhill skis	**горные лыжи** *GORniye LYzhi*
■ poles	**палки** *PALki*
■ figure skates	**фигурные коньки** *fiGURniye kan'KI*
■ hockey skates	**хоккейные коньки** *khaKYEYniye kan'KI*

IN THE COUNTRYSIDE

Let's go to the country.	**Поедем в деревню.** *paYEdim v diRYEVnyu*
Do you have a dacha in the country?	**У вас есть дача в деревне?** *u VAS YEST' DAcha v diRYEVnye*
How long does it take to get there?	**Сколко времени туда ехать?** *SKOL'ka VRYEmini tuDA YEkhat'*
How beautiful!	**Как красиво!** *KAK kraSIva*
Look at the _____.	**Посмотрите на _____.** *pasmaTRItye na*
■ birds	**птиц** *PTITS*
■ bridge	**мост** *MOST*
■ brook	**ручей** *ruCHYEY*

▪ fields	**поля**	*paLYA*
▪ flowers	**цветы**	*tsviTY*
▪ forest	**лес**	*LYES*
▪ hills	**холмы**	*khalMY*
▪ lake	**озеро**	*Ozira*
▪ mountains	**горы**	*GOry*
▪ plants	**растения**	*raSTYEniya*
▪ pond	**пруд**	*PRUT*
▪ river	**реку**	*RYEku*
▪ sea	**море**	*MOrye*
▪ trees	**деревья**	*diRYEv'ya*
▪ village	**село**	*siLO*
▪ valley	**долину**	*daLInu*

I'm lost.

Я потерялся. *YA patiRYALsya*

Where does _____ lead?

Куда идёт _____? *kuDA iDYOT*

▪ this road	**эта дорога**	*Eta daROga*
▪ this path	**эта тропинка**	*Eta traPINka*

Can you show me the way?

Вы можете мне показать дорогу?
*VY MOzhitye MNYE pakaZAT"
daROgu*

FOOD AND DRINK

A restaurant meal in Russia is an event to be enjoyed and savored for the better part of an evening. For a quick bite to eat, visit one of the local **Пельменная** *pil'MYEnaya* (Siberian dumpling), **Шашлычная** *shaSHLYCHnaya* (shish-kabob), or **Гриль** *GRIL'* (grill) establishments. When dining out you will have the choice not only of Russian cuisine, but also of exceptional national cuisines such as Armenian, Georgian, and Uzbek. The Russian breakfast tends to be simple, but hearty. You might have a pastry or the famous Russian dark bread with butter and marmalade. You can also have **каша** *KAsha* (a warm cereal), **сосиски** *saSISki* (hot dogs), or **яйца** *YAYtsa* (eggs), accompanied by a glass of **русский чай** *RUski CHAY* (Russian tea) with plenty of **сахар** *SAkhar* (sugar). Because lunch tends to be the main meal of the day, Russians typically will have a **салат** *saLAT* (salad), **суп** *SUP* (soup), a main course, and a light dessert, accompanied by more **чёрный хлеб** *CHORny KHLYEP* (black bread). An excellent selection for lunch is offered at the major hotels, which often feature a smorgasbord (**Шведский стол** *SHVYETski STOL*) for lunch at reasonable prices. Thus, you can sample a variety of dishes. In the evening you might have a light snack of **бутерброды** *butirBROdy* (open-faced sandwiches), with **икра** *iKRA* (caviar), **сыр** *SYR* (cheese), **рыба** *RYba* (fish), or **мясо** *MYAsa* (meat), and a **пирожное** *piROZHnaye* (sweet pastry) at one of the theater buffets. If you go to a restaurant, there will likely be elaborate **закуски** *zaKUSki* (hors d'œuvres) including assorted meats, fish, patés, and cucumbers and tomatoes with sour cream, with ample amounts of vodka, wine, or champagne for the numerous toasts normally accompanying such a feast.

Most restaurants now accept reservations and you should call ahead, or have your hosts or someone at the hotel make those arrangements. Moscow and St. Petersburg are now very cosmopolitan and you will have your choice of cuisine, decor, and price category including a growing number of familiar Western-style fast food chains.

EATING OUT

The main Russian meals are

breakfast	завтрак	*ZAFtrak*
lunch	обед	*aBYET*
supper	ужин	*Uzhin*

You will probably come across the following establishments serving food.

buffet	буфет	*buFYET*
cafe	кафе	*kaFYEY*
cafeteria	столовая	*staLOvaya*
grill	гриль	*GRIL'*
ice cream parlor	кафе мороженое	*kaFYEY maROzhinaye*
pancake house	блинная	*BLInaya*
pelmennaya (Siberian dumpling shop)	пельменная	*pil'MYEnaya*
restaurant	ресторан	*ristaRAN*
shashlychnaya (shish-kabob)	шашлычная	*shaSHLYCHnaya*
snack bar	закусочная	*zaKUsachnaya*

Do you know a good restaurant?	Вы знаете хороший ресторан? *VY ZNAyitye khaROshi ristaRAN*
Is it very expensive?	Он очень дорогой? *ON Ochin' daraGOY*
Can I sample Russian cuisine there?	Там можно попробовать русскую кухню? *TAM MOZHna paPRObavat' RUskuyu KUKHnyu*

I'd like to reserve a table _____.	**Я хочу заказать стол _____.** *YA khaCHU zakaZAT' STOL*
■ for tonight	**на сегодня** *na siVODnya*
■ for tomorrow evening	**на завтра** *na ZAFtra*
■ for two (three, four) persons	**на двоих (троих, четверых)** *na dvaIKH (traIKH, chitviRYKH)*
■ at 8:00 PM (20:00)	**в двадцать часов** *v DVAtsat' chiSOF*
Waiter!	**Молодой человек!** *malaDOY chilaVYEK*
Miss!	**Девушка!** *DYEvushka*

The customs surrounding a Russian restaurant meal deserve a minute of your attention. You should be attentive to signs posted on the front door. **Перерыв** *piriRYF* indicates that the restaurant is closed for a break between meals. **Свободных мест нет** *svaBODnykh MYEST NYET* means no free places at the moment. You might want to wait, but in the evening most Russians will stay until closing time. When you get past the doorman, check your coat and hat at the **Гардероб** *gardiROP*. From there you proceed to the *maitre d'hotel* (**метрдотель** *mitrdaTYEL'*), who will escort you to a table. Unless your party is large enough to fill an entire table, strangers may be seated next to you. If you are alone, there will be a wait until all the seats at the table are occupied; thus it is in your interest to pick a place at a partially occupied table that has not yet been served. When the waiter (**официант** *afitsiANT*) or waitress (**официантка** *afitsiANTka*) approaches, you will hear "**Я вас слушаю** *YA VAS SLUshayu*," literally, "I am listening," which means, "I am ready to take your order." Normally you will order the entire meal at that time, including dessert (**сладкое** *SLATkaye*) and coffee or tea.

Is this table being served?	**Этот стол обслуживается?** *Etat STOL apSLUzhivayitsa*
Please bring the menu.	**Меню, пожалуйста.** *miNYU paZHAlusta*
What is your specialty?	**Какое у вас фирменное блюдо?** *kaKOye u VAS FIRminaye BLYUda*
I'm (not) very hungry. (*m*)	**Я (не) очень голоден.** *YA (NYE) Ochin' GOladin*
I'm (not) very hungry. (*f*)	**Я (не) очень голодна.** *YA (NYE) Ochin' galadNA*
To begin with, bring us _____.	**Для начала, принесите нам _____.** *dlya naCHAla priniSItye NAM*
▨ some vodka (100 grams)	**сто грамм водки** *STO GRAM VOTki*
▨ some cognac (100 grams)	**сто грамм коньяка** *STO GRAM kan'yaKA*
▨ a bottle of red wine	**бутылку красного вина** *buTYLku KRASnava viNA*
▨ a bottle of white wine	**бутылку белого вина** *buTYLku BYElava viNA*
▨ a bottle of beer	**бутылку пива** *buTYLku PIva*
▨ a bottle of mineral water	**бутылку минеральной воды** *buTYLku miniRAL'nay vaDY*
▨ a bottle of soft drink	**бутылку лимонада** *buTYLku limaNAda*
I'm ready to order now.	**Я готов заказать.** *YA gaTOF zakaZAT'*
What do you recommend?	**Что вы рекомендуете?** *SHTO VY rikaminDUyitye*
Please, also bring us _____.	**Принесите, пожалуйста _____.** *priniSItye paZHAlusta*
▨ some bread	**хлеба** *KHLYEba*

■ some butter	масла	*MAsla*
■ some more ____	ещё ____	*yiSHO*
■ an ashtray	пепельницу	*PYEpil'nitsu*
■ a knife	нож	*NOSH*
■ a fork	вилку	*VILku*
■ a spoon	ложку	*LOSHku*
■ a glass	стакан	*staKAN*
■ a vodka glass	рюмку	*RYUMku*
■ a plate	тарелку	*taRYELku*
■ a napkin	салфетку	*salFYETku*

I'll have the ____.   Я возьму ____.   *YA vaz'MU*

THE MENU

Russian menus are pre-printed and are often several pages long. Only those selections with a price indicated are available. Even so, you might ask whether your favorite dish can be ordered.

APPETIZERS (ЗАКУСКИ)
COLD (ХОЛОДНЫЕ) AND WARM (ЖАРКИЕ)

At banquets and formal dinners great care, attention, and expense are devoted to appetizers (закуски *zaKUSki*), which accompany the obligatory toasts with Russian vodka. It is important to dig in and help yourself. Russians recommend black bread spread with lots of butter and cucumbers sprinkled with salt as a way to compensate for the alcohol. You will be delighted by the variety of items, which can range from elaborate fish trays to exquisite caviar. But if you are on a tight budget, be sure to ask in advance what all this costs.

assorted fish	ассорти рыбное	*asarTI RYBnaye*
assorted meats	ассорти мясное	*asarTI misNOye*

caviar	икра *iKRA*
black caviar	зернистая икра *zirNIStaya iKRA*
red caviar	кетовая икра *KYEtavaya iKRA*
mushrooms	грибы *griBY*
mushrooms julienne	жульен из грибов *zhuL'YEN iz griBOF*
sandwich	бутерброд *butirBROT*

THE EGG (ЯЙЦО)

hard-boiled eggs	яйца вкрутую *YAYtsa frkuTUyu*
soft-boiled eggs	яйца всмятку *YAYtsa FSMYATku*
fried eggs	яичница-глазунья *yaICHnitsa glaZUn'ya*
scrambled eggs	яичница-болтунья *yaICHnitsa balTUn'ya*

THE SALAD (САЛАТ)

In addition to the standard salad dishes, almost every restaurant has its house specialty salad (**салат** *saLAT*). Ask the waiter about the ingredients, and wait to be pleasantly surprised, visually and gastronomically.

crab salad	салат из крабов *saLAT is KRAbof*
tomato salad	салат из помидоров *saLAT is pamiDOraf*
cucumber salad	салат из огурцов *saLAT iz agurTSOF*

THE SOUP (СУП)
THE FIRST COURSE (ПЕРВОЕ)

Soup (**суп** *SUP*) is an absolute must in the winter, but even in the summer months Russians enjoy their soups. The most frequently encountered soups are **борщ** *BORSH*, made of beets, **щи** *SHI*, made from cabbage, and **солянка** *saLYANka*, made from fish or meat.

beet soup	**борщ**	*BORSH*
bouillon	**бульон**	*buL'YON*
cabbage soup	**щи**	*SHI*
fish soup	**рыбный суп**	*RYBny SUP*
kidney soup	**рассольник**	*raSOL'nik*
mushroom soup	**грибной суп**	*gribNOY SUP*
noodle soup	**суп-лапша**	*SUP-lapSHA*
solyanka	**солянка**	*saLYANka*

THE MAIN (SECOND) COURSE (ВТОРОЕ)

For the main course, much will depend upon the availability of different fish (**рыба** *RYba*) and meat (**мясо** *MYAsa*) dishes. Here too, you might inquire about the **фирменные блюда** *FIRminiye BLYUda* (house specialties).

FISH (РЫБА)

carp	**карп**	*KARP*
cod	**треска**	*triSKA*
herring	**селёдка**	*siLYOTka*
pike, perch	**судак**	*suDAK*
salmon	**сёмга**	*SYOMga*
sturgeon	**осетрина**	*asiTRIna*
filet of sturgeon	**балык**	*baLYK*
trout	**форель**	*faRYEL'*

MEAT (МЯСО)

beef Stroganoff	**беф-строганов**	*bif-STROganaf*
steak	**бифштекс**	*bifSHTYEKS*
cutlets	**котлеты**	*katLYEty*

golubtsy (stuffed cabbage)	голубцы	*galupTSY*
roast beef	ростбиф	*ROSTbif*
lamb	баранина	*baRAnina*
liver	печень	*PYEchin'*
pelmeni (Siberian dumplings)	пельмени	*pil'MYEni*
pork chops	свиные отбивные котлеты	*sviNIye atbivNIye katLYEty*
ragout	рагу	*raGU*
schnitzel	шницель	*SHNItsil'*
veal	телятина	*tiLYAtina*
fried	жареный	*ZHAriny*
grilled	обжаренный	*abZHAriny*
baked	печёный	*piCHOny*

| boiled | варёный *vaRYOny* |
| stewed | тушёный *tuSHOny* |

POULTRY (ПТИЦА)

chicken	курица / цыплёнок *KUritsa / tsyPLYOnak*
duck	утка *UTka*
goose	гусь *GUS'*
pheasant	фасан *faSAN*
poultry	птица *PTItsa*
turkey	индейка *inDYEYka*

DESSERTS (СЛАДКОЕ)
THE THIRD COURSE (ТРЕТЬЕ)

stewed fruit	компот *kamPOT*
ice cream	мороженое *maROzhinaye*
fresh fruits	свежие фрукты *SVYEzhiye FRUKty*
whipped cream	взбитые сливки *VZBItiye SLIFki*

BEVERAGES (НАПИТКИ)

A word should be said about beverages (**напитки** *naPITki*), especially alcoholic ones. Whether at a restaurant, an official function, or just being hosted in someone's home, vodka, wine, champagne, and cognac may be available in liberal quantities. Drinking for Russians is surrounded with ceremony, including the obligation for the host to raise a toast, after which most Russians empty their glasses by drinking **до дна** *da DNA* (bottoms up, literally "to the bottom"). You should not feel compelled after the first toast to keep pace with your hosts. Remember to eat something for every glass and to follow the lead of the Russians and drink liberal amounts of **минеральная вода** *miniRAL'naya vaDA* (mineral water) between toasts.

Alcohol can be purchased almost anywhere—in grocery stores, supermarkets, and even kiosks on the street. To be safe, purchase only at legitimate outlets, and beware of bargains. If it looks too good (or inexpensive) to be real, then it probably isn't.

beer	пиво	*PIva*
champagne	шампанское	*shamPANskaye*
■ very dry	сухое	*suKHOye*
■ semi-dry	полусухое	*palusuKHOye*
■ sweet	сладкое	*SLATkaye*
cognac	коньяк	*kaN'YAK*
coffee	кофе	*KOfye*
■ with milk	с молоком	*s malaKOM*
_____ juice	_____ сок	*SOK*
■ apple	яблочный	*YAblachny*
■ grape	виноградный	*vinaGRADny*
■ orange	апельсиновый	*apil'SInavy*
kvass	квас	*KVAS*
milk	молоко	*malaKO*
mineral water	минеральная вода	*miniRAL'naya vaDA*
soft drink	лимонад	*limaNAT*
tea	чай	*CHAY*
■ with lemon	с лимоном	*s liMOnam*
■ with sugar	с сахаром	*s SAkaharam*
_____ wine	_____ вино	*viNO*
■ Armenian	армянское	*arMYANskaya*
■ Georgian	грузинское	*gruZINskaye*

■ dry	**сухое**	*suKHOye*
■ red	**красное**	*KRASnaye*
■ sweet	**сладкое**	*SLATkaye*
■ white	**белое**	*BYElaye*

SETTLING UP

Your bill, especially in major cities, will probably include a service charge. Be sure to look for it or ask the waiter. Beyond that charge, be guided by your satisfaction with the service. Something between 10 and 20 percent of the bill total is appropriate.

The check, please.	**Счёт, пожалуйста.** *SHOT paZHAlusta*
Separate checks, please.	**Посчитайте отдельно, пожалуйста.** *pashiTAYtye aDYEL'na paZHAlusta*
Is service included?	**Обслуживание входит в счёт?** *apSLUzhivaniye FKHOdit f SHOT*
I didn't order this.	**Я этого не заказывал.** *YA Etava NYE zaKAzyval*
Please check the bill.	**Проверьте счёт, пожалуйста.** *praVYER'tye SHOT paZHAlusta*
It appears you've made an error.	**Кажется, что вы ошиблись.** *KAzhitsa SHTO VY aSHYblis'*
We are in a hurry.	**Мы спешим.** *MY spiSHYM*
Will it take long?	**Нам долго ждать?** *NAM DOLga ZHDAT'*
This is for you.	**Это для вас.** *Eta dlya VAS*

SHOPPING FOR FOOD

Sometime during your stay you'll probably want to purchase something for a midnight snack or an early morning start. You might visit a bakery (**булочная** *BUlachnaya*) or a pastry shop (**кондитерская** *kanDItirskaya*), try out a Russian style supermarket (**гастроном** *gastraNOM*), or buy something at an outdoor market (**рынок** *RYnak*) or the stands on the street corners. Most items are sold by weight, and you'll purchase many things by the hundred grams (about one quarter of a pound) or by the kilogram (two and one quarter American pounds).

BREADS (ХЛЕБ)
THE BAKERY (БУЛОЧНАЯ)

a loaf of white bread	**батон белого хлеба** *baTON BYElava KHLYEba*
dark bread	**чёрный хлеб** *CHORny KHLYEP*
rye bread	**ржаной хлеб** *rzhaNOY KHLYEP*
a roll	**булочка** *BUlachka*

DAIRY PRODUCTS
MILK AND CHEESE (МОЛОКО И СЫР)

Russian cheese	**российский сыр** *raSIYski SYR*
Dutch cheese	**голландский сыр** *gaLANTski SYR*
creamy butter	**сливочное масло** *SLIvachnaye MAsla*
chocolate butter	**шоколадное масло** *shakaLADnaye MAsla*
cream cheese	**творог** *tvaROK*
sour cream	**сметана** *smiTAna*
kefir (a yogurt-like beverage)	**кефир** *kiFIR*

CAKES (ТОРТЫ)
THE PASTRY SHOP (КОНДИТЕРСКАЯ)

jelly	**варенье** *vaRYEn'ye*
muffins/cupcakes	**кекс** *KYEKS*
a round cookie	**кольцо** *kal'TSO*
oatmeal cookies	**овсянное печенье** *afSYAnaye piCHEn'ye*
a cake	**торт** *TORT*
a pie	**пирог** *piROK*
pastry	**пирожное** *piROZHnaye*

SEASONINGS (ПРИПРАВА)

saccharin	**сахарин** *sakhaRIN*
sugar	**сахар** *SAkhar*
salt	**соль** *SOL'*
pepper	**перец** *PYErits*
horseradish	**хрен** *KHRYEN*
mayonnaise	**майонез** *mayaNYES*
mustard	**горчица** *garCHItsa*
garlic	**чеснок** *chiSNOK*
vegetable oil	**растительное масло** *raSTItil'naye MAsla*
vinegar	**уксус** *UKsus*

COLD CUTS

ham	**ветчина** *vichiNA*
salami	**колбаса** *kalbaSA*

FRUITS (ФРУКТЫ)

apple	**яблоко**	*YAblaka*
apricot	**абрикос**	*abriKOS*
banana	**банан**	*baNAN*
cherry	**вишня**	*VISHnya*
currants	**смородина**	*smaROdina*
date	**финик**	*FInik*
fig	**фига**	*FIga*
grapefruit	**грейпфрут**	*GRYEYPfrut*
grapes	**виноград**	*vinaGRAT*
lemon	**лимон**	*liMON*
melon	**дыня**	*DYnya*
orange	**апельсин**	*apil'SIN*
pear	**груша**	*GRUsha*
peach	**персик**	*PYERsik*
pineapple	**ананас**	*anaNAS*
plum	**слива**	*SLIva*
pomegranate	**гранат**	*graNAT*
raspberries	**малина**	*maLIna*
strawberries	**клубник**	*klubNIK*
tangerine	**мандарин**	*mandaRIN*
watermelon	**арбуз**	*arBUS*
almonds	**миндаль**	*minDAL'*
chestnuts	**каштан**	*kaSHTAN*
nuts	**орехи**	*aRYEkhi*

ICE CREAM (МОРОЖЕНОЕ)

_____ ice cream	_____ **мороженое** _maROzhinaye_
■ chocolate	**шоколадное** _shakaLADnaye_
■ vanilla	**сливочное** _SLIvachnaye_

VEGETABLES (ОВОЩИ)

asparagus	**спаржа** _SPARzha_
beets	**свёкла** _SVYOkla_
cabbage	**капуста** _kaPUSta_
carrots	**морковь** _marKOF"_
cauliflower	**цветная капуста** _tsvitNAya kaPUSta_
cucumbers	**огурцы** _agurTSY_
eggplant	**баклажан** _baklaZHAN_
lettuce	**салат** _saLAT_
mushrooms	**грибы** _griBY_
noodles	**лапша** _lapSHA_
onions	**лук** _LUK_
potatoes	**картофель** _karTOfil'_
pumpkin	**тыква** _TYKva_
radishes	**редиска** _riDISka_
rice	**рис** _RIS_
sauerkraut	**квашенная капуста** _KVAshinaya kaPUSta_
spinach	**шпинат** _shpiNAT_
string beans	**стручковая фасоль** _struchKOvaya faSOL'_
tomatoes	**помидоры** _pamiDOry_
turnips	**репька** _RYEP'ka_

MEETING PEOPLE

GREETINGS AND INTRODUCTIONS

Hello!	**Здравствуйте!** *ZDRASTvuytye*
My name is ____.	**Меня зовут ____.** *miNYA zaVUT*
What is your name?	**Как вас зовут?** *KAK VAS zaVUT*

Russians use three names, a first name (**имя** *Imya*), a patronymic derived from one's father's name (**отчество** *Ochistva*), and a family name (**фамилия** *faMIliya*). It is polite to refer to recent acquaintances with the name and patronymic. Thus one would address even the president of the country as **Владимир Владимирович** *vlahDEEmeer vlahDEEmeerovich*. Russians are likely to have a nickname. For example, Ivan—**Иван** *iVAN* becomes Vanya—**Ваня** *Vanya*, Aleksandr—**Александр** *alikSANDR* becomes Sasha—**Саша** *Sasha*.

Pleased to meet you.	**Очень приятно.** *Ochin' priYATna*
I am from ____.	**Я из ____.** *YA iz*
■ Australia	**Австралии** *afSTRAlii*
■ Canada	**Канады** *kaNAdy*
■ England	**Англии** *ANglii*
■ the USA	**США** *SA SHA A*
I like ____ very much.	**Мне очень нравится ____.** *MNYE Ochin' NRAvitsa*
■ Moscow	**Москва** *maskVA*
■ St. Petersburg	**Санкт Петербург** *SANKT pitirBURK*

■ your country	ваша страна	*VAsha straNA*
■ your republic	ваша республика	*VAsha riSPUblika*

May I introduce myself.	**Разрешите мне представиться.** *razriSHYtye MNYE pritSTAvitsa*

May I introduce my _____.	**Разрешите мне представить _____.** *razriSHYtye MNYE pritSTAvit'*
■ brother	**брата** *BRAta*
■ colleague	**коллегу** *kaLYEgu*
■ daughter	**дочь** *DOCH*
■ father	**отца** *aTSA*
■ friend	**друга** *DRUga*
■ husband	**мужа** *MUzha*
■ mother	**мать** *MAT'*

■ sister	**сестру**	*siSTRU*
■ wife	**жену**	*zhiNU*
■ son	**сына**	*SYna*

I am _____.	**Я _____.**	*YA*
■ an artist	**художник**	*khuDOZHnik*
■ a builder	**строитель**	*straItel'*
■ a businessman	**бизнесмен**	*biznisMYEN*
■ a correspondent	**корреспондент**	*karispanDYENT*
■ a diplomat	**дипломат**	*diplaMAT*
■ a doctor	**врач**	*VRACH*
■ a dentist	**зубной врач**	*zubNOY VRACH*
■ a lawyer	**адвокат**	*advaKAT*
■ a teacher	**преподаватель**	*pripadaVAtil'*
■ a student	**студент**	*stuDYENT*
■ a nurse	**медсестра**	*medsiSTRA*
■ a writer	**писатель**	*piSAtil'*

Where are you from?	**Откуда вы?** *atKUda VY*
Where do you work?	**Где вы работаете?** *GDYE VY raBOtayitye*
What is your profession?	**Кто вы по профессии?** *KTO VY pa praFYEsii*
I will be staying _____.	**Я здесь буду _____.** *YA ZDYES' BUdu*
■ a few days	**несколько дней** *NYEskal'ka DNYEY*
■ a week	**неделю** *niDYElyu*
■ a month	**месяц** *MYEsits*
Would you like a picture?	**Хотите фотографию?** *khaTItye fataGRAfiyu*

Stand there.	**Стойте там.** *STOYtye TAM*
Smile!	**Улыбайтесь!** *ulyBAYtis'*
Say "cheese"! ("raisin")	**Скажите "изюм"!** *skaZHYtye iZYUM*
I want a photo of you.	**Я хочу фотографию вас.** *YA khaCHU fataGRAfiyu VAS*
◼ as a remembrance	**на память** *na PAmit'*

SOCIALIZING

May I have this dance? (May I invite you?)	**Разрешите вас пригласить?** *razriSHYtye VAS priglaSIT'*
All right. With pleasure.	**Хорошо. С удовольствием.** *kharaSHO s udaVOL'STviyim*
Would you like a cigarette?	**Закурите?** *zaKUritye*
Would you like a drink?	**Что-нибудь выпьете?** *SHTO-nibut' VYpitye*
Do you mind if I smoke?	**Ничего если я закурю?** *nichiVO YEsli YA zakuRYU*
May I take you home?	**Можно вас домой проводить?** *MOZHna VAS daMOY pravaDIT'*
May I call you?	**Можно вам позвонить?** *MOZHna VAM pazvaNIT'*
What is your telephone number?	**Какой ваш номер телефона?** *kaKOY VASH NOmir tiliFOna*

Here is my telephone number.	**Вот мой номер телефона.** *VOT MOY NOmir tiliFOna*
Here is my address.	**Вот мой адрес.** *VOT MOY Adris*
Will you write to me?	**Вы мне напишете?** *VY MNYE naPIshitye*
Are you married? (of a man)	**Вы женаты?** *VY zhiNAty*
Are you married? (of a woman)	**Вы замужем?** *VY ZAmuzhim*
Are you alone? (of a man)	**Вы один?** *VY aDIN*
Are you alone? (of a woman)	**Вы одна?** *VY adNA*
Is your husband here?	**Ваш муж здесь?** *VASH MUSH ZDYES'*
Is your wife here?	**Ваша жена здесь?** *VAsha zhiNA ZDYES'*
I'm here with my family.	**Я здесь с семьёй.** *YA ZDYES' s siM'YOY*
Do you have children?	**У вас есть дети?** *u VAS YEST" DYEti*
How many?	**Сколько?** *SKOL'ka*
How old are they?	**Сколько им лет?** *SKOL'ka IM LYET*
What are you doing tomorrow?	**Какие у вас планы на завтра?** *kaKIye u VAS PLAny na ZAFtra*
Are you free this evening?	**Вы свободны сегодня вечером?** *VY svaBODny siVODnya VYEchiram*

Would you like to go together?	**Хотите пойти вместе?** *khaTItye payTI VMYEStye*
I'll wait for you in front of the hotel.	**Я вас жду у входа гостиницы.** *YA VAS ZHDU u FKHOda gaSTInitsy*
I'll pick you up.	**Я за вами заеду.** *YA za VAmi zaYEdu*

SAYING GOOD-BYE

Thank you for your hospitality.	**Спасибо за гостеприимство.** *spaSIba za gastipriIMstva*
Nice to have met you.	**Очень приятно с вами познакомиться.** *Ochin' priYATna s VAmi paznaKOmitsa*
Regards to _____.	**Привет _____.** *priVYET*
Until tomorrow.	**До завтра.** *da ZAFtra*
Until later.	**Пока.** *paKA*
Until this evening.	**До вечера.** *da VYEchira*
Good-bye.	**До свидания.** *da sviDAniya*
Goodnight.	**Спокойной ночи.** *spaKOYnay NOchi*
Farewell.	**Прощайте.** *praSHAYtye*
I wish you _____.	**Я желаю вам _____.** *YA zhiLAyu VAM*
■ all the best	**всего доброго** *fsiVO DObrava*
■ bon voyage	**счастливого пути** *shastLIvava puTI*

SHOPPING

SHOPS AND STORES

To sample the wide variety of consumer items, you might begin with a visit to one of the large department stores in Moscow. Located on Red Square, the most famous store is GUM (**ГУМ**), the State Department Store. Just a few blocks away you can visit TSUM (**ЦУМ**), the Central Department Store, and Children's World (**Детский мир** *DYETski MIR*). As with any major city, Moscow and St. Petersburg offer a variety of shops, many of them aimed at visitors, and where prices might be higher than in stores frequented by the local citizens. Russian stores open around 9:00 AM and remain open until about 8:00 PM. Many close for an hour during the lunch period. Signs posted on the door indicate the opening and closing times as well as the lunch break (**перерыв на обед** *piriRYF na aBYET*), but they will be listed according to the twenty-four hour clock. Thus 1:00 PM is 13:00 and 7:30 PM is 19:30. In addition to the stores you might try the farmers' market (**рынок** *RYnak*). Don't miss the fashionable shops in Moscow on Novy Arbat and Tverskaya Street, or Russia's premier shopping mall on Manezhnaya Square. In St. Petersburg you must stroll and shop on Nevsky Prospect.

GOING SHOPPING

I'd like to go shopping today.	**Сегодня я хочу пойти по магазинам.** *siVODnya YA khaCHUpayTI pa magaZInam*
Where is a nearby _____?	**Где поблизости _____?** *GDYE paBLIzasti*
■ antique shop	**комиссионный магазин** *kamisiOny magaZIN*
■ bakery	**булочная** *BUlachnaya*

▪ barber shop	парикмахерская *parikMAkhirskaya*	
▪ beauty parlor	женский салон *ZHENski saLON*	
▪ bookstore	книжный магазин *KNIZHny magaZIN*	
▪ butcher shop	магазин "Мясо" *magaZIN MYAsa*	
▪ camera shop	магазин "Фототовары" *magaZIN fotataVARY*	
▪ candy store	магазин "Конфеты" *magaZIN kanFYEty*	
▪ clothing store	магазин "Одежда" *magaZIN aDYEZHda*	
▪ department store	универмаг *univirMAK*	
▪ drugstore	аптека *apTYEka*	
▪ dry cleaner's	химчистка *khimCHISTka*	
▪ fabric store	магазин "Ткани" *magaZIN TKAni*	
▪ florist	магазин "Цветы" *magaZIN tsviTY*	
▪ fruit and vegetable store	магазин "Овощи и Фрукты" *magaZIN Ovashi I FRUKty*	
▪ furrier	магазин "Меха" *magaZIN miKHA*	
▪ gift (souvenir) store	магазин "Подарки" *magaZIN paDARki*	
▪ hardware store	хозяйственный магазин *khaZYAYSTviny magaZIN*	
▪ health-food store	магазин "Диета" *magaZIN diYEta*	
▪ jewelry store	ювелирный магазин *yuviLIRny magaZIN*	
▪ laundry	прачечная *PRAchichnaya*	
▪ liquor store	магазин "Вино" *magaZIN viNO*	
▪ newsstand	газетный киоск *gaZYETny kiOSK*	
▪ optician	оптика *OPtika*	
▪ pastry shop	кондитерская *kanDItirskaya*	
▪ record store	магазин "Пластинки" *magaZIN plaSTINki*	

■ shoe store **магазин "Обувь"** *magaZIN Obuf'*

■ shoe repair shop **ремонт обуви** *riMONT Obuvi*

■ sporting goods store **магазин "Спорттовары"** *magaZIN sparttaVAry*

■ stationery store **канцелярские товары** *kantsiLYARskiye taVAry*

■ supermarket **гастроном** *gastraNOM*

■ tailor **ателье мод** *atiL'YE mot*

■ tobacco shop **магазин "Табак"** *magaZIN taBAK*

■ toiletries shop **парфюмерия** *parfyuMYEriya*

■ toy store **магазин "Игрушки"** *magaZIN iGRUSHki*

■ travel agent **бюро путешествий** *byuRO putiSHESTvi*

■ watchmaker **ремонт часов** *riMONT chiSOF*

Young man! **Молодой человек!** *malaDOY chilaVYEK*

Young lady! **Девушка!** *DYEvushka*

Can you help me? **Вы можете мне помочь _____?** *VY MOzhitye MNYE paMOCH'*

In most Russian shops you first examine the articles with the help of the salesperson behind the counter. When you decide on your purchase, you need to find out the price. Then you go to the cashier and tell him or her the total cost and the department. After paying you receive a receipt (**чек** *CHEK*), which you bring back to the original counter, where your purchase will be waiting for you. If you feel unsure of the Russian number system, you might have the salesperson write down the price. The personnel are scrupulously honest, and if you smile and show courtesy and good humor you are likely to be helped through the process.

BOOKSTORE (КНИЖНЫЙ МАГАЗИН)

Where is the biggest (best) bookstore?	**Где самый большой (лучший) книжный магазин?** *GDYE SAmy bal'SHOY (LUCHshi) KNIZHny magaZIN*
How may I help you?	**Как вам помочь?** *KAK VAM paMOCH*
Go ahead! I'm listening.	**Говорите! Я вас слушаю.** *gavaRItye YA VAS SLUshayu*
Do you have books in English?	**У вас есть книги на английском языке?** *u VAS YEST" KNIgi na anGLIYskam yizyKYE*
The title of the book is _____.	**Название книги _____.** *naZVAniye KNIgi*
The author of the book is _____.	**Автор книги _____.** *AFtar KNIgi*
I don't know the title.	**Я не знаю названия.** *YA NYE ZNAyu naZVAniya*
I don't know the author.	**Я не знаю автора.** *YA NYE ZNAyu AFtara*
I'm just looking.	**Я только смотрю.** *YA TOL'ka smaTRYU*
I would like to buy _____.	**Я хотел бы купить _____.** *YA khaTYEL BY kuPIT"*
■ a guide book	**путеводитель** *putivaDItil'*
■ a map of this city	**план города** *PLAN GOrada*
■ a pocket dictionary	**карманный словарь** *karMAny slaVAR'*

■ a Russian-English dictionary	**русско-английский словарь** *Ruska-anGLIYski slaVAR'*
Where can I find _____?	**Где можно наити _____?** *GDYE MOZHna nayTI*
■ children's books	**детские книги** *DYETskiye KNIgi*
■ art books	**книги по искусству** *KNIgi pa iSKUSTvu*
■ a collection of stories	**сборник рассказов** *ZBORnik raSKAzaf*
■ a collection of poetry	**сборник стихотворений** *ZBORnik stikhatvaRYEni*
■ a history book	**книгу по истории** *KNIgu pa iSTOrii*
■ a novel in translation	**роман в переводе** *raMAN f piriVOdye*
I'll take these books.	**Я возьму эти книги.** *YA vaz'MU Eti KNIgi*
How much do they cost?	**Сколько они стоят?** *SKOL'ka aNI STOyit*
Could you write it down, please.	**Запишите мне это, пожалуйста.** *zapiSHYtye MNYE Eta paZHAlusta*
Wrap them up, please.	**Заверните их, пожалуйста.** *zavirNItye IKH paZHAlusta*

CLOTHING (ОДЕЖДА)

Would you please show me _____.	**Покажите мне, пожалуйста _____.** *pakaZHYtye MNYE paZHAlusta*
■ a belt	**пояс (ремень)** *POyas (riMYEN')*
■ a blouse	**блузку** *BLUSku*
■ a bra	**бюстгальтер** *byustGAL'tir*
■ a dress	**платье** *PLAt'ye*

■ a coat	пальто	*pal'TO*
■ a fur coat	шубу	*SHUbu*
■ a fur hat	меховую шапку	*mikhaVUyu SHAPku*
■ gloves	перчатки	*pirCHATki*
■ a handkerchief	носовой платок	*nasaVOY plaTOK*
■ a jacket	пиджак	*pidZHAK*
■ jeans	джинсы	*DZHYNsy*
■ mittens	рукавицы	*rukaVItsy*
■ panties (ladies')	трусики	*TRUsiki*
■ pants	брюки	*BRYUki*
■ pantyhose	колготки	*kalGOTki*
■ a raincoat	плащ	*PLASH*
■ a robe	халат	*khaLAT*
■ a scarf	шарф	*SHARF*
■ a shirt	сорочку (рубашку)	*saROCHku (ruBASHku)*
■ (a pair of) shoes	обувь	*Obuf'*
■ a skirt	юбку	*YUPku*

shorts (men's briefs)	**трусы** *truSY*
a slip	**комбинацию** *kambiNAtsiyu*
a half-slip	**нижнюю юбку** *NIZHnyuyu YUPku*
slippers	**тапочки** *TApachki*
socks	**носки** *naSKI*
stockings	**чулки** *chulKI*
a suit	**костюм** *kaSTYUM*
a sweater	**свитер** *SVItir*
a tie	**галстук** *GALstuk*
an undershirt	**майку** *MAYku*
a wallet	**бумажник** *buMAZHnik*

Do you have anything _____? | **У вас есть что-нибудь _____?** *u VAS YEST' SHTO-nibut'*

with long sleeves	**с длинными рукавами** *z DLInymi rukaVAmi*
with short sleeves	**с короткими рукавами** *s kaROTkimi rukaVAmi*
cheaper	**подешевле** *padiSHEvlye*
else	**ещё** *yiSHO*
larger	**побольше** *paBOL'she*
more expensive	**подороже** *padaROzhe*
longer	**подлиннее** *padliNYEye*
of better quality	**лучшего качества** *LUCHshiva KAchistva*
shorter	**покороче** *pakaROche*
smaller	**поменьше** *paMYEN'she*

Where are the sale items? | **Где товары по сниженным ценам?** *GDYE taVAry pa SNIzhinym tsiNAM*

I don't like the color. | **Мне не нравится цвет.** *MNYE NYE NRAvitsa TSVYET*

Do you have it in _____?	У вас есть _____? *u VAS YEST'*
■ black	**чёрный** *CHORny*
■ dark blue	**синий** *SIni*
■ light blue	**голубой** *galuBOY*
■ brown	**коричневый** *kaRICHnivy*
■ gray	**серый** *SYEry*
■ green	**зелёный** *ziLYOny*
■ pink	**розовый** *ROzavy*
■ red	**красный** *KRASny*
■ white	**белый** *BYEly*
■ yellow	**жёлтый** *ZHOLty*

It doesn't fit me.	**Это не мой размер.** *Eta NYE MOY razMYER*
It fits me well.	**Это на меня сидит хорошо.** *Eta na miNYA siDIT kharaSHO*
I take size _____.	**Мой размер _____.** *MOY razMYER*
May I try it on?	**Можно примерить?** *MOZHna priMYErit'*
Where are the changing rooms?	**Где примерочные кабины?** *GDYE priMYErachniye kaBIny*
I need a _____.	**Мне нужен _____.** *MNYE NUzhin*
■ small	**маленький размер** *MAlin'ki razMYER*
■ medium	**средний размер** *SRYEDni razMYER*
■ large	**большой размер** *bal'SHOY razMYER*
I'll take it.	**Я возьму.** *YA vaz'MU*

FABRICS (ТКАНИ)

chiffon	**шифон** *shiFON*
corduroy	**рубчатый вельвет** *RUPchaty vil'VYET*
cotton	**хлопчатобумажная ткань** *khlapchatabuMAZHnaya TKAN'*
felt	**войлок** *VOYlak*
flannel	**фланель** *flaNYEL'*
fur	**мех** *MYEKH*
■ fox	**лиса** *liSA*
■ rabbit	**кролик** *KROlik*
■ mink	**норка** *NORka*
■ sheepskin	**овчина** *afCHIna*
■ marmot	**сурок** *suROK*
■ sable	**соболь** *SObal'*
■ wolf	**волк** *VOLK*
gabardine	**габардин** *gabarDIN*
lace	**кружева** *kruzhiVA*
leather	**кожа** *KOzha*
linen	**полотно** *palatNO*
nylon	**нейлон** *niyLON*
permanent press	**плиссированная ткань** *plisiROvanaya TKAN'*
polyester	**полиэфир** *palieFIR*
poplin	**поплин** *paPLIN*

rayon	**вискоза** *viSKOza*
sateen	**сатин** *saTIN*
satin	**атлас** *atLAS*
silk	**шёлк** *SHOLK*
suede	**замша** *ZAMsha*
terrycloth	**махровая ткань** *maKHROvaya TKAN'*
velvet	**бархат** *BARkhat*
velveteen	**вельвет** *vil'VYET*
wash-and-wear	**немнущаяся ткань** *niMNUshayasya TKAN'*
wool	**шерсть** *SHERST'*
Show me something ____.	**Покажите мне что-нибудь ____.** *pakaZHYtye MNYE SHTO-nibut'*
■ in a solid color	**однотонное** *adnaTOnaye*
■ with stripes	**в полоску** *f paLOSku*
■ with polka dots	**в горошек** *v gaROshik*
■ in plaid	**в клетку** *f KLYETku*
■ in herringbone	**в ёлочку** *v YOlachku*
■ checked	**в шашечку** *f SHAshichku*

SHOES AND BOOTS (ОБУВЬ)

I want to look at (men's) shoes.	**Я хочу смотреть ботинки.** *YA khaCHU smaTRYET' baTINki*
I want to look at (women's) shoes.	**Я хочу смотреть туфли.** *YA khaCHU smaTRYET' TUfli*

I want to buy a pair of boots.	**Я хочу купить пару сапог.** *YA khaCHU kuPIT' PAru saPOK*
I don't know my size.	**Я не знаю какой размер.** *YA NYE ZNAyu kaKOY razMYER*
These are too big.	**Они мне велики.** *aNI MNYE viliKI*
These are too narrow.	**Они мне тесны.** *aNI MNYE tiSNY*
These are too small	**Они мне малы.** *aNI MNYE maLY*
These are too wide.	**Они мне широки.** *aNI MNYE shiraKI*
They pinch me.	**Они меня жмут.** *aNI miNYA ZHMUT*
They fit me.	**Они мне как раз.** *aNI MNYE KAK RAS*
I'll take them.	**Я их возьму.** *YA IKH vaz'MU*
I also need shoelaces.	**Мне также нужны шнурки.** *MNYE TAGzhe nuzhNY shnurKI*

When you shop for clothes in Russia you must be aware that there are great variations in sizes. It is helpful if you know your height (**рост** *ROST*) and chest (**обхват груди** *apKHVAT GRUdi*) and waist (**обхват талии** *apKHVAT TAlii*) measurements in centimeters in order to use the conversion charts found in many department and clothing stores. In any case, you should try on the item. Ask for the changing booths—**примерочные кабины** *priMYErachniye kaBIny*.

ELECTRICAL APPLIANCES
(ЭЛЕКТРОТОВАРЫ)

Russian electrical appliances operate on 220-volt current, except for some outlets for electric shavers and hair dryers in hotel rooms. To use 110-volt electrical appliances you will need a converter, and you will also need an adapter plug to enable European or American plugs to fit Russian sockets. Alternatively, you might purchase a hair dryer or electric shaver with dual voltage.

I want to buy _____.	**Я хочу купить _____.**	*YA khaCHU kuPIT'*
an adapter	**адаптер**	*aDAPtir*
a battery	**батарею**	*bataRYEyu*
a blender	**сокавыжиматель**	*sakavyzhiMAtil'*
an electric shaver	**электрическую бритву**	*elikTRIchiskuyu BRITvu*
an extension cord	**шнур-удлинитель**	*SHNUR-udliNItil'*
a hair dryer	**фен**	*FYEN*
a plug	**вилку**	*VILku*
a radio	**радио**	*RAdio*
a record player	**проигриватель**	*praIgrivatil'*
a cassette recorder	**магнитофон**	*magnitaFON*
a television set	**телевизор**	*tiliVIzar*
a VCR	**видео-магнитофон**	*VIdio-magnitaFON*
a toaster	**тостер**	*TOStir*
a transformer	**трансформатор**	*transfarMAtar*
It doesn't work.	**Он не работает.**	*ON NYE raBOtayit*
Can you repair this?	**Вы можете это починить?**	*VY MOzhitye Eta pachiNIT'*

FOOD (ГАСТРОНОМ) AND HOUSEHOLD ITEMS (ХОЗЯЙСТВЕННЫЕ ТОВАРЫ)

When you set out for the stores, bring along a plastic bag or, even better, a net bag. Russians have a name for this bag—**авоська** *aVOS'ka* (just in case). Some items will be wrapped in plain gray or brown paper, but you'll find it more convenient to carry them in the bag. Many food stores are self-service, but in others you'll need to determine the price of what you want, then tell the cashier and pay. Only after you have a receipt can you line up to obtain the item.

Please give me _____.	**Дайте мне, пожалуйста, _____.** *DAYtye MNYE paZHAlusta*
■ a bar of soap	**кусок мыла** *kuSOK MYla*
■ a bottle of juice	**бутылку сока** *buTYLku SOka*
■ a box of cereal	**пакет крупы** *paKYET kruPY*
■ a can of tomato sauce	**банку томатного соуса** *BANku taMATnava SOUsa*
■ ten eggs	**десяток яиц** *diSYAtak yaITS*
■ a jar of coffee	**банку кофе** *BANku KOfye*
■ a kilo of potatoes	**кило картошки** *kiLO karTOSHki*
■ a half-kilo of cherries	**пол-кило вишни** *POL-kiLO VISHni*
■ a liter of milk	**литр молока** *LITR malaKA*
■ a box of candy	**коробку конфет** *kaROPku kanFYET*
■ 100 grams of cheese	**сто грамм сыра** *STO GRAM SYra*
■ 200 grams of salami	**двести грамм колбасы** *DVYESti GRAM kalbaSY*
■ a roll of toilet paper	**рулон туалетной бумаги** *ruLON tuaLYETnay buMAgi*

METRIC WEIGHTS AND MEASURES

Solid Measures (approximate measurements only)			
OUNCES	GRAMS (ГРАММ)	GRAMS (ГРАММ)	OUNCES
¼	7	10	⅓
½	14	100	3½
¾	21	300	10½
1	28	450	16 (1 lb.)
POUNDS	KILOGRAMS (КИЛОГРАММ)	KILOGRAMS (КИЛОГРАММ)	POUNDS
1	½	1	2¼
5	2¼	3	6½
10	4½	5	11
20	9	10	22
50	23	50	110
100	45	100	220

Liquid Measures (approximate measurements only)			
OUNCES	MILLILITERS (ГРАММ)	MILLILITERS (ГРАММ)	OUNCES
1	30	10	⅓
6	175	50	1½
12	350	100	3½
16	475	150	5
32	900	250	8½
GALLONS	LITERS (ЛИТР)	LITERS (ЛИТР)	GALLONS
1	3¾	1	¼ (1 quart)
5	19	5	1⅓
10	38	10	2½

NOTE: Common measurements for purchasing food are one kilo (one kilogram = one thousand grams) or some multiple of one hundred grams: **сто грамм, двести грамм.** Russians also use grams instead of milliliters for liquid measurement. A common measure of vodka is 100 grams.

THE JEWELRY STORE
(ЮВЕЛИРНЫЙ МАГАЗИН)

We would like to see _____.	**Мы хотели бы посмотреть _____.** *MY khaTYEli BY pasmaTRYET'*
▓ some beads	**бусы** *BUsy*
▓ a bracelet	**браслет** *braSLYET*
▓ a brooch	**брошь** *BROSH*
▓ a chain	**цепочку** *tsiPOCHku*
▓ a charm	**брелок** *briLOK*
▓ some earrings	**серьги** *SYER'gi*
▓ a necklace	**ожерелье** *azhiRYEl'ye*
▓ a pin	**булавку** *buLAFku*
▓ a ring	**кольцо** *kal'TSO*
▓ a wedding/ engagement ring	**обручальное кольцо** *abruCHAL'naye kal'TSO*
▓ a watch	**часы** *chiSY*
▓ a digital watch	**электронные часы** *elikTROniye chiSY*
Is this _____?	**Это _____?** *Eta*
▓ gold	**золото** *ZOlata*
▓ platinum	**платина** *PLAtina*
▓ silver	**серебро** *siriBRO*
▓ stainless steel	**нержавейка** *nirzhaVYEka*
Is it sold gold or gold plated?	**Это золото или позолоченое?** *Eta ZOlata Ili pazaLOchinaye*
How many carats?	**Сколько каратов?** *SKOL'ka kaRAtaf*

What is this stone?	**Что это за камень?** *SHTO Eta za KAmin'*
I like _____.	**Я люблю _____.** *YA lyuBLYU*
■ amber	**янтарь** *yanTAR'*
■ amethyst	**аметист** *amiTIST*
■ aquamarine	**аквамарин** *akvamaRIN*
■ diamond	**бриллиант** *briliANT*
■ emerald	**изумруд** *izumRUT*
■ ivory	**слоновую кость** *SLOnavuyu KOST'*
■ jade	**нефрит** *niFRIT*
■ jasper	**яшму** *YASHmu*
■ malachite	**малахит** *malaKHIT*
■ onyx	**оникс** *Oniks*
■ pearls	**жемчуг** *zhimCHUK*
■ sapphire	**сапфир** *sapFIR*
■ topaz	**топаз** *taPAS*
■ tourmaline	**турмалин** *turmaLIN*
■ turquoise	**бирюзу** *biRYUzu*
I like this ring.	**Мне нравится это кольцо.** *MNYE NRAvitsa Eta kal'TSO*
How much does it cost?	**Сколько оно стоит?** *SKOL'ka aNO STOit*

AUDIO AND VIDEO EQUIPMENT
(АУДИО-ВИДЕО ТОВАРЫ)

Is there an audio-video store nearby?	**Есть поблизости магазин аудио-видео?** *YEST' paBLIzasti magaZIN AUdio-VIdio*

Do you have _____?	У вас есть _____? *U VAS YEST'*
▪ a camcorder	**видеокамера** *vidioKAmera*
▪ a digital camcorder	**цифровая видеокамера** *tsifraVAya vidioKAmera*
▪ a CD player	**CD-плеер** *SI-DI PLYEyer*
▪ a CD recorder	**CD-магнитофон** *SI-DI magnitaFON*
▪ CDs	**компактдиски** *kampakDISki*
▪ DAT cassettes	**DAT-кассеты** *DI-AY-TI kaSYEty*
▪ DVD movies	**DVD-видеофильмы** *DI-VI-DI vidioFIL'M*
▪ a DVD player	**DVD-плеер** *DI-VI-DI PLEyer*
▪ digital videofilm	**пленка для цифрового видео** *PLYONka DLYA tsifraVOva VIdio*
▪ a minidisk player	**плеер для миникассет** *PLEyer DLYA minikaSYET*
▪ minidisks	**миникассеты** *minikaSYEty*
▪ recordable CDs	**чистые компактдиски** *CHIStye kampakDISki*
▪ a small cassette player	**маленький аудиоплеер** *MAlen'ki audioPLEyer*
▪ VCR movies	**видеофильмы** *vidioFIL'my*
▪ blank VCR tape	**чистая видеокассета** *CHIStaya vidiokaSYEta*
▪ films with English subtitles	**фильмы с английскими титрами** *FIL'my s anGLIYskimi TItrami*
Where is the _____ section?	Где отдел _____? *GDYE aDYEL*
▪ "Rock"	**Рок** *ROK*
▪ "Russian Music"	**Русская музыка** *RUskaya MUzyka*
▪ "Classical Music"	**Классическая музыка** *klaSIchiskaya MUzyka*

- "Folk Music" **Народная музыка** *naRODnaya MUzyka*

- "Latest Hits" **Популярная (современная) музыка** *papuLYARnaya (savriMYEnaya) MUzyka*

- "Opera and Ballet" **Опера и балет** *Opira I baLYET*

THE NEWSSTAND

| Do you have any newspapers in English? | **У вас есть газеты на английском?** *U VAS YEST' gaZYEty na anGLIYskam* |

| Show me some magazines in English. | **Покажите мне журналы на английском.** *pakaZHYtye MNYE zhurNAly na anGLIYskam* |

| These postcards, please. | **Эти открытки, пожалуйста.** *Eti atKRYTki paZHAlusta* |

| Do you have stamps? | **У вас есть марки?** *u VAS YEST' MARki* |

| How much do I owe? | **Сколько с меня?** *SKOL'ka s miNYA* |

Russian kiosks are little booths that sell everything from postcards and stamps to computer programs and videotapes. Most cassettes and CDs will work fine when you return home. But be advised that Russian television and videocassettes use a different standard than American television. Don't purchase videocassettes unless they are clearly marked for use with the NTSC standard.

PHOTOGRAPHIC EQUIPMENT
(ФОТОГРАФИЧЕСКИЕ ТОВАРЫ)

Where is a camera shop?	**Где здесь фототовары?** *GDYE ZDYES' fotataVAry*
Do you develop film?	**Вы проявляете плёнку?** *VY prayaVLYAyitye PLYONku*
Do you have _____?	**У вас есть _____?** *U VAS YEST'*
■ a digital camera	**цифровая камера** *tsifroVAya KAmera*
■ a flash	**вспышка** *FSPYSHka*
■ compact camera	**компактный фотоаппарат** *kamPAKTny fotoapaRAT*
■ different lenses	**разные обьективы** *RAZnye abyekTIvy*
■ an SLR camera	**зеркальный фотоаппарат** *Z'ERkal'ny fotoapaRAT*
■ a tripod	**треножник** *triNOZHnik*
■ a zoom lens	**обьектив зум** *abyekTIF ZOOM*
I have two rolls.	**У меня две плёнки.** *U miNYA DVYE PLYONki*
Please print them all!	**Напечатайте все!** *napiCHAtaytye FSYE*
Can you enlarge this one?	**Вы можете эту увеличить?** *VY MOzhitye Etu uviLIchit'*
glossy finish	**гланц** *GLANTS*
matte finish	**матовый** *MAtavy*

color film, 20 exposures	**цветную плёнку, двадцать кадров** *tsvitNUyu PLYONku, DVAtsat' KAdraf*
black and white film, 36 exposures	**черно-белую плёнку, тридцать шесть кадров** *CHORna-BYEluyu PLYONku, TRItsat' SHEST" KAdraf*
for slides	**на слайды** *na SLAYdy*
ASA 100	**ГОСТ 100** *GOST STO*

If you forget to bring enough film, don't be too concerned. In major cities there are numerous outlets selling film that will develop your pictures overnight or within the hour. It may be a bit more expensive, but you will be able to know if that once-in-a-lifetime shot on Red Square has really been captured.

Do you repair cameras?	**Вы чините фотоаппараты?** *VY chiNItye fotoapaRAty*
I need a battery for my flash.	**Мне нужна батарея для вспышки.** *MNYE nuzhNA bataRYEya dlya FSPYSHki*

SOUVENIRS

For fine Russian souvenirs, check the specialty shops, and don't forget the one at the airport before you depart. Some of the traditional Russian handicrafts are painted wooden dishes from the city of Khokhloma and exquisite lacquered boxes from Palekh and Mstyora. You may also want to buy some of the fine linen items or filigree work, and you certainly don't want to forget caviar and vodka for friends back home. The quality of goods at the airport duty-free shops is excellent, but prices may be higher than in town.

I want to purchase a _____.	Я хочу купить _____.	*YA khaCHU kuPIT'*
■ special gift	особый подарок	*aSOby paDArak*
■ small souvenir	маленький сувенир	*MAlin'ki suviNIR*

It's for _____.	Он для _____.	*ON dlya*
■ my daughter	моей дочки	*maYEY DOCHki*
■ my father	моего отца	*mayiVO aTSA*
■ my husband	моего мужа	*mayiVO MUzha*
■ my mother	моей матери	*maYEY MAtiri*
■ my son	моего сына	*mayiVO SYna*
■ my wife	моей жены	*maYEY zhiNY*

Would you show me some _____.	Покажите мне _____.	*pakaZHYtye MNYE*
■ blown glass	художественное стекло	*khuDOzhistvinaye stiKLO*
■ carved objects	резьбу	*riz'BU*
■ crystal	хрусталь	*khruSTAL'*
■ nested dolls	матрёшки	*maTRYOSHki*
■ ceramics	керамику	*kiRAmiku*
■ fans	веера	*viyiRA*
■ jewelry	ювелирные изделия	*yuviLIRniye izDEYliya*
■ lace	кружева	*kruzhiVA*
■ leather goods	изделия из кожи	*izDYEliya is KOzhi*

liqueurs	**ликёры** *liKYOry*
musical instruments	**музыкальные инструменты** *muzyKAL'niye instruMYENty*
perfumes	**духи** *duKHI*
pictures	**картины** *karTIny*
posters	**плакаты** *plaKAty*

How do you want to pay?	**Чем вы будете платить?** *CHEM VY BUditye plaTIT'*
With cash.	**Наличными.** *naLICHnymi*
With a credit card.	**Кредитной карточкой.** *kriDITnay KARtachkay*

OFFICE SUPPLIES
(КАНЦЕЛЯРСКИЕ ТОВАРЫ)

I want to buy ____.	**Я хочу купить ____.** *YA khaCHU kuPIT'*
a ball-point pen	**ручку** *RUCHku*
a deck of cards	**колоду карт** *kaLOdu KART*
drawing paper	**бумагу для рисования** *buMAgu dlya rasaVAniya*
an envelope	**конверт** *kanVYERT*
an eraser	**ластик** *LAStik*
glue	**клей** *KLYEY*
a notebook	**тетрадь** *tiTRAT'*
a pencil	**карандаш** *karanDASH*
a pencil sharpener	**точилку** *taCHILku*

■ a ruler	**линейку**	*liNYEYku*
■ Scotch tape	**скотч (клеющую ленту)**	*SKOTCH (KLYEyushuyu LYENtu)*
■ string	**шпагат**	*shpaGAT*
■ typing paper	**бумагу для пишущей машинки**	*buMAgu dlya PIshushey maSHYNki*
■ a writing pad	**блокнот**	*blakNOT*
■ writing paper	**бумагу для писем**	*buMAgu dlya PIsim*
■ thumbtacks	**кнопки**	*KNOPki*
■ paperclips	**скрепки**	*SKRYEPki*
■ rubber bands	**резинки**	*riZINki*

TOBACCO (ТАБАК)

A pack of cigarettes, please.	**Пачку сигарет, пожалуйста.**	*PACHku sigaRYET paZHAlusta*
■ filtered	**с фильтром**	*s FIL'tram*
■ unfiltered	**без фильтра**	*byes FIL'tra*
■ menthol	**с ментолом**	*s minTOlam*
■ king-size (long)	**кинг-сайз (длинные)**	*KING-SAYS (DLIniye)*
Are these cigarettes strong?	**Эти сигареты крепкие?**	*Eti sigaRYEty KRYEPkiye*
Are they mild?	**Они слабые?**	*aNI SLAbiye*
Do you have American cigarettes?	**У вас есть американские сигареты?**	*u VAS YEST" amiriKANskiye sigaRYEty*

What brands?	**Какие марки?** *kaKIye MARki*
And a pack of matches, please.	**И спички, пожалуйста.** *I SPICHki paZHAlusta*
Do you carry _____?	**У вас есть _____?** *u VAS YEST'*
butane gas	**газ** *GAS*
chewing tobacco	**махорка** *maKHORka*
cigarette holders	**мундштуки** *muntSHTUki*
cigars	**сигары** *siGAry*
flints	**кремни** *krimNI*
lighters	**зажигалки** *zazhiGALki*
pipes	**трубки** *TRUPki*
pipe tobacco	**трубочный табак** *TRUbachny taBAK*

TOILETRIES
(ПАРФЮМЕРИЯ)

Do you have _____?	**У вас есть _____?** *u VAS YEST'*
aftershave	**лосьон после бритья** *laS'YON POslye briT'YA*
bobby pins	**шпильки заколки** *SHPILki zaKOLki*
a brush	**щётка** *SHOTka*
cleansing cream	**крем для очистки кожи** *KRYEM dlya aCHISTki KOzhi*
nourishing cream	**питательный крем** *piTAtil'ny KRYEM*
cologne	**одеколон** *adikaLON*
a comb	**расчёска** *rasCHOSka*
condoms	**презервативы** *prizirvaTIvy*

▓ a deodorant	**дезодорант**	*dizadaRANT*
▓ disposable diapers	**бумажные пелёнки**	*buMAZHniye piLYONki*
▓ eye liner	**карандаш для бровей**	*karanDASH dlya braVYEY*
▓ eyebrow pencil	**карандаш для век**	*karanDASH dlya VYEK*
▓ eye shadow	**тени**	*TYEni*
▓ face lotion	**лосьон**	*laS'YON*
▓ hair spray	**лак для волос**	*LAK dlya vaLOS*
▓ lip gloss	**блеск для губ**	*BLYESK dlya GUP*
▓ lipstick	**губная помада**	*gubNAya paMAda*
▓ make-up	**крем-пудра (мэйк-ап)**	*KRYEM-PUdra (meyk-AP)*
▓ mascara	**тушь для ресниц**	*TUSH dlya riSNITS*
▓ a mirror	**зеркало**	*ZYERkala*
▓ mouthwash	**зубной эликсир**	*zubNOY elikSIR*
▓ nail clippers	**кусачки**	*kuSACHki*
▓ a nail file	**пилка**	*PILka*
▓ nail polish	**лак для ногтей**	*LAK dlya nakTYEY*
▓ nail polish remover	**ацетон**	*atsiTON*
▓ a razor	**бритва**	*BRITva*
▓ razor blades	**лезвия**	*LYEZviya*
▓ rouge	**румяна**	*ruMYAna*
▓ sanitary napkins	**гигиенические салфетки**	*gigiyiNIchiskiye salFYETki*

■ (cuticle) scissors	**маникюрные ножницы** *maniKYURniye NOZHnitsy*
■ shampoo	**шампунь** *shamPUN'*
■ a sponge	**губка** *GUPka*
■ talcum powder	**тальк** *TAL'K*
■ tampons	**тампоны (марлевые салфетки)** *tamPOny (MARliviye salFYETki)*
■ tissues	**салфетки** *salFYETki*
■ toilet paper	**туалетная бумага** *tuaLYETnaya buMAga*
■ a toothbrush	**зубная щётка** *zubNAya SHOTka*
■ toothpaste	**зубная паста** *zubNAya PASta*
■ tweezers	**щипчики** *SHIPchiki*

PERSONAL CARE AND SERVICES

If your hotel doesn't offer these services, ask the desk clerk to recommend a place nearby.

BARBER SHOP (ПАРИКМАХЕРСКАЯ)

Where is a good barber shop?	**Где хорошая парикмахерскиая?** *GDYE khaROshaya parikMAkhirskaya*
Does the hotel have a barber shop?	**В гостинице есть парикмахерская?** *v gaSTInitse YEST' parikMAkhirskaya*
Do I have to wait long?	**Надо долго ждать?** *NAda DOLga ZHDAT'*
Whose turn is it?	**Чья очередь?** *CH'YA Ochirit'*
I want a shave.	**Я хочу побриться.** *YA khaCHU paBRItsa*
I want a haircut.	**Я хочу постричься.** *YA khaCHU paSTRICHsa*
A shampoo, please.	**Помойте, пожалуйста, голову.** *paMOYtye paZHAlusta GOlavu*
Short in back, long in front.	**Сзади коротко, спереди длинно.** *ZAdi KOratka SPYEridi DLIna*
Leave it long.	**Оставьте эту длину.** *aSTAF'tye Etu dliNU*
I want it (very) short.	**(Очень) коротко.** *(Ochin') KOratka*

You can cut a little ____.	**Можно покороче ____.** *MOZHna pakaROche*
■ in back	**сзади** *ZAdi*
■ in front	**спереди** *SPYEridi*
■ off the top	**сверху** *SFYERkhu*

I have a part ____.	**У меня пробор ____.** *u miNYA praBOR*
■ on the left	**слева** *SLYEva*
■ on the right	**справа** *SPRAva*
■ in the middle	**прямой** *priMOY*

I comb my hair ____.	**Я зачёсываю волосы ____.** *YA zaCHOsyvayu VOlasy*
■ straight back	**прямо назад** *PRYAma naZAT*
■ without a part	**без пробора** *byes praBOra*

Cut a little bit more here.	**Здесь чуть-чуть покороче.** *ZDYES' CHUT'-CHUT' pakaROche*
That's fine.	**Так хорошо.** *TAK kharaSHO*

I don't want ____.	**Не надо ____.** *NYE NAda*
■ a wash	**мытья** *myT'YA*
■ eau de cologne	**одеколона** *adikaLOna*

Use the scissors only.	**Только ножницами.** *TOL'ka NOZHnitsami*
A razor cut.	**Бритвой, пожалуйста.** *BRITvay paZHAlusta*
You can use the electric razor.	**Можно электрической бритвой.** *MOZHna elikTRIchiskay BRITvay*
Please trim ____.	**Подстригите ____.** *padstriGItye*

Please even out _____.	Подравняйте _____. *padravNYAYtye*
■ my beard	бороду *BOradu*
■ my moustache	усы *uSY*
■ my sideburns	височки *viSOCHki*

Please shave the back of
Побрейте шею. *paBRYEYtye SHEyu*

Where is a mirror?
Где здесь зеркало? *GDYE ZDYES' ZYERkala*

I want to look at myself.
Хочу на себя взглянуть. *khaCHU na siBYA vzgliNUT"*

How much do I owe you?
Сколько я вам должен? *SKOL'ka YA VAM DOLzhin*

BEAUTY PARLOR
(ЖЕНСКАЯ ПАРИКМАХЕРСКАЯ)

Is there a beauty parlor near here?
Поблизости есть женская парикмахерская? *paBLIzasti YEST" ZHENskaya parikMAkhirskaya*

Can I make an appointment _____?	Можно записаться _____? *MOZHna zapiSAtsa*
■ for today	на севодня *na siVODnya*
■ after lunch	после обеда *POslye aBYEda*
■ tomorrow	на завтра *na ZAFtra*

What would you like to have done?
Что вам сделать? *SHTO VAM ZDYElat'*

A color rinse?
Окраску волос? *aKRASku vaLOS*

A facial massage?
массаж лица? *maSASH liTSA*

A haircut?
Стрижку? *STRISHku*

A manicure?	**Маникюр?**	*maniKYUR*
A permanent?	**Химическую завивку?** *khiMIchiskuyu zaVIFku*	
A shampoo?	**Мытьё?**	*myT'YO*
A tint?	**Тон?**	*TON*
A touch up?	**Поправку?**	*paPRAFku*
A wash and set?	**Мытьё и укладку?** *myT'YO I uKLATku*	
No, don't cut it.	**Нет, стричь не надо.** *NYET STRICH NYE NAda*	
What color?	**Какого цвета?**	*kaKOva TSYEta*

What color? **Какого цвета?** *kaKOva TSYEta*
- ◼ auburn — **каштановый** *kashTAnavy*
- ◼ blond — **белокурый** *bilaKUry*
- ◼ brunette — **брюнетка** *bryuNYETka*
- ◼ a darker color — **потемнее** *patimNYEye*

◼ a lighter color	**посветлее** *pasvitLYEye*
◼ the same color	**такой же цвет** *taKOY zhe TSVYET*

Don't use any hair spray.	**Без лака, пожалуйста.** *byez LAka paZHAlusta*
Just a little.	**Совсем мало.** *safSYEM MAla*
A little more.	**Побольше.** *paBOL'she*
Give me a new (stylish) hairdo.	**Сделайте мне модную причёску.** *ZDYElaytye MNYE MODnuyu priCHOSku*
Something striking _____.	**Что-нибудь экстравагантное _____.** *SHTO-nibut' ekstravaGANTnaye*
◼ with curls	**с кудрями** *s KUdryami*
◼ with waves	**с волнами** *s valNAmi*
◼ with bangs	**с чёлкой** *s CHOLkay*
In a bun on top.	**Пучок.** *puCHOK*
A pony tail?	**Хвост?** *KHVOST*

THE BATHHOUSE (БАНЯ)

One of the true pleasures in Russia is a visit to the bathhouse, or **баня** *BAnya*. Bathhouses range from the super-luxurious and expensive to the old-fashioned and more reasonable. Before you set out on your own, ask your host or the hotel concierge for his or her recommendations and any concerns or reservations he or she might have. Take shampoo, soap, a change of underwear, and a towel with you. Be prepared to spend a few hours spoiling yourself. At the entrance to the bathhouse you'll see vendors selling bunches of oak or birch twigs (**веник** *VYEnik*). These are a must, so buy a bunch. Inside, you purchase a ticket, then proceed to the changing rooms, where you can leave your clothes in a locker. Find a wash-basin (**тазик** *TAzik*), and you are ready to begin. Wet yourself down, then go into the steam room (**парильня** *paRIL'nya*). It is hottest at the top, so move up gradually. After a few minutes of sweating, go outside and take a cool dip in the pool, then return to the steam room. Russians suggest that this ritual be performed three times. Finally, you'll bathe and shampoo your hair. Then the old-timers recommend that you sit a while (maybe have a cool drink) so your body can adjust to normal room temperature. Oh, yes! Smack the twigs against your skin to improve the circulation. For hard-to-reach places, it is acceptable to ask your neighbor for assistance. The baths can also provide a number of services, such as pressing clothes and doing minor repairs. Some may offer a barber shop and beauty parlor with manicures and pedicures.

I'll take some twigs.	**Веник, пожалуйста.** *VYEnik paZHAlusta*
One ticket, please.	**Один билет, пожалуйста.** *aDIN biLYET paZHAlusta*
Can I leave my valuables?	**Можно сдавать ценные вещи?** *MOZHna zdaVAT' TSEniye VYEshi*
Please bring me _____.	**Принесите мне, пожалуйста _____.** *priniSItye MNYE paZHAlusta*
▊ some slippers	**тапочки** *TApachki*
▊ a bar of soap	**кусок мыла** *kuSOK MYla*
▊ a linen towel	**простыню** *praSTYnyu*
▊ a sponge	**мочалку** *maCHALku*
▊ some shampoo	**шампунь** *shamPUN'*
▊ a wrap-around	**накидку** *naKITku*
May I take this washbasin?	**Можно взять этот тазик?** *MOZHna VZYAT' Etat TAzik*
Where is the steam room?	**Где парильня?** *GDYE paRIL'nya*

It's too hot for me up there.	**Там мне слишком жарко.** *TAM MNYE SLISHkam ZHARka*
Where is the swimming pool?	**Где бассейн?** *GDYE baSYEYN*
Where are the showers?	**Где душ?** *GDYE DUSH*
Is there a sauna here?	**Здесь есть сауна?** *ZDYES' YEST' SAUna*
Do you have a buffet?	**У вас есть буфет?** *u VAS YEST' buFYET*

LAUNDRY AND DRY CLEANING
(ПРАЧЕЧНАЯ И ХИМЧИСТКА)

You may be able to have shirts, blouses, and underwear washed at the hotel. Usually one of the maids will do it for a modest price. There also will probably be an ironing board and iron on your floor. Simply ask the "key lady" (**дежурная** *diZHURnaya*). Otherwise you can use the laundromat and dry cleaner's.

Where is the nearest laundry?	**Где ближайшая прачечная?** *GDYE bliZHAYshaya PRAchichnaya*
Where is a laundromat?	**Где прачечная самообслуживания?** *GDYE PRAchichnaya samaapSLUzhivaniya*
I have a lot of clothes to be _____.	**У меня набралась большая _____.** *U miNYA nabraLAS' bal'SHAya*
■ dry cleaned	**чистка** *CHISTka*
■ washed	**стирка** *STIRka*
■ ironed	**глажка** *GLASHka*

Here's the list: **Вот список:** *VOT SPIsak*

- three shirts **три рубашки** *TRI ruBASHki*
- ten handkerchiefs **десять носовых платков** *DYEsit' nasaVYKH platKOF*
- six pairs of socks **шесть пар носков** *SHEST' PAR naSKOF*
- one blouse **одна блузка** *aDNA BLUSka*
- panties **трусики** *TRUsiki*
- three pajamas **три пижамы** *TRI piZHAmy*
- one suit **один костюм** *aDIN kaSTYUM*
- five ties **пять галстуков** *PYAT' GALstukaf*
- two dresses **два платья** *DVA PLAt'ya*
- one sweater **один свитер** *aDIN SVItir*
- a pair of gloves **перчатки** *pirCHATki*

I need them _____. **Мне нужно _____.** *MNYE NUZHna*

- tonight **к вечеру** *k VYEchiru*
- tomorrow **завтра** *ZAFtra*
- the day after tomorrow **послезавтра** *pasliZAFtra*

When will you bring them back? **Когда вы их принесёте?** *kagDA VY IKH priniSYOtye*

When will it be ready? **Когда будет готово?** *kagDA BUdit gaTOva*

There is a spot on the blouse. **На блузке есть пятно.** *na BLUSkye YEST' pitNO*

There's a button missing. **Здесь нет пуговицы.** *ZDYES' NYET PUgavitsy*

Can you sew it back on? **Не могли бы вы пришить?** *NYE maGLI BY VY priSHYT'*

These aren't my things. **Это не мои вещи.** *Eta NYE maYI VYEshi*

SHOE REPAIRS (РЕМОНТ ОБУВИ)

All around town you are likely to see tiny shoe shine and repair booths. Why not step inside and treat yourself to a shine? At the booths you can have minor repairs performed. For major repairs, bring your shoes or boots to the shoe repair shops.

A shoe shine please.	**Почистите, пожалуйста.** *paCHIStitye paZHAlusta*
Can you fix these _____?	**Вы можете починить _____?** *VY MOzhitye pachiNIT"*
■ ladies' shoes	**туфли** *TUfli*
■ shoes	**ботинки** *baTINki*
■ boots	**сапоги** *sapaGI*
Just soles.	**Только подмётки.** *TOL'ka padMYOTki*
Heels, please.	**Каблуки, пожалуйста.** *kabluKI paZHAlusta*
Can you do it now?	**Вы можете сейчас?** *VY MOzhitye siyCHAS*
A pair of shoelaces.	**Шнурки.** *shnurKI*
A pair of insoles.	**Стельки.** *STYEL'ki*

WATCH REPAIRS (РЕМОНТ ЧАСОВ)

Can you repair this _____?	**Вы можете починить _____?** *VY MOzhitye pachiNIT"*
■ clock/watch	**часы** *chiSY*

▦ alarm clock	**будильник**	*buDIL'nik*
▦ digital watch	**электронные часы**	*elikTROniye chiSY*
▦ quartz watch	**кварцовые часы**	*KVARtsaviye chiSY*
▦ wristwatch	**наручные часы**	*naRUCHniye chiSY*

There's something wrong with the _____.	**Проблема с _____.**	*praBLYEma s*
▦ glass	**стеклом**	*stiKLOM*
▦ hour hand	**часовой стрелкой**	*chisaVOY STRYELkay*
▦ minute hand	**минутной стрелкой**	*miNUTnay STRYELkay*
▦ second hand	**секундной стрелкой**	*siKUNDnay STRYELkay*
▦ stem (screw)	**головкой**	*gaLOFkay*

Could you look at it?	**Вы могли бы посмотреть?**	*VY maGLI BY pasmaTRYET'*
Can you replace the battery?	**Можно поставить новую батарейку?**	*MOZHna paSTAvit' NOvuyu bataRYEYku*
Can you clean it?	**Можно их почистить?**	*MOZHna IKH paCHIStit'*
I dropped it.	**Я их уронил.**	*YA IKH uraNIL*
It doesn't run well.	**Они плохо идут.**	*aNI PLOkha iDUT*
It's fast.	**Они спешат.**	*aNI spiSHAT*
It's slow.	**Они отстают.**	*aNI atstaYUT*

It's stopped running.	**Они стоят.** *aNI staYAT*
I wind it every day.	**Я завожу их каждый день.** *YA zavaZHU IKH KAZHdy DYEN'*

CAMERA REPAIRS
(РЕМОНТ ФОТОАППАРАТОВ)

Can you fix this camera?	**Вы можете починить этот фотоаппарат?** *VY MOzhitye pachiNIT' Etat fotaapaRAT*
It doesn't work well.	**Он плохо работает.** *ON PLOkha raBOtayit*
How much will it cost?	**Сколько стоит ремонт?** *SKOL'ka STOit riMONT*
When can I come and get it?	**Когда за ним прийти?** *kagDA za NIM priyTI*
I need it as soon as possible.	**Мне нужно как можно скорее.** *MNYE NUZHna KAK MOZHna skaRYEye*

Travel Tips A good rule of thumb about purchases is "If you see it, buy it!" You can never be certain in Russia that an item will be there the next day or that a store will be open. A variety of things—a lunch break (**перерыв на обед** *piriRYF na aBYET*), closure for inventory (**закрыт на учёт** *zaKRYT na uCHOT*), or the periodical cleaning day (**санитарный день** *saniTARny DYEN'*)—may interfere with your intentions.

MEDICAL CARE

If you are given a prescription you will need to go to a pharmacy—**аптека** *apTYEka*. Here you can also find nonprescription remedies for what ails you. Most medicines are very inexpensive. In major cities several pharmacies provide round-the-clock emergency services.

PHARMACY

Where is the nearest pharmacy?	**Где ближайшая аптека?** *GDYE bliZHAYshaya apTYEka*
When does the pharmacy _____?	**Когда аптека _____?** *kagDA apTYEka*
open	**открывается** *atkryVAyitsa*
close	**закрывается** *zakryVAyitsa*
Where is the prescription section?	**Где рецептный отдел?** *GDYE riTSEPTny aDYEL*
Where are the nonprescription medicines?	**Где безрецептные лекарства?** *GDYE byezriTSEPTniye liKARSTva*
I need something for _____.	**Мне нужно что-нибудь от _____.** *MNYE NUZHna SHTO-nibut' at*
a cold	**насморка** *NASmarka*
constipation	**запора** *zaPOra*
a cough	**кашля** *KASHlya*
diarrhea	**поноса** *paNOsa*
a fever	**жара** *ZHAra*
hay fever	**сенной лихорадки** *SYEnay likhaRATki*

a headache	**головной боли**	*galavNOY BOli*
insomnia	**бессоницы**	*biSOnitsy*
nausea	**тошноты**	*tashnaTY*
sunburn	**солнечного ожога**	*SOLnichnava aZHOga*
a toothache	**зубной боли**	*zubNOY BOli*
an upset stomach	**желудочного расстройства**	*zhiLUdachnava raSTROYSTva*

Is a prescription necessary?	**Нужен рецепт?** *Nuzhin riTSEPT*
Can you fill this prescription for me?	**У вас есть лекарство по этому рецепту?** *u VAS YEST' liKARSTva pa Etamu riTSEPtu*
It's an emergency.	**Это срочно.** *Eta SROCHna*
Should I wait for it?	**Мне подождать?** *MNYE padaZHDAT'*
How long will it take?	**Сколько ждать?** *SKOL'ka ZHDAT'*
When can I come for it?	**Когда мне прийти?** *kagDA MNYE priyTI*
When should I come back?	**Когда мне вернуться?** *kagDA MNYE virNUtsa*
Do you have _____?	**У вас есть _____?** *u VAS YEST'*
adhesive tape	**пластырь** *plaSTYR'*
alcohol	**спирт** *SPIRT*
an antacid	**щёлочь** *SHOlach*
an antiseptic	**антисептик** *antiSYEPtik*
aspirin	**аспирин** *aspiRIN*
bandages	**бинт** *BINT*

cotton	**вата** *VAta*
cough drops	**таблетки от кашля** *taBLYETki at KASHlya*
cough syrup	**микстура от кашля** *mikSTUra at KASHlya*
ear drops	**ушные капли** *ushNIye KApli*
eye drops	**глазные капли** *glazNIye KApli*
iodine	**йод** *YOT*
a mild laxative	**(лёгкое) слабительное** *(LYOkaye) slaBItil'naye*
magnesia	**магнезия** *magNYEziya*
mustard plaster	**горчичник** *garCHICHnik*
an ointment	**мазь** *MAS'*
a sedative	**успокаивающее** *uspaKAivayushiye*
sleeping pills	**снотворное** *snaTVORnaye*
suppositories	**свечи** *SVEchi*
a thermometer	**термометр** *tirMOmitr*
vitamins	**витамины** *vitaMIny*

DOCTORS

In an emergency call the number for immediate care—**Скорая помощь** *SKOraya POmash*. The number in Moscow and St. Petersburg is **03**. Identify yourself as a foreigner and describe the problem, and within minutes a physician will be at your hotel. Western-style medical and dental centers have also appeared in large cities. Check at the hotel reception desk.

I don't feel well.	**Я чувствую себя плохо.** *YA CHUSTvuyu siBYA PLOkha*
I feel sick. (*m*)	**Я заболел.** *YA zabaLYEL*

I feel sick. (*f*)	**Я заболела.** *YA zabaLYEla*
Please call a doctor.	**Вызовите, пожалуйста, врача.** *VYzavitye paZHAlusta vraCHA*
Is there a doctor who speaks English?	**Есть врач, который говорит по-английски?** *YEST" VRACH kaTOry gavaRIT pa-anGLIYski*
I'm dizzy. (My head is spinning.)	**Голова кружится.** *galaVA KRUzhitsa*
I feel weak.	**Я чувствую слабость.** *YA CHUSTvuyu SLAbast'*
I want to sit down for a while.	**Мне нужно посидеть.** *MNYE NUZHna pasiDYET"*
My temperature is normal.	**У меня нормальная температура.** *u miNYA narMAL'naya timpiraTUra*
I have a high temperature.	**У меня высокая температура.** *u miNYA vySOkaya timpiraTUra*

PARTS OF THE BODY

It hurts here.	**Болит здесь.** *baLIT ZDYES'*
My _____ hurts.	**У меня болит _____.** *u miNYA baLIT*
abdomen	**живот** *zhiVOT*
arm	**рука** *ruKA*
back	**спина** *spiNA*
breast	**грудь** *GRUT'*
cheek	**щека** *shiKA*
ear	**ухо** *Ukha*

■ elbow	локоть	*LOkat'*
■ eye	глаз	*GLAS*
■ face	лицо	*liTSO*
■ finger	палец	*PALits*
■ foot	ступня	*stupNYA*
■ hand	кисть	*KIST"*
■ head	голова	*galaVA*
■ heart	сердце	*SYERtse*
■ hip	бедро	*biDRO*
■ knee	колено	*kaLYEna*
■ leg	нога	*naGA*
■ lip	губа	*GUba*
■ mouth	рот	*ROT*
■ neck	шея	*SHEya*
■ nose	нос	*NOS*
■ rib	ребро	*riBRO*
■ shoulder	плечо	*pliCHO*
■ skin	кожа	*KOzha*
■ stomach	желудок	*zhiLUdak*
■ throat	горло	*GORla*
■ tooth	зуб	*ZUP*
■ wrist	запястье	*zaPYASt'ye*

WHAT'S WRONG

I have _____.	У меня _____.	*u miNYA*
■ an abscess	нарыв	*naRYV*
■ a broken bone	перелом	*piriLOM*
■ a bruise	ушиб	*uSHYP*

◼ a burn	**ожог** *aZHOK*
◼ something in my eye	**что-нибудь в глазу** *SHTO-nibut' v glaZU*
◼ the chills	**озноб** *aZNOP*
◼ a chest cold	**бронхит** *branKHIT*
◼ a head cold	**насморк** *NASmark*
◼ a cough	**кашель** *KAshil'*
◼ cramps	**судороги** *SUdaragi*
◼ a cut	**порез** *paRYES*
◼ diarrhea	**понос** *paNOS*
◼ a fever	**температура** *timpiraTUra*
◼ a headache	**головная боль** *galavNAya BOL'*
◼ an infection	**инфекция** *inFYEKtsiya*
◼ a lump/swelling	**опухоль** *Opukhal'*
◼ a sore throat	**ангина** *anGIna*
◼ a wound	**рана** *RAna*

I'm allergic to _____. **У меня аллергия от _____.** *U miNYA alirGIya at*

◼ penicillin   **пеницилина** *pinitsiLIna*

I am taking this medicine.   **Я принимаю это лекарство.** *YA priniMAyu Eta liKARSTva*

I feel better.   **Я чувствую себя лучше.** *YA CHUSTvuyu siBYA LUCHshe*

I feel worse.   **Я чувствую себя хуже.** *YA CHUSTvuyu siBYA KHUzhe*

DOCTOR'S INSTRUCTIONS

Open your mouth!   **Откройте рот!** *atKROYtye ROT*

Stick out your tongue!	**Покажите язык!** *pakaZHYtye yiZYK*
Cough!	**Покашляйте!** *paKASHlyaytye*
Breathe deeply!	**Дышите глубоко!** *dySHYtye glubaKO*
Breathe normally!	**Дышите нормально!** *dySHYtye narMAL'na*
Undress (to the waist)!	**Разденьтесь (до пояса)!** *razDYEN'tis' (da POyasa)*
Lie down!	**Ложитесь!** *laZHYtis'*
Stand up!	**Вставайте!** *fstaVAYtye*
You may get dressed!	**Одевайтесь** *adiVAYtis'*

PATIENT'S CONCERNS

Is it serious?	**Это серьёзно?** *Eta siR'YOZna*
Do I have to go to the hospital?	**Мне нужно лечь в больницу?** *MNYE NUZHna LYECH v bal'NItsu*
Are you giving me a prescription?	**Вы мне выпишете лекарство?** *VY MNYE VYpishitye liKARSTva*
How often should I take the medicine?	**Как часто принимать лекарство?** *KAK CHASta priniMAT' liKARSTva*
How long must I stay in bed?	**Сколько времени мне лежать?** *SKOL'ka VRYEmini MNYE liZHAT'*
Thank you for everything.	**Спасибо за всё.** *spaSIba za FSYO*

ACCIDENTS

Help!	**Помогите!** *pamaGItye*
Call a doctor!	**Вызовите врача!** *VYzavitye vraCHA*
Call an ambulance!	**Вызовите скорую помощь!** *VYzavitye SKOruyu POmash*
Take me to a hospital!	**Отвезите меня в больницу!** *atviZItye miNYA v bal'NItsu*
I fell.	**Я упал.** *YA uPAL*
I was knocked over.	**Меня сбили с ног.** *miNYA ZBIli s NOK*
I was hit by a car	**Меня сбила машина.** *miNYA zbiLA maSHYna*
I'm having a heart attack.	**У меня сердечный приступ.** *u miNYA sirDYECHny PRIstup*

I burned myself.	**Я обварился.** *YA abvaRILsya*
I cut myself.	**Я порезался.** *YA paRYEzalsya*
I'm bleeding.	**У меня кровотечение.** *u miNYA kravatiCHEniye*
I've lost a lot of blood.	**Я потерял много крови.** *YA patiRYAL MNOga KROvi*
I think the bone is broken.	**Я думаю, у меня перелом.** *YA DUmayu u miNYA piriLOM*
The leg is swollen.	**Нога вздута.** *naGA VZDUta*
The wrist is twisted.	**Запястье растянуто.** *zaPYASt'ye raSTYAnuta*
My ankle is dislocated.	**Лодыжка вывыхнута.** *laDYSHka VYvykhnuta*

DENTISTS

I have a terrible toothache.	**У меня страшно болит зуб.** *u miNYA STRASHna baLIT ZUP*
Where is the nearest dental clinic?	**Где ближайшая зубная поликлиника?** *GDYE bliZHAYshaya zubNAya paliKLInika*
I've lost a filling.	**Я потерял пломбу.** *YA patiRYAL PLOMbu*
I've broken a tooth.	**Я сломал зуб.** *YA slaMAL ZUP*
I can't chew.	**Я не могу жевать.** *YA NYE maGU zhiVAT"*

My gums hurt.	**Болят дёсны.**	*baLYAT DYOSny*
Is there an infection?	**Это инфекция?**	*Eta inFYEKtsiya*
Do you have to pull the tooth?	**Вам надо зуб удалить?** *VAM NAda ZUP udaLIT'*	
Can you put in a filling?	**Можете поставить пломбу?** *MOzhitye paSTAvit' PLOMbu*	

- an amalgam one   **амальгаму**   *amal'GAmu*
- a gold one   **золотую**   *zalaTUyu*
- a porcelain one   **фарфоровую**   *farFOravuyu*
- a silver one   **серебряную**   *siRYEbryanuyu*
- a temporary one   **временную**   *VRYEminuyu*

Can you fix _____?	**Вы можете починить _____?** *VY MOzhitye pachiNIT'*

- this bridge   **этот мост**   *Etat MOST*
- this crown   **эту коронку**   *Etu kaRONku*
- my denture   **зубной протез**   *zubNOY praTYES*
- this false tooth   **этот вставной зуб**   *Etat fstavNOY ZUP*

When should I return?	**Когда мне вернуться?** *kagDA MNYE virNUtsa*
How much will it cost?	**Сколько это стоит?** *SKOL'ka Eta STOit*

OPTICIANS

Can you repair these glasses?	**Вы можете починить эти очки?** *VY MOzhitye pachiNIT' Eti achKI*

I've broken a lens.	**Я разбил стекло.** *YA razBIL stiKLO*
The frame broke.	**Разбилась оправа.** *razBIlas' aPRAva*
The arm is broken.	**Сломан заушник.** *SLOman zaUSHnik*
Can you put in a new lens?	**Можно вставить новое стекло?** *MOZHna FSTAvit' NOvaye stiKLO*
Can you tighten the screw?	**Можно подвернуть винтик?** *MOZHna padvirNUT' VINtik*
I need them urgently.	**Мне нужно срочно.** *MNYE NUZHna SROCHna*
I don't have an extra pair.	**У меня нет запасных.** *u miNYA NYET zapasNYKH*
Do you have contact lenses?	**У вас есть контактные линзы?** *u VAS YEST' kanTAKTniye LINzy*
Can you replace it immediately?	**Можете заменить сейчас?** *MOzhitye zamiNIT' siyCHAS*
Do you sell sunglasses?	**У вас продаются солнечные очки?** *u VAS pradaYUtsa SOLnichninye achKI*

THE HANDICAPPED

What's the Russian for ____?	**Как по-русски ____?** *KAK pa-RUSki*
■ cane	**палка** *PALka*

■ crutches	**костыли** *kostyLI*
■ glasses	**очки** *achKI*
■ hearing aid	**слуховой аппарат** *slukhaVOY apaRAT*
■ sign language	**немая азбука** *nyeMAya AZbuka*
■ walker	**ходунки** *khadunKI*
■ wheelchair	**инвалидное кресло** *invaLIDnaye KRESla*

Handicapped Accessibility

Persons with physical challenges will find many individuals willing to help, but, as previously mentioned, the basic infrastructure for handicapped accessibility is still lacking in most places in Russia. You will find signs setting seats aside in busses, trolleys, and on the metro (**Места для инвалидов** *myeSTA GLYA invaLIdaf*). You will find Russians generally solicitous to your needs in theaters, hotels, museums, and so on, but you should expect to have yourself and your wheelchair carried up and down stairs and onto public transportation. Remember also that you must be able to cover long distances on foot even to reach public transportation or to transfer from one station or stop to another. Elevators are not available in the metro systems.

NOTE: The contemporary Russian language has not developed a vocabulary sensitive to people with physical challenges. Expressions increasingly common in English such as "visually impaired," "hearing impaired," and even "physically challenged" are simply not in current usage. The following basic phrases are provided to communicate your needs and situation to your Russian hosts.

I am blind. (*f*)	**Я слепая.**	*YA slyePAya*
I am blind. (*m*)	**Я слепой.**	*YA slyePOY*
He is deaf.	**Он глухой.**	*ON gluKHOY*
She is deaf.	**Она глухая.**	*aNA gluKHAya*
She is lame.	**Она хромая.**	*aNA khraMAya*
He is lame.	**Он хормой.**	*ON khraMOY*

Travel Tips Experienced travelers to Russia always carry a packet of tissues with them to use as napkins and to wipe their glasses, which fog up when going from the outdoor chill into the warmth of the metro stations. In an emergency the tissues can substitute for toilet paper, sometimes in short supply. Other useful items are a pocket knife with screwdriver and corkscrew, plastic bags for wet clothes or shoes, a tube of spot remover, rubber bands, small packets of laundry detergent, a travel clothesline, and a sink stopper.

COMMUNICATIONS

Most post offices are open from 9:00 AM to 6:00 PM with a one-hour break for lunch. The main post, telegraph, and telephone office on Tverskaya Street is open around the clock. Mail boxes are painted bright blue. Stamps are also available at many newsstands and kiosks. You might consider mailing home books that you purchase as gifts: the cost is minimal, and you will be less burdened on the way home. In addition, you'll delight your friends with colorful, varied stamps from Russia. They make great collector's items.

POST OFFICE (ПОЧТА)

I want to mail a letter.	**Я хочу послать письмо.** *YA khaCHU paSLAT' piS'MO*
Where's a post office?	**Где почта?** *GDYE POCHta*
Where's the mailbox?	**Где почтовый ящик?** *GDYE pachTOvy YAshik*
What is the postage on ____?	**Сколько стоит ____?** *SKOL'ka STOit*
▪ a letter	**письмо** *piS'MO*
▪ an airmail letter	**авиаписьмо** *aviapiS'MO*
▪ an insured/ certified letter	**ценное письмо** *TSEnaye piS'MO*
▪ a registered letter	**заказное письмо** *zakazNOye piS'MO*
▪ a special delivery letter	**письмо с доставкой** *piS'MO z daSTAFkay*
▪ a package	**посылка** *paSYLka*
▪ a postcard	**открытка** *atKRYTka*

▣ printed matter	**бандероль**	*bandiROL'*
to the USA	**в США**	*f SA SHA A*
to Canada	**в Канаду**	*f kaNAdu*
to Australia	**в Австралию**	*v afSTRAliyu*
to England	**в Англию**	*v ANgliyu*

When will it arrive?
(be received)
Когда получат? *kagDA paLUchat*

Which window is
for _____?
Какое окно за _____? *kaKOye akNO za*

▣ general delivery
до востребования *da vasTREYbavaniya*

▣ money order
денежный перевод *DYEnizhny piriVOT*

▣ stamps
марки *MARki*

▣ collector's
stamps
коллекционные марки *kaliktsiOniye MARki*

Are there any
letters for me?
Есть письма для меня? *YEST' PIS'ma dlya miNYA*

My name is _____.
Меня зовут _____. *miNYA zaVUT*

Please give
me _____.
Дайте мне, пожалуйста _____. *DAYte MNYE paZHAlusta*

▣ ten postcards
десять открыток *DYEsit' atKYRtak*

▣ five 20-kopeck
stamps
пять марок по двадцать *PYAT' MArak pa DVAtsat'*

TELEPHONES (ТЕЛЕФОНЫ)

You usually can place local calls from your hotel room,
either by dialing directly or by first dialing a single number
for an outside line. For most calls within Russia you can also
dial direct.

For international calls it may be less expensive to use your credit card and one of the major carriers, such as ATT, MCI, Sprint, that have local access lines in Moscow and St. Petersburg. Call your credit card company before leaving for Russia to obtain those local numbers, or have your relatives and friends call you. Send them your local number using e-mail!

Telephone booths (sometimes marked **ТАКСОФОН**) are likely to require tokens that can be obtained at many kiosks around town or telephone cards. Cellular phones (**сотовый телефон** *SO-tavy tiliFON*) are increasingly popular and yours might even work there.

You won't always have a telephone book at hand, so be sure to have your own private paper or electronic notebook to record the numbers of friends, colleagues, and new business acquaintances.

Where is _____?	**Где _____?** *GDYE*
■ a pay telephone	**телефон-автомат** *tiliFON-aftaMAT*
■ a telephone booth	**телефонная кабина** *tiliFOnaya kaBIna*
I need a telephone card.	**Мне нужна телефонная карта.** *MNYE nuzhNA tiliFOnaya KARta*
Can I use your phone?	**Можно от вас позвонить?** *MOZHna at VAS pazvaNIT"*
Here is the number.	**Вот номер.** *VOT NOmir*
Can you help me?	**Вы можете мне помочь?** *VY MOzhitye MNYE paMOCH*
I want to order _____.	**Я хочу заказть _____.** *YA khaCHU zakaZAT"*
■ a long-distance call	**междугородный разговор** *mizhdugaRODny razgaVOR*
■ an international call	**мездународный разговор** *mizhdunaRODny razgaVOR*

■ a person-to-person call	**на человека** *na chilaVYEka*
■ a station-to-station call	**на номер** *na NOmir*

What is your telephone number?
Какой у вас номер телефона?
kaKOY u VAS NOmir tiliFOna

And the area code?
И код города? *I KOT GOrada*

Operator, please dial this number for me.
Девушка, набирайте, пожалуйста, этот номер. *DYEvushka, nabiRAYtye paZHAlusta Etat NOmir*

I've been disconnected.
Меня разъединили. *miNYA razyidiNIli*

May I speak with _____?
Можно говорить с _____?
MOZHna gavaRIT' s

I can barely hear you.
Плохо слышно. *PLOkha SLYSHna*

Speak louder!	**Говорите громче!** *gavaRItye GROMche*
Speak slowly!	**Говорите медленно!** *gavaRItye MYEDlina*
Who is speaking?	**Кто говорит?** *KTO gavaRIT*
Who is calling?	**Кто спрашивает?** *KTO SPRAshivayit*
Don't hang up!	**Не кладите трубку!** *NYE klaDItye TRUPku*
The line is busy.	**Занято.** *ZAnyata*
No one answers.	**Никто не подойдёт.** *niKTO NYE padaDYOT*
You've reached a wrong number.	**Вы не туда попали.** *VY NYE tuDA paPAli*
Call back later.	**Перезвоните позже.** *pirizvaNItye POzhe*
Please give him a message.	**Передайте ему, пожалуйста.** *piriDAYtye yiMU paZHAlusta*

FAXES (ТЕЛЕФАКСЫ)

Do you have a fax machine?	**У вас есть телефакс?** *U VAS YEST' tiliFAKS*
What is your fax number?	**Какой у вас номер факса?** *kaKOY U VAS NOmir FAKsa*
I'd like to send you a fax	**Я хотел бы послать вам факс.** *YA khaTYEL BY paSLAT' VAM FAKS*

May I fax this please?	**Можно послать этот факс?** *MOZHna poSLAT" Etat FAKS*
Fax it to me.	**Пошлите мне факсом.** *paSHLIti MNYE FAKsam*
I didn't get your fax.	**Я не получил ваш факс.** *YA NYE paluCHIL VASH FAKS*
Did you receive my fax?	**Вы получили мой факс?** *VY paluCHIli MOY FAKS*
I can't read your fax.	**Я не могу читать ваш факс.** *YA NYE maGU chiTAT" VASH FAKS*
Send it again.	**Пошлите его еще раз.** *paSHLIti yiVO yiSHO RAS*

TELEGRAMS (ТЕЛЕГРАММЫ)

Where do they accept telegrams?	**Где принимают телеграммы?** *GDYE priniMAyut tiliGRAmy*
I want to send _____.	**Я хочу послать _____.** *YA khaCHU paSLAT"*
a fax	**телефакс** *tiliFAKS*
a telegram	**срочную телеграмму** *SROCHnuyu tiliGRAmu*
an international telegram	**международную телеграмму** *mizhdunaRODnuyu tiliGRAmu*
a telex	**телекс** *TYEliks*
How much per word?	**Сколько стоит слово?** *SKOL'ka STOit SLOva*
Where are the forms?	**Где бланки?** *GDYE BLANki*

Can I send it collect?	**Можно послать доплатно?** *MOZHna paSLAT" daPLATna*
How long does a telegram take?	**Сколько времени идёт телеграмма?** *SKOL'ka VRYEmini iDYOT tiliGRAma*

COMPUTERS (КОМПЬЮТЕРЫ)

Personal computers (**персональные компьютеры** *persaNAL'niye kamPYUtery*) and cellular telephones (**сотовые телефоны** *SOtavye teleFOny*) have helped to redefine the world of communication in the twenty-first century. Russians, like people everywhere, want access to the internet (**интернет**) and depend more and more on e-mail (**электронная почта** *elikTROnaya POCHta*). You'll certainly want to know the words and phrases connected with the new technologies.

Where can I buy ____?	**Где можно купить ____?** *GDYE MOZHna kuPIT"*
a desktop computer	**настольный компьютер** *naSTOL'ny kamPYUter*
a portable computer	**переносный компьютер** *piriNOSny kamPYUter*
a laptop	**ноутбук** *NOTbuk*
I need a new ____.	**Мне нужен новый ____.** *MNYE NUzhen NOvy*
printer	**принтер** *PRINter*
modem	**модем** *MOdem*
scanner	**сканер** *SKAner*
hard disk	**жесткий диск** *ZHOski DISK*
monitor	**монитор** *MOnitar*
CPU	**системный блок** *siSTYEMny BLOK*
laptop	**ноутбук** *NOTbuk*

What's the Russian for _____?	**Как но-русски _____?** *KAK pa-RUski*
mouse	**мышь** *MYSH*
keyboard	**клавиатура** *klaviaTUra*
desktop	**рабочий стол** *raBOchi STOL*
file	**файл** *FAIL*
folder	**папка** *PAPka*
enter text	**водить текст** *vaDIT" TYEKST*
delete	**удалить** *udaLIT"*
open	**открыть** *atKRYT"*
close	**закрыть** *zaKRYT"*
save	**сохранить** *sakhraNIT"*
print	**напечатать** *napiCHAtat'*
copy	**скопировать** *skaPIravat'*
cut	**вырезать** *VYrezat'*
paste	**вставить** *FSTAvit'*

How do I connect to the internet?	**Как подключиться к сети интернет?** *KAK potklyuCHItsa k SYEti INternet?*
Who is your provider?	**Кто ваш провайдер?** *KTO VASH praVAIdyer?*

Please help me _____.	**Помогите, пожалуйста _____.** *pamaGItye paZHAlusta*
read my e-mail	**читать электронную почту** *chiTAT" elikTROnuyu POCHtu*
print a text	**печатать текст** *piCHAtat' TYEKST*
find a web page	**найти web страницу*** *NAIti WEB straNItsu*

* NOTE: Many words and expressions related to e-mail, addresses, and web page URLs are written with the Roman alphabet.

GENERAL INFORMATION

Since Russians use the twenty-four hour clock, the PM hours are designated by the numbers thirteen to twenty.

TELLING TIME

What time is it?	**Который сейчас час?**	*kaTOry siyCHAS CHAS*
One o'clock.	**Час.**	*CHAS*
Two o'clock.	**Два часа.**	*DVA chiSA*
Three o'clock.	**Три часа.**	*TRI chiSA*
Four o'clock.	**Четыре часа.**	*chiTYRrye chiSA*
Five o'clock.	**Пять часов.**	*PYAT' chiSOF*
Six o'clock.	**Шесть часов.**	*SHEST' chiSOF*
Seven o'clock.	**Семь часов.**	*SYEM' chiSOF*
Eight o'clock.	**Восемь часов.**	*VOsim' chiSOF*
Nine o'clock.	**Девять часов.**	*DYEvit' chiSOF*
Ten o'clock.	**Десять часов.**	*DYEsit' chiSOF*
Eleven o'clock.	**Одиннадцать часов.**	*aDInatsat' chiSOF*
Twelve o'clock.	**Двенадцать часов.**	*dviNAtsat' chiSOF*

One o'clock PM.	**Тринадцать часов.**	*triNAtsat' chiSOF*
Noon.	**Полдень.**	*POLdyen'*
Midnight.	**Полночь.**	*POLnach*

Once an hour has begun, Russians look forward to the next hour. Thus, 1:05 is "five minutes of the second hour."

1:05	**пять минут второго**	*PYAT miNUT ftaROva*
2:10	**десять минут третьего**	*DYEsit' miNUT TRYET'yiva*
a quarter past three	**четверть четвёртого**	*CHETvirt' chitVYORtava*
4:20	**двадцать минут пятого**	*DVAtsat' miNUT PYAtava*
5:25	**двадцать пять минут шестого**	*DVAtsat' PYAT' miNUT shiSTOva*
half past six	**половина седьмого**	*palaVIna sid'MOva*

After the half hour Russians count backwards from the *next* hour; thus 7:35 is eight minus twenty-five minutes.

7:35	**без двадцати пяти восемь** *byez dvatsaTI piTI VOsim'*
8:40	**без двадцати девять** *byez dvatsaTI DYEvit'*
9:45	**без четверти десять** *byes CHETvirti DYEsit'*
10:50	**без десяти одиннадцать** *byez disiTI aDInatsat'*
11:55	**без пяти двенадцать** *byes piTI dviNAtsat'*

EXPRESSIONS OF TIME

When?	**Когда?** *kagDA*
At what time?	**В котором часу?** *f kaTOram chiSU*
at five o'clock	**в пять часов** *f PYAT' chiSOF*
in an hour	**через час** *CHEris CHAS*
before two	**до двух** *da DVUKH*
after six	**после шести** *POslye shiSTI*
about seven	**около семи** *Okala siMI*
by eight	**к восьми** *k vas' MI*
From what time?	**С какого времени?** *s kaKOva VRYEmini*
Until what time?	**До какого времени?** *da kaKOva VRYEmini*

per hour	за час *za CHAS*
an hour ago	час назад *CHAS naZAT*
late	поздно *POZna*
early	рано *RAna*
on time	вовремя *VOvrimya*
in the morning	утром *Utram*
in the afternoon	днём *DNYOM*
in the evening	вечером *VYEchiram*
a second	секунда *siKUNda*
Just a minute!	**Минуточку!** *miNUtachku*
Right away!	**Сейчас!** *siyCHAS*

DAYS

What day is today?	**Какой сегодня день?** *kaKOY siVODnya DYEN'*
Today is _____.	**Сегодня _____.** *siVODnya*
■ Monday	понедельник *paniDYEL'nik*
■ Tuesday	вторник *FTORnik*
■ Wednesday	среда *sriDA*
■ Thursday	четверг *chitVERK*
■ Friday	пятница *PYATnitsa*
■ Saturday	суббота *suBOta*
■ Sunday	воскресенье *vaskriSYEn'ye*
today	сегодня *siVODnya*
yesterday	вчера *fchiRA*

tomorrow	завтра *ZAFtra*
the day after tomorrow	послезавтра *pasliZAFtra*
the day before yesterday	позавчера *pazafchiRA*
on Wednesday	в среду *f SRYEdu*
a week from Tuesday	во вторник через неделю *va FTORnik CHEris niDYElyu*
a day	день *DYEN'*
a week	неделя *niDYElya*
a month	месяц *MYEsits*
a year	год *GOT*
a working day	рабочий день *raBOchi DYEN'*
a day off	выходной день *vykhadNOY DYEN'*
a holiday	праздник *PRAZnik*

MONTHS

January	январь *yanVAR'*
February	февраль *fiVRAL'*
March	март *MART*
April	апрель *aPRYEL'*
May	май *MAY*
June	июнь *iYUN'*
July	июль *iYUL'*

August	**август** *AVgust*
September	**сентябрь** *sinTYABR'*
October	**октябрь** *akTYABR'*
November	**ноябрь** *naYABR'*
December	**декабрь** *diKABR'*

DATES

What's today's date?	**Какое сегодня число?** *kaKOye siVODnya chiSLO*
The fifth of May.	**Пятое мая.** *PYAtaya MAya*
When did it happen?	**Когда это случилось?** *kagDA Eta sluCHIlas'*
On June 1, 1991.	**Первого июня, девяноста первого года.** *PYERvava iYUnaya diviNOSta PYERvava GOda*

SEASONS

in the spring	**весной** *viSNOY*
in the summer	**летом** *LYEtam*
in the fall	**осенью** *Osin'yu*
in the winter	**зимой** *ziMOY*
every summer	**каждое лето** *KAZHdaye LYEta*
last year	**в прошлом году** *f PROSHlam gaDU*
next year	**в будущем году** *v BUdushim gaDU*

WEATHER

How is the weather today?	**Какая сегодня ногода?** *kaKAya siVODnya paGOda*
The weather today is ____.	**Сегодня погода ____.** *siVODnya paGOda*
■ good	**хорошая** *khaROshaya*
■ bad	**плохая** *plaKHAya*
What splendid weather!	**Какая прекрасная погода!** *kaKAya priKRASnaya paGOda*
Today it's ____.	**Сегодня ____.** *siVODnya*
■ hot	**жарко** *ZHARka*
■ warm	**тепло** *tiPLO*
■ cold	**холодно** *KHOladna*
■ cool	**прохладно** *praKHLADna*
The sun is shining.	**Светит солнце.** *SVYEtit SONtsa*
The wind is blowing.	**Дует ветер.** *DUyit VYEtir*
It's raining.	**Идёт дождь.** *iDYOT DOSH*
It's snowing.	**Идёт снег.** *iDYOT SNYEK*

TEMPERATURE CONVERSIONS

To change degrees Fahrenheit to Centigrade, subtract 32 and multiply by $5/9$.

$$41°F - 32 = 9 \times 5/9 = 5°C$$

To convert from Centigrade to Fahrenheit, multiply by $\frac{5}{9}$ and add 32.

$$10°C \times \frac{9}{5} = 18 + 32 = 50°F$$

To get an approximate temperature quickly, take the degrees Fahrenheit, subtract 30 and divide by 2, or, take the degrees Centigrade, multiply by 2, and add 30.

Most seasoned travelers know a few temperatures for reference.

DEGREES	
FAHRENHEIT	CELSIUS
212	100
98.6	37
86	30
77	25
68	20
50	10
32	0
14	−10
−4	−20
−22	−30
−40	−40

It is small consolation that at minus 40 degrees, Fahrenheit and Centigrade temperatures are identical.

OFFICIAL HOLIDAYS

January 1—New Year's Day

1 января   Новый год

January 7—Russian Orthodox Christmas

7 января   Рождество Христово

March 8—International Women's Day

8 марта   Международный женский день

May 1—May Day Workers' Day	**1 мая Праздник весны и труда**
May 9—Victory Day	**9 мая День победы**
June 14—Russian Independence Day	**14 июня Декларация о государственном суверенитете**
November 7—Day of Conciliation*	**7 ноября День согласия и примирения**

* In the Soviet era the day to celebrate the Great October Socialist Revolution.

Happy birthday!	**С днём рождения!** *z DNYOM raZHDYEniya*
Happy holiday!	**С праздником!** *s PRAZnikam*
Happy New Year!	**С Новым годом!** *s NOvym GOdam*

The Russian Orthodox Church still observes Christmas and Easter according to the pre-revolutionary calendar.

| Merry Christmas! (with the birth of Christ) | **С Рождеством Христовым!** *s razhdiSTVOM khriSTOvym* |
| Happy Easter! (Christ is risen) | **Христос воскресе!** *khriSTOS vaSKRYEs'ye* |

RUSSIA AND ITS NEIGHBORS

Until 1991 there were fifteen republics in what was then known as the Soviet Union (**Советский Союз** *saVYETski saYUS*), officially the Union of Soviet Socialist Republics, abbreviated in Russian as **CCCP** (*ES-ES-ES-ER*). There are now fifteen independent countries, with several of them belonging to a loose Confederation of Independent States (CIS), abbreviated **СНГ** (**Содружество Независимых Государтсв** *saDRUzhestva nyezaVIsimykh gasuDARTSF*). The official name of what we call "Russia" is the Russian Federation (**Российская Федерация** *raSIskaya fidiRAtsiya*) with its capital in Moscow (**Москва** *maskVA*).

Armenia (capital, Yerevan)	**Армения (Ереван)**
Azerbaijan (Baku)	**Азербайджан (Баку)**
Belarus (Minsk)	**Беларусь (Минск)**
Estonia (Tallinn)	**Эстония (Таллинн)**
Georgia (Tbilisi)	**Грузия (Тбилиси)**
Kazakhstan (Almaty)	**Казахстан (Алма-Ата)**
Kyrgyzstan (Bishkek)	**Кыргызстан (Бишкек)**
Latvia (Riga)	**Латвия (Рига)**
Lithuania (Vilnius)	**Литва (Вильнюс)**
Moldova (Chisinau)	**Молдова (Кишинёв)**
Russia (Moscow)	**Россия (Москва)**
Tajikistan (Dushanbe)	**Таджикистан (Душанбе)**
Turkmenistan (Ashgabat)	**Туркменистан (Ашхабад)**
Ukraine (Kiev)	**Украина (Киев)**
Uzbekistan (Tashkent)	**Узбекистан (Ташкент)**

Only since 1991 have Russians distinguished between citizenship and nationality. A citizen of the Russian Federation says:

| I'm a Russian citizen. | **Я россиянин.** *(m)* *YA rasiYAnin* |
| | **Я россиянка.** *(f)* *YA rasiYANka* |

But to speak of his or her nationality he or she says:

I'm a Russian.	**Я русский.** *(m)* *YA RUski*
	Я русская. *(f)* *YA RUskaya*
I'm an Estonian.	**Я эстонец.** *(m)* *YA eSTOnits*
	Я эстонка. *(f)* *YA eSTONka*
I'm a Ukrainian.	**Я украинец.** *(m)* *YA ukraInits*
	Я украинка. *(f)* *YA ukraINka*

Using the same principles, you can identify yourself.

I'm American.	**Я американец.** *(m)* *YA amiriKAnits*
	Я американка. *(f)* *YA amiriKANka*
I'm Australian.	**Я австралиец.** *(m)* *YA afstraLIyits*
	Я австралийка. *(f)* *YA afstraLIYka*
I'm British.	**Я англичанин.** *(m)* *YA angliCHAnin*
	Я англичанка. *(f)* *YA angliCHANka*
I'm Canadian.	**Я канадец.** *(m)* *YA kaNAdits*
	Я канадка. *(f)* *YA kaNATka*

COUNTRIES AND NATIONALITIES

Where are you from?	**Откуда вы?** *otKUda VY*
I'm from _____ (plus genitive case).	**Я из _____.** *YA IS*
Africa	**Африка** *AFrika*
Asia	**Азия** *Aziya*
Australia	**Австралия** *afSTRAliya*
Europe	**Европа** *yiVROpa*
America	**Америка** *aMYErika*
Austria	**Австрия** *AFstriya*
Belgium	**Бельгия** *BYEL'giya*
Canada	**Канада** *kaNAda*
China	**Китай** *kiTAY*
England	**Англия** *ANgliya*
France	**Франция** *FRANtsiya*
Germany	**Германия** *girMAniya*
Greece	**Греция** *GRYEtsiya*
Hungary	**Венгрия** *VYENgriya*
India	**Индия** *INdiya*
Ireland	**Ирландия** *irLANdiya*
Israel	**Израиль** *izraIL'*
Italy	**Италия** *iTAliya*

Japan	**Япония**	*yaPOniya*
Norway	**Норвегия**	*narVYEgiya*
Poland	**Польша**	*POL'sha*
Portugal	**Португалия**	*partuGAliya*
Russia	**Россия**	*raSIya*
Scotland	**Шотландия**	*shatLANdiya*
Spain	**Испания**	*iSPAniya*
Sweden	**Швеция**	*SHVEtsiya*
Switzerland	**Швейцария**	*shviyTSAriya*
the United States	**Соединённые Штаты**	*sayidiNYOniye SHTAty*

DIRECTIONS

north	**север**	*SYEvir*
south	**юг**	*YUK*
east	**восток**	*vaSTOK*
west	**запад**	*ZApat*

IMPORTANT SIGNS

Вверх	*VVYERKH*	Up
Вниз	*VNIS*	Down
Вход	*FKHOT*	Entrance

Выход	*VYkhat*	Exit
Женщины	*ZHENshiny*	Women
Заказано	*zaKAzana*	Reserved
Закрыто	*zaKRYta*	Closed
Занято	*ZAnita*	Occupied
Запасный выход	*zaPASny VYkhat*	Emergency Exit
Идите	*iDItye*	Go
К себе	*k siBYE*	Pull
Касса	*KAsa*	Cashier
Лифт	*LIFT*	Elevator
Мест нет	*MYEST NYET*	No Vacancies (no places)
Мужчины	*mushCHIny*	Men
Не курить	*NYE kuRIT'*	No Smoking
Не трогать	*NYE TROgat'*	Don't Touch
Остановка автобуса	*astaNOFka aFTObusa*	Bus Stop
Осторожно	*astaROZHna*	Caution
От себя	*at siBYA*	Push
Открыто	*atKRYta*	Open
Перерыв	*piriRYF*	On Break
Стойте	*STOYtye*	Wait
Туалет	*tuaLYET*	Toilet

ABBREVIATIONS

АН	Академия Наук	Academy of Sciences
АЭС	атомная электростанция	atomic power station
АО	акционерное общество	joint stock company
ГАИ	Государственная автомобильная инспекция	State Automobile Inspection
ГУМ	Государственный универсальный магазин	State Department Store
ГЭС	гидроэлектрическая станция	hydroelectric station
ин.	иностранный	foreign
и т.д.	и так далее	et cetera (etc.)
и т.п.	и тому подобное	and so forth
к.	копейка	kopeck
кг.	килограмм	kilogram
КП	Коммунистическая партия	Communist Party
гр.	гражданин *(m)*	citizen
гр-ка	гражданка *(f)*	citizen
МГУ	Московский государственный университет	Moscow State University
мл.	младший	junior
мм.	миллиметр	millimeter
пк	персональный компьютер	PC—personal computer
р.	рубль	ruble
РФ	Российская Федерация	Russian Federation
СНГ	Содружество Независимых Государтсв	Confederation of Independent States
ст.	старший	senior
ст.	станция	station
стр.	страница	page
США		USA
ц.	цена	price
ч.	час	o'clock
шт.	штука	an item

METRIC CONVERSIONS

If you are not used to the metric system, you'll need the following tables and conversion charts during your visit to Russia.

SOME CONVENIENT ROUGH EQUIVALENTS

These are rough approximations, but they'll help you to "think metric" when you don't have a pocket calculator handy.

3 километра (kilometers) = 2 miles
30 грамм (grams) = 1 ounce
100 грамм (grams) = 3.5 ounces
1 килограмм (kilogram) = 2 pounds
1 литр (liter) = 1 quart
1 гектар (hectare) = 1 acre

CENTIMETERS/INCHES

It is usually unnecessary to make exact conversions from inches to the metric system, but to give you an approximate idea of how they compare, we give the following guide.

To convert **сантиметры** *santiMYEtry* (centimeters) to **дюймы** *DYUYmy* (inches), multiply by 0.39.

To convert inches (**дюймы**) to centimeters (**сантиметры**), multiply by 2.54.

Сантиметры

Дюймы

METERS/FEET

1 **метр** (meter) = **39.37 дюймов** (inches)
1 **фут** (foot) = **0.3 метр** (meter)
1 **метр** (meter) = **3.28 фута** (feet)
1 **ярд** (yard) = **0.9 метр** (meter)
1 **метр** (meter) = **1.09 ярд** (yard)

How tall are you in meters? See for yourself.

ФУТЫ/ДЮЙМЫ (FEET/INCHES)	МЕТРЫ/САНТИМЕТРЫ (METERS/CENTIMETERS)
5	1.52
5 1	1.545
5 2	1.57
5 3	1.595
5 4	1.62
5 5	1.645
5 6	1.68
5 7	1.705
5 8	1.73
5 9	1.755
5 10	1.78
5 11	1.805
6	1.83
6 1	1.855

WHEN YOU WEIGH YOURSELF

1 килограмм (kilogram) = **2.2 фунта** (pounds)
1 фунт (pound) = **0.45 килограмма** (kilogram)

КИЛОГРАММЫ KILOGRAMS	ФУНТЫ POUNDS
40	88
45	99
50	110
55	121
60	132
65	143
70	154
75	165
80	176
85	187
90	198
95	209
100	220

LIQUID MEASUREMENTS

1 литр (liter) = **1.06 кварта** (quart)
4 литра (liters) = **1.06 галлон** (gallon)
For quick approximate conversion, multiply the number of gallons (**галлоны**) by 4 to get liters (**литры**). Divide the number of **литры** (liters) by 4 to get **галлоны** (gallons).

EMERGENCY TELEPHONE NUMBERS

Fire	**Пожарная охрана 01**
Police	**Милиция 02**
Medical care	**Скорая помощь 03**
Gas leaks	**Газ 04**

MINI-DICTIONARY FOR BUSINESS TRAVELERS

amount	сумма	*SUma*
appraise	оценивать	*aTSEnivat'*
authorize	уполномочивать	*upalnaMOchivat'*
authorized edition	авторизованное издание	*avtariZOvanaye izDAniye*
bill	счёт	*SHOT*
bill of exchange	вексель	*VYEKsil'*
bill of lading	коносамент	*kanasaMYENT*
bill of sale	товарный чек	*taVARny CHEK*
business operation	дело	*DYEla*
buy	купить	*kuPIT'*
cash payment	наличный расчёт	*naLICHny raSHOT*
cash a check	получить деньги по чеку	*paluCHIT' DYEN'gi pa CHEku*
certified check	расчётный чек	*raSHOTny CHEK*
chamber of commerce	торговая палата	*tarGOvaya paLAta*
compensation for damages	возмещение убытков	*vazmiSHEniye uBYTkaf*
competition	конкуренция	*kankuRYENtsiya*
competitive price	конкурентоспо-собная цена	*kankurintaspa-SOBnaya tsiNA*

contract	контракт	*kanTRAKT*
contractual obligations	контрактные обязательства	*kanTRAKTniye abiZAtil'stva*
controlling interest	контрольный пакет акций	*kanTROL'ny paKYET AKtsi*
co-owner	совладелец	*savlaDYElits*
co-partner	партнёр	*partNYOR*
delivery	поставка	*paSTAFka*
down payment	первоначальный платёж	*pirvanaCHAL'ny plaTYOSH*
(payment) due	подлежит оплате	*padliZHYT" aPLAtye*
enterprise	предприятие	*pritpriYAtiye*
expedite delivery	продвинуть поставку	*praDVInut' paSTAFku*
expenses	затраты / расходы	*zaTRAty / rasKHOdy*
goods	товары	*taVAry*
hard currency	валюта	*vaLYUta*
infringement of patent rights	нарушение патентных прав	*naruSHEniye paTYENTnykh PRAF*
installment	рассрочка	*raSROCHka*
insurance	страхование	*strakhaVAniye*
international law	международное право	*mizhdunaROD-naye PRAva*
lawful possessions	законное имущество	*zaKOnaye iMUshistva*

lawsuit	судебный процесс	*suDYEBny praTSES*
lawyer	адвокат	*advaKAT*
letter of credit	аккредитив	*akridiTIF*
mail-order business	посылочная фирма	*paSYlachnaya FIRma*
manager	директор / заведующий	*diRYEKtar / zaVYEdushi*
market value (price)	рыночная цена	*RYnachnaya tsiNA*
overdue	просроченный	*praSROchiny*
payment	платёж	*plaTYOSH*
partial payment	частичный платёж	*chiSTICHny plaTYOSH*
price	цена	*tsiNA*
property	имущество	*iMUshistva*
purchasing agent	покупателный агент	*pakuPAtil'ny aGYENT*
put on the market	поставить на рынок	*paSTAvit' na RYnak*
retail price	розничная цена	*ROZnichnaya tsiNA*
sale	продажа	*praDAzha*
sales tax	налог на полупки	*naLOK na paKUPki*
to sell	продавать	*pradaVAT"*
to send	послать	*paSLAT"*
to send back	возвращать	*vazvraSHAT"*

to send COD	послать наложенным платежом	*paSLAT" naLOzhinym platiZHOM*
shipment	отправка / отгрузка	*atPRAFka / adGRUSka*
tax	налог	*naLOK*
tax-exempt	освобождённый от налогов	*asvabazhDYOny at naLOgaf*
trade	торговля	*tarGOvlya*
transact business	вести дела	*viSTI diLA*
transfer	перевод	*piriVOT*
transportation charges	плата на транспорт / на перевозку	*PLAta na TRANSport / na piriVOSku*
via	через	*CHEris*
yield a profit	приносить прибыль	*prinaSIT" PRIbyl'*

председатель

Travel Tips Russia is not the place to show
off your new wardrobe. Often you will be wrapped in a
warm overcoat. Why not take along some well-worn
items that you are tired of and planning to part with
anyway? Before departure you can leave the items
with the maid or "key lady," who will find good use for
them. This way you save on laundry and make some
room for the souvenirs that you are bound to
accumulate during the trip.

QUICK GRAMMAR GUIDE

Russian is an inflected language. Nouns, pronouns, modifiers, and verbs change their forms to convey different meanings. Normally, the lexical meaning of the word is in the root, the beginning part of a word. The grammatical meaning is contained in the different endings.

NOUNS

Russian nouns are classed according to their gender, number, and case. They can be masculine, feminine, or neuter. Gender is a grammatical category not necessarily coinciding with biological reality. Masculine nouns usually end in a consonant. Feminine nouns often end in **-a** or **-я**. Neuter nouns generally end in **-o** or **-e**.

Russian nouns can be singular or plural in each of the six cases: nominative, accusative, genitive, prepositional, dative, and instrumental. (Tip: It suffices in most situations to know the nominative and accusative cases.)

MASCULINE NOUNS

SINGULAR	HARD CONSONANTS	SOFT CONSONANTS
Nominative	журнал	портфель
Accusative	журнал	портфель
Genitive	журнала	портфеля
Prepositional	журнале	портфеле
Dative	журналу	портфелю
Instrumental	журналом	портфелем

PLURAL		
Nominative	журналы	портфели
Accusative	журналы	портфели
Genitive	журналов	портфелей
Prepositional	журналах	портфелях
Dative	журналам	портфелям
Instrumental	журналами	портфелями

The accusative singular and plural forms for Russian animate (i.e. persons and animals) masculine nouns are the same as the genitive case forms.

NEUTER NOUNS

SINGULAR	ENDING IN -o	ENDING IN -e
Nominative	письмо	здание
Accusative	письмо	здание
Genitive	письма	здания
Prepositional	письме	здании
Dative	письму	зданию
Instrumental	письмом	зданием
PLURAL		
Nominative	письма	здания
Accusative	письма	здания
Genitive	писем	зданий
Prepositional	письмах	зданиях
Dative	письмам	зданиям
Instrumental	письмами	зданиями

FEMININE NOUNS

SINGULAR	ENDING IN -a	ENDING IN -я
Nominative	телеграмма	тётя
Accusative	телеграмму	тётю
Genitive	телеграммы	тёти
Prepositional	телеграмме	тёте
Dative	телеграмме	тёте
Instrumental	телеграммой	тётей
PLURAL		
Nominative	телеграммы	тёти
Accusative	телеграммы	тётей
Genitive	телеграмм	тётей
Prepositional	телеграммах	тётях
Dative	телеграммам	тётям
Instrumental	телеграммами	тётями

The accusative plural forms for Russian animate (i.e. persons) feminine nouns are the same as the genitive case plural forms. Some Russian feminine nouns end in the soft sign -ь, and a few neuter nouns end in -я. In both instances the nominative and accusative cases are identical.

You may see some variations of the above endings caused by spelling rules in Russian. The three key rules are

"8" rule: After these eight letters (г, к, х, ж, ч, ш, щ, ц) you may not write the letters я or ю, but must replace them with а or у.

"7" rule: After these seven letters (г, к, х, ж, ч, ш, щ) you may not write the letter ы, but must write и.

"5" rule: After these five letters (ж, ч, ш, щ, ц) you may write the letter о only if it is accented. When it is not accented, you replace the expected о with the letter е.

PRONOUNS

Pronouns replace, or stand in for, nouns. They also have gender, number, and case. The following personal pronouns are important for travelers.

SINGULAR	I	YOU	HE (IT)	SHE
Nom.	я	ты	он (оно)	она
Acc.	меня	тебя	его	её
Gen.	меня	тебя	его	её
Prep.	мне	тебе	нём	ней
Dat.	мне	тебе	ему	ей
Instr.	мной	тобой	им	ей

PLURAL	WE	YOU	THEY
Nom.	мы	вы	они
Acc.	нас	вас	их
Gen.	нас	вас	их
Prep.	нас	вас	них
Dat.	нам	вам	им
Instr.	нами	вами	ими

	WHO?	WHAT?
Nom.	кто	что
Acc.	кого	что
Gen.	кого	чего
Prep.	ком	чём
Dat.	кому	чему
Inst.	кем	чем

ADJECTIVES/POSSESSIVE MODIFIERS

Modifiers in Russian agree with the noun in gender, number, and case. Knowing the spelling rule will help you figure out these endings. (Hint: When the ending of the noun changes, the ending of the modifier is also likely to change.)

	SINGULAR Masculine	Neuter	Feminine	PLURAL All Genders
Nom.	новый	новое	новая	новые
Acc.	новый	новое	новую	новые
Gen.	нового	нового	новой	новых
Prep.	новом	новом	новой	новых
Dat.	новому	новому	новой	новым
Instr.	новым	новым	новой	новыми
Nom.	мой	моё	моя	мои
Acc.	мой	моё	мою	мои
Gen.	моего	моего	моей	моих
Prep.	моём	моём	моей	моих
Dat.	моему	моему	моей	моим
Instr.	моим	моим	моей	моими
Nom.	наш	наше	наша	наши
Acc.	наш	наше	нашу	наши
Gen.	нашего	нашего	нашей	наших
Prep.	нашем	нашем	нашей	наших
Dat.	нашему	нашему	нашей	нашим
Instr.	нашим	нашим	нашей	нашими

ADVERBS

Russian adverbs do not change their form. Most are readily identifiable by the endings **-ое/-е** or **-и**. Some examples are

quickly	**быстро**
slowly	**медленно**
of course	**конечно**
automatically	**автоматически**

To make the comparative adverbs (quicker, slower, etc.) you change the **-о** into **-ее**

quicker	**быстрее**
slower	**медленнее**

To make the comparative of adverbs ending in **-и** you add **более** (more) or **менее** (less) before the word.

more automatically	**более автоматически**
less practically	**менее практически**

VERBS

The dictionary form of most verbs (the infinitive) ends in **-ть**. All Russian verbs have aspect, a grammatical category rendered in other ways in English. Russian aspect can be perfective or imperfective and reflects a Russian's way of looking at the world.

THE PAST TENSE

The past tense is formed by replacing the **-ть** of the infinitive form with **-л** for the masculine singular or adding

-ла for the feminine singular, -ло for the neuter singular, or
-ли for all plurals.

TO SELL	ПРОДАВАТЬ
I was selling.	Я продавал.
Masha was selling.	Маша продавала.
We, You, They sold.	Мы, Вы, Они продавали.

TO BUY	КУПИТЬ
Ivan bought.	Иван купил.
Irina bought.	Ирина купила.
We, You, They bought.	Мы, Вы, Они купили.

IMPERFECTIVE PRESENT/ PERFECTIVE FUTURE

Russian verbs belong to one of two conjugations (verb classes). The final consonants in both conjugations are the same: only the vowels **e** or **и** change to indicate that a verb belongs to the first or second conjugation. If the verb is imperfective, the conjugated form is in the present tense. The conjugated form of a perfective verb signifies the future.

FIRST CONJUGATION		SECOND CONJUGATION	
TO WORK	РАБОТАТЬ	TO SPEAK WITH	ПОГОВОРИТЬ
I work.	Я работаю.	I'll speak.	Я поговорю.
You work.	Ты работаешь.	You'll speak.	Ты поговоришь.
He works.	Он работает.	She'll speak.	Она поговорит.
We work.	Мы работаем.	We'll speak.	Мы поговорим.
You work.	Вы работаете.	You'll speak.	Вы поговорите.
They work.	Они работают.	They'll speak.	Они поговорят.

THE IMPERFECTIVE FUTURE

To form the future of imperfective verbs, add the future forms of the verb "to be" **быть** to the imperfective infinitive.

TO BE	БЫТЬ	TO WORK	РАБОТАТЬ
I will be	**я буду**	I will be working.	**Я буду работать.**
you will be	**ты будешь**	You will be working.	**Ты будешь работать.**
she will be	**она будет**	He will be working.	**Он будет работать.**
we will be	**мы будем**	We will be working.	**Мы будем работать.**
you will be	**бы будете**	You will be working.	**Вы будете работать.**
they will be	**они будут**	They will be working.	**Они будут работать.**

COMMANDS

Most commands will be easily identifiable. Almost all have the ending **-айте/-яйте** or **-ите**.

Listen!	**Слушайте!**
Repeat!	**Повторяйте!**
Look!	**Смотрите!**
Help!	**Помогите!**
Go away!	**Отойдите!**

QUESTIONS

Most questions in Russian can be formed by using one of the interrogative pronouns (question words).

Who?	**Кто?**	*KTO*
What?	**Что?**	*SHTO*
Where?	**Где?**	*GDYE*
Where to?	**Куда?**	*kuDA*
When?	**Когда?**	*kagDA*
Why?	**Почему?**	*pachiMU*
How?	**Как?**	*KAK*
How much?	**Сколько?**	*SKOL'ka*

In a sentence without an interrogative, Russians use a rising tone on the word in question.

Are you working <u>on</u> Saturday?	**Вы работаете в субботу?**
Do you want to go?	**Вы хотите <u>пойти</u>?**

NEGATIONS

Form the negative by placing **не** before the verb or any other word you wish to negate.

I don't speak Ukrainian.	**Я не говорю по-украински.**
No, not that one.	**Нет, не это.**

You can always use the famous Russian "NO"—**НЕТ** for emphasis.

WORD ORDER

In general, Russian word order is freer than English. A basic rule is that any new information and consequently the most important facts are found at the end of the sentence.

PREPOSITIONS

Most prepositions are not accented in speech but are pronounced together with the following word. The list below should be helpful.

about	о	*a*
according to	по	*pa*
across	через	*CHEris*
after	после	*POslye*
among	среди	*sriDI*
around	вокруг	*vaKRUK*
at	у	*u*
before	до / перед	*da / PYErit*
behind	за	*za*
between	между	*MYEZHdu*
down	вниз	*VNIS*
during	во время	*va VRYEmya*
except	кроме	*KROmye*
for	для	*dlya*
from	из / с / от	*is / s / at*
in	в	*v*
in front of	перед	*PYErit*
inside	внутри	*vnuTRI*
on	на	*na*
on top	над	*nat*
opposite	напротив	*naPROtif*
outside	вне	*vnye*

through	**через**	*CHEris*
to	**в / на**	*v / na*
toward	**к**	*k*
under	**под**	*pat*
until	**до**	*da*
with	**с**	*s*
without	**без**	*byes*

Travel Tips Russians love winter and impatiently await its arrival. Dress warmly and wear waterproof shoes or boots because the distances between buildings are great and the streets and sidewalks tend to be slushy from October through May. You might purchase a fur hat with ear flaps (**ушанка** *uSHANka*) as a practical addition to your wardrobe and a great souvenir of your visit.

READY REFERENCE KEY

Here are some phrases and words from the book that you are likely to use often. For a more extensive list of phrases, refer to the appropriate chapter in the book.

SIMPLE WORDS AND PHRASES

Do you speak English?	**Вы говорите по-английски?** *VY gavaRItye pa-anGLIYski*
I speak a little Russian.	**Я говорю немного по-русски.** *YA gavaRYU niMNOga pa-RUski*
Do you understand?	**Вы понимаете?** *VY paniMAyitye*
I understand.	**Я понимаю.** *YA paniMAyu*
I don't understand.	**Я не понимаю.** *YA NYE paniMAyu*
How do you say _____ in Russian?	**Как _____ по-русски?** *KAK pa-RUski*
Please repeat.	**Повторите, пожалуйста.** *paftaRItye paZHAlusta*

BEING POLITE

Hello.	**Здравствуйте.** *ZDRASTvuytye*
Yes.	**Да.** *DA*
No.	**Нет.** *NYET*

Please.	**Пожалуйста.** *paZHAlusta*
Thank you.	**Спасибо.** *spaSIba*
Excuse me!	**Извините!** *izviNItye*
That's all right.	**Хорошо.** *kharaSHO*
It doesn't matter.	**Ничего.** *nichiVO*
Good-bye.	**До свидания.** *da sviDAniya*

BASIC NEEDS

What is it?	**Что это?** *SHTO Eta*
When?	**Когда?** *kagDA*
Where?	**Где?** *GDYE*
Where to?	**Куда?** *kuDA*
■ to the right	**направо** *naPRAva*
■ to the left	**налево** *naLYEva*
■ straight ahead	**прямо** *PRYAma*
How much does it cost?	**Сколько стоит?** *SKOL'ka STOit*
I'd like _____.	**Мне хочется _____.** *MNYE KHOchitsa*
Please bring me _____.	**Принесите мне, пожалуйста _____.** *priniSItye MNYE paZHAlusta*
Please show me _____.	**Покажите мне, пожалуйста _____.** *pakaZHYtye MNYE paZHAlusta*

ENGLISH-RUSSIAN DICTIONARY

Accented syllables are indicated by capital letters in the italicized phonetic transcription. Verbs are identified according to their aspects: (*i*) imperfective; (*p*) perfective. Nouns that end in the soft sign "**ь**" are either (*m*) masculine or (*f*) feminine; neuter nouns that do not end in **o** or **e** are indicated by an (*n*). All definitions reflect only the usage(s) actually presented in the chapters of this book.

A

abdomen живот *zhiVOT*

able мочь (i) *MOCH*

about о / об *O / OP*

above над *NAT*

abscess нарыв *naRYF*

accept принимать (i) *priniMAT'*

accepted, acceptable принято *PRInita*

according to по *PO*

account счёт *SHOT*

accumulate набраться (p) *naBRAtsa*

ace (cards) туз *TUS*

achievement достижение *dastiZHEniye*

get acquainted познакомиться (p) *paznaKOmitsa*

across через *CHEris*

active действующий *DYEYSTvuyushi*

adapter адаптер *aDAPtir*

address адрес *Adris*

adhesive tape пластырь (m) *plaSTYR'*

administrator администратор *adminiSTRAtar*

advance: in advance заранее *zaRAniye*

Africa Африка *Afrika*

after после *POslye*

afternoon: in the afternoon днём *DNYOM;* **good afternoon.** добрый день. *DObry DYEN'*

ago назад *naZAT*

ahead: straight ahead прямо *PRYAma*

aid помощь (f) *POmash*

air mattress надувной матрац *naduvNOY maTRATS*

aircraft самолёт *samaLYOT*

airmail letter авиаписьмо *aviapiS'MO*

airport аэропорт *aeraPORT*

aisle проход *praKHOT*

alarm clock будильник *buDIL'nik*

alcohol спирт *SPIRT*

all (everything) всё *FSYO*

all (everyone) все *FSYE*

allergy аллергия *alirGIya*

allow (may I) разрешить (p) *razriSHYT'*

almonds миндаль (m) *minDAL'*

almost чуть *CHUT'*

alone (m) один *aDIN*

alone (f) одна *aDNA*

already уже *uZHE*

also также *TAKzhe*

amalgam амальгама
amal'GAma

amber янтарь (m) *yanTAR'*

ambulance скорая помощь
SKOraya POmash

America Америка *aMYErika*

American (m) американец
amiriKAnits

American (f) американка
amiriKANka

American американский
amiriKANski

amethyst аметист *amiTIST*

among среди *sriDI*

amount сумма *SUma*

and и / а *I /A*

ankle лодышка *laDYSHka*

anniversary годовщина
gadafSHIna

another (more) ещё *yiSHO*

antacid щёлочь (f) *SHOlach*

antique store комиссионный
магазин *kamisiOny*
magaZIN

antiseptic антисептик
antiSYEPtik

anyone кто-нибудь *KTO-*
nibut'

appetizer закуска *zaKUSka*

apple яблоко *YAblaka*

make an appointment (sign up) записаться (p)
zapiSAtsa

appraise оценивать (i)
aTSEnivat'

approach подойти (p)
padayTI

apricot абрикос *abriKOS*

April апрель (m) *aPRYEL'*

aquamarine аквамарин
akvamaRIN

area code код города *KOT*
GOrada

arm рука *ruKA*

around вокруг *vaKRUK*

arrive прибывать (i)
pribyVAT'

art искусство *isKUSTva*

artist художник
khuDOZHnik

ASA ГОСТ *GOST*

ashtray пепельница
PYEpil'nitsa

ask спрашивать (i)
SPRAshivat'

asparagus спаржа *SPARzha*

aspirin аспирин *aspiRIN*

assortment ассорти (n)
asarTI

at у *U*

ATM (automatic teller machine) банкомат
bankaMAT

attack приступ *PRIstup*

attraction
достопримечательность (f)
dastaprimiCHAtil'nast'

auburn каштановый
kaSHTAnavy

August август *AVgust*

Australia Австралия
afSTRAliya

Australian (m) австралиец
afstraLIyets

Australian (f) австралийка
afstraLIYka

author автор *AFtar*

authorized авторизованный
aftariZOvany

automatic автоматический
aftamaTIchiski

awful ужасно *uZHASna*

B

back спина *spiNA*

back (in the back) сзади
ZAdi

backwards назад *naZAT*

bad плохой *plaKHOY*

baggage багаж *baGASH*;
check baggage сдать в
багаж *ZDAT v baGASH*

baggage claim check
багажная бирка
baGAZHnaya BIRka

baked печёный *piCHOny*
bakery булочная *BUlachnaya*
balcony балкон *balKON*
ball мяч *MYACH*
ballet балет *baLYET*
banana банан *baNAN*
bandage бинт *BINT*
bangs чёлка *CHOLka*
bank банк *BANK*
bar бар *BAR*
bar (of soap, etc.) кусок *kuSOK*
barber shop парикмахерская *parikMAkhirskaya*
bathhouse баня *BAnya*
bathing suit купальник *kuPAL'nik*
bathing trunks плавки *PLAFki*
bathroom туалет *tuaLYET*
battery батарея *bataRYEya*
battery (car) аккумулятор *akumuLAYtar*
be быть (i) *BYT'*
beach пляж *PLYASH*
beads бусы *BUsy*
beans фасоль (f) *faSOL'*
beard борода *baraDA*
beautiful красивый *kraSIvy*
beauty parlor женский салон *ZHENski saLON*
beef Stroganoff беф-строганов *bif-STROganaf*
beer пиво *PIva*
beets свёкла *SVYOkla*
beet soup борщ *BORSH*
before до / перед *DO / PYErit*
begin начинать(ся) (i) *nachiNAtsa*
beginning (starting time) начало *naCHAla*
behind за *ZA*
bellboy швейцар *shviyTSAR*
belt пояс *POyas*, ремень (m) *riMYEN'*
best лучший *LUchshy*
better лучше *LUche*

between между *MYEZHdu*
beverage напиток *naPItak*
big большой *bal'SHOY*
bill (check) чек *CHEK*
bill (paper currency) купюра *kuPYUra*
billion миллиард *miliART*
bindings крепления *kriPLYEniya*
bird птица *PTItsa*
birthday день рождения *DYEN' razhDYEniya;* **Happy Birthday!** С днём рождения! *z DNYOM razhDYEniya*
bishop (chess) слон *SLON*
black чёрный *CHORny*
blank form бланк *BLANK*
blanket одеяло *adiYAla*
bleeding кровотечение *kravatiCHEniye*
blender сокавыжиматель (m) *sakavyzhiMAtil'*
blind (f) слепая *slyePAya*
blind (m) слепой *slyePOY*
blond белокурый *bilaKUry*
blood кровь (f) *KROF'*
blouse блузка *BLUSka*
blow дуть (i) *DUT'*
blown glass художественное стекло *khuDOzhistvinaye stiKLO*
blue: dark blue синий *SIni;* **light blue** голубой *galuBOY*
board доска *daSKA*
boarding pass посадочный талон *paSAdachny taLON*
boat лодка *LOTka,* теплоход *tiplaKHOT*
bobby pin шпилька *SHPILka*
body тело *TYEla*
boiled варёный *vaRYOny*
boiling water кипяток *kipiTOK*
Bolshoi Theater Большой театр *bal'SHOY tiATR*
bolt (fastener) болт *BOLT*

Bon voyage! Счастливого пути! *shastLIvava puTI*
bone кость (f) *KOST'*
book книга *KNIga*
bookstore книжный магазин *KNIZHny magaZIN*
booth кабина *kaBIna*
boot сапог *saPOK*
bottle бутылка *buTYLka*
bottom дно *DNO*
bouillon бульон *buL'YON*
box ящик *YAshik*, коробка *kaROPka*
box (packet) пакет *paKYET*
box (loge) ложа *LOzha*
bra бюстгалтер *byustGAL'tir*
bracelet браслет *braSLYET*
brake тормоз *TORmas*
brand марка *MARka*
bread хлеб *KHLYEP*
break (recess) перерыв *piriRYF*
break сломать (p) *slaMAT'*
breakfast завтрак *ZAFtrak*
breast грудь (f) *GRUT'*
breathe дышать (i) *dySHAT'*
bridge мост *MOST*
briefcase портфель (m) *partFYEL'*
bring принести (p) *priniSTI*
British (m) англичанин *angliCHAnin*
British (f) англичанка *angliCHANka*
British (English) английский *anGLIYski*
broken bone перелом *piriLOM*
brooch брошь (f) *BROSH*
brook ручей *ruCHEY*
brother брат *BRAT*
brown коричневый *kaRICHnivy*
bruise ушиб *uSHYP*
brunette брюнетка *bryuNYETka*
brush щётка *SHOTka*

buffet, snack bar буфет *buFYET*
builder строитель (m) *straItil'*
building здание *ZDAniye*
bulb лампочка *LAMpachka*
bumper бампер *BAMpir*
bun (hairdo) пучок *puCHOK*
bunch of twigs веник *VYEnik*
bureau (office) бюро *byuRO*
burn ожог *aZHOK*
burn oneself обвариться (p) *obvaRItsa*
bus автобус *aFTObus*
business бизнес *BIZnis*
businessman бизнесмен *biznisMYEN*
but а / но *A / NO*
butane gas газ *GAS*
butcher shop магазин "Мясо" *magaZIN MYAsa*
butter масло *MAsla*
button пуговица *PUgavitsa*
buy купить (p) *kuPIT'*

C

cabbage капуста *kaPUSta*
cabbage soup щи *SHI*
cabin каюта *kaYUta*
cafe кафе *kaFYEY*
cafeteria столовая *staLOvaya*
cake торт *TORT*
call (summon) позвать (p) *paZVAT'*
call (telephone) позвонить (p) *pazvaNIT'*
camera фотоаппарат *fotoapaRAT*
can банка *BANka*
can мочь (i) *MOCH*; **I can** я могу *YA maGU*; **you can** ты можешь *TY MOzhish*; **he/she can** он/она может *ON/aNA MOzhit*; **we can** мы можем *MY MOzhim*; **you can** вы можете *VY MOzhitye*; **they can** они могут *aNI MOgut*

Canada Канада *kaNAda*
Canadian (m) канадец *kaNAdits*
Canadian (f) канадка *kaNATka*
Canadian канадский *kaNATski*
candy конфета *kanFYEta*
cane палка *PALka*
cap шапочка *SHApachka*
car автомобиль (m) *aftamaBIL'*, машина *maSHYna*
carat карат *kaRAT*
carburetor карбюратор *karbyuRAtar*
card карта *KARta*
carefully осторожно *astaROZHna*
carp карп *KARP*
carrots морковь (f) *marKOF''*
carry понести (p) *paniSTI*
cart тележка *tiLYEZHka*
carved object резьба *riz'BA*
cash наличные (деньги) *naLICHniye (DYEN'gi)*
cashier касса *KAsa*
casino казино *kaziNO*
cassette кассета *kyaSYEta*
cassette recorder магнитофон *magnitaFON*
cathedral собор *saBOR*
Catholic католический *kataLIchiski*
cauliflower цветная капуста *tsvitNAya kaPUSta*
caution! опасность! (f) *aPASnast'*
caviar икра *iKRA; black caviar* зернистая икра *zirNIStaya iKRA; red caviar* кетовая икра *KYEtavaya iKRA*
CD (compact disc) компактный диск *kamPAKTny DISK*
cellular phone сотовый телефон *SOtavy tiliFON*

cemetery кладбище *KLADbishe*
center середина *siriDIna*
centimeter сантиметр *santiMYETR*
central центральный *tsinTRAL'ny*
century век *VYEK*
ceramics керамика *kiRAmika*
cereal (cold) крупа *kruPA*
cereal (warm) каша *KAsha*
certified letter ценное письмо *TSEnaye piS'MO*
chain цепочка *tsiPOCHka*
chaise longue шезлонг *shizLONG*
champagne шампанское *shamPANskaye*
change размен *razMYEN*
change разменять (i) *razmiNYAT*
changing room примерочная кабина *priMYErachnaya kaBIna*
charge the battery зарядить аккумулятор *zariDIT' akumuLYAtar*
charm (jewelry) брелок *briLOK*
chassis шасси (n) *shaSI*
cheap, inexpensive дешёвый *diSHOvy*
cheaper, less expensive подешевле *padiSHEvlye*
check (bill) чек *CHEK*
check проверить (p) *praVYErit'*
Check! Шах! *SHAKH*
checked в шашечку *f SHAshichku*
checkers шашки *SHASHki*
check-in регистрация *rigiSTRAtsiya*
Checkmate! Мат! *MAT*
check-out time расчётный час *rasSHOTny CHAS*
checkroom камера хранения *KAmira khraNYEniya*

cheek щека *shiKA*
Cheers! На здоровье! *na zdaROv'ye*
cheese сыр *SYR*
cherry вишня *VISHnya*
chess шахматы *SHAKHmaty*
chest cold бронхит *branKHIT*
chestnut каштан *kaSHTAN*
chew жевать (i) *zhiVAT"*
chewing tobacco махорка *maKHORka*
chicken курица *KUritsa*, цыплёнок *tsyPLYOnak*
chiffon шифон *shiFON*
children дети *DYEti*
chills озноб *aZNOP*
chocolate шоколадный *shakaLADny*
chop/cutlet отбивная котлета *atbivNAya katLYEta*
church церковь (f) *TSERkaf'*
cigarette сигарета *sigaRYEta*
cigar сигар *siGAR*
circle кольцо *kal'TSO*
circle (theater) ярус *YArus*
circus цирк *TSYRK*
CIS (Confederation of Independent States) СНГ *ES-EN-GE*
citizen (m) гражданин *grazhdaNIN*
citizen (f) гражданка *grazhDANka*
city город *GOrat*
city tour экскурсия по городу *ekSKURsiya pa GOradu*
class класс *KLAS*; **economy class** туристический класс *turiSTIchiski KLAS*
classical классический *klaSIchiski*
clean почистить (p) *paCHIStit'*
cleaned убран *Ubran*
cleansing cream крем для очистки кожи *KRYEM dlya aCHISTki KOzhi*

clinic поликлиника *paliKLInika*
clock часы *chiSY*
close закрывать(ся) (i) *zakryVAt(sa)*, закрыть(ся) (p) *zaKRYt(sa)*
closed закрыто *zaKRYta*
clothing одежда *aDYEZHda*
clubs (cards) трефы *TRYEfy*
clutch pedal сцепление *tsiPLYEniye*
coat пальто *pal'TO*
coatroom гардероб *gardiROP*
cod треска *triSKA*
coffee кофе (m) *KOfye*
cognac коньяк *kaN'YAK*
cold (in the head) насморк *NASmark*
cold холодный *khaLODny*
colleague коллега *kaLYEga*
collect (telegram) доплатно *daPLATna*
collection сборник *ZBORnik*
collector's stamps коллекционные марки *kaliktsiOniye MARki*
cologne одеколон *adikaLON*
color цвет *TSVYET*
color(ed) цветной *tsvitNOY*
color rinse окраска *aKRASka*
comb расчёска *rasCHOSka*
comb зачёсывать (i) *zaCHOsyvat'*
come прийти (p) *priyTI*
comedy комедия *kaMYEdiya*
committee комитет *kamiTYET*
communist коммунистический *kamuniSTIchiski*
company фирма *FIRma*
compartment купе *kuPYE*
competition конкуренция *kankuRYENtsiya*
completely совсем *saFSYEM*
computer (adj) компьютерный *kamP'YUtirny*

computer (n) компьютер
kamPYUter

comrade товарищ *taVArish*

concert концерт *kanTSERT*

conductor (musical)
дирижёр *diriZHOR*

**Confederation of
Independent States**
Содружество Независимых
Государств *saDRUzhestva
nyezaVIsimykh
gasuDARTSF*

confirm потвердить (p)
patvirDIT

connect to the internet
подключиться к сети
интернет *potklyuCHItsa k
SYEti INternet*

constipation запор *zaPOR*

contact lens контактная
линза *kanTAKTnaya LINza*

contract контракт *kanTRAKT*

control контроль (m)
kanTROL'

conventional units у.е.

conversation разговор
razgaVOR

cookie печенье *piCHEn'ye*

cool прохладный
praKHLADny

cop милиционер
militsiaNYER

copy скопировать
skaPIravat'

cord шнур *SHNUR*

corduroy рубчатый вельвет
RUPchaty vil'VYET

correct правильный
PRAvil'ny

correspondent корреспондент
karispanDYENT

cosmonaut космонавт
kasmaNAFT

cosmos космос *KOSmas*

cost стоить (i) *STOit'*

cot раскладушка
rasklaDUSHka

cotton вата *VAta*

cotton fabric
хлопчатобумажная ткань
*khlapchatabuMAZHnaya
TKAN'*

cough кашель (m) *KAshil'*

cough покашлять (p)
paKASHlit'

cough drops таблетки от
кашля *taBLYETki at
KASHlya*

cough syrup микстура от
кашля *mikSTUra at
KASHlya*

count посчитать (p)
pashiTAT

country страна *straNA*

countryside деревня
diRYEVnya

coupon, ticket талон *taLON*

**course (currency exchange
rate)** курс *KURS*

cover charge входный билет
FKHODny biLYET

CPU (central processing unit)
системный блок *siSTYEMny
BLOK*

crab краб *KRAP*

cramp судорога *SUdaraga*

crazy: are you crazy? вы с
ума сошли? *VY s uMA
saSHLI*

cream сливки *SLIFki;*
whipped cream взбитые
сливки *VZBItiye SLIFki*

cream cheese творог *tvaROK*

credit card кредитная
карточка *kriDITnaya
KARtachka*

cross-country skis беговые
лыжи *bigaVIye LYzhi*

crossing (pedestrian)
переход *piriKHOT*

crossing (vehicular) переезд
piriYEST

crown (dental) коронка
kaRONka

crutches костыли *kostyLI*

crystal хрусталь (m)
khruSTAL'

cucumber огурец *aguRYETS*

cuisine кухня *KUKHnya*
cupcake кекс *KYEKS*
curls кудри *KUdri*
currants смородина *smaROdina*
currency (foreign—freely convertible) валюта *vaLYUta*
currency exchange обмен валюты *abMYEN vaLYUty*
currency exchange point обменный пункт *abMYEny PUNKT*
curve поворот *pavaROT*
customs declaration декларация *diklaRAtsiya*
cut порез *paRYES*
cut (v) вырезать *VYrezat'*
cut oneself порезаться (p) *paRYEzatsa*
cuticle scissors маникюрные ножницы *maniKYURniye NOZHnitsy*
cutlet котлета *katLYEta*

D

dacha (country home) дача *DAcha*
dance танцевать (i) *tantsiVAT'*
dangerous опасный *aPASny*
dark (adj) тёмный *TYOMny*
darkly (adv) темно *timNO*
darker потемнее *patimNYEye*
darn it! чёрт возьми! *CHORT vaz'MI*
date (calendar) число *chiSLO*
date (fruit) финик *FInik*
daughter дочка *DOCHka*, дочь (f) *DOCH*
day день (m) *DYEN'*
dead end тупик *tuPIK*
deaf (f) глухая *gluKHAya*
deaf (m) глухой *gluKHOY*
deal (cards) сдавать (i) *zdaVAT'*

December декабрь (m) *diKABR'*
deck of cards колода *kaLOda*
declaration декларация *diklaRAtsiya*
declare декларировать (i) *diklaRIravat'*
deeply глубоко *glubaKO*
degree (of temperature) градус *GRAdus*
delete, pull (a tooth) удалить (p) *udaLIT'*
delivery доставка *daSTAFka*, поставка *paSTAFka*
deluxe люкс *LYUKS*
dental зубной *zubNOY*
dentist зубной врач *zubNOY VRACH*
denture зубной протез *zubNOY praTYES*
deodorant дезодорант *dizadaRANT*
depart отправляться (i) *atpraVLYAtsa*, уезжать (i) *uyiZHAT'*
department store универмаг *univirMAK*
deposit (security) залог *zaLOK*
deposit slip приходный ордер *priKHODny ORdir;* **make a deposit** выдать вклад *VYdat' FKLAT*
desk стол *STOL*
desktop рабочий стол *raBOchi STOL*
desktop computer настольный компьютер *naSTOL'ny kamPYUter*
dessert сладкое *SLATkaye*
detour объезд *aBYEST*
develop (film) проявлять (i) *prayiVLYAT'*
devil чёрт *CHORT*
dial набирать (i) *nabiRAT'*
diamond бриллиант *briliANT*
diamonds (cards) бубны *BUBny*

diaper пелёнка *piLYONka*
diarrhea понос *paNOS*
dictionary словарь (m) *slaVAR'*
digital watch электронные часы *elikTRONiye chiSY*
dinner ужин *Uzhin*
diplomat дипломат *diplaMAT*
direction направление *napravLYEniye*
directional signal сигнальный огонь *sigNAL'ny aGON'*
disconnect разъединить (p) *razyidiNIT'*
discotheque дискотека *diskaTYEka*
disc, disk диск *DISK*
dish блюдо *BLYUda*
dislocated вывыхнут *VYvykhnut*
disposable diapers бумажная пелёнка *buMAZHnaya piLYONka*
dizzy: I'm dizzy голова кружится *galaVA KRUzhitsa*
do сделать (p) *ZDYElat'*
dock пристань (f) *PRIstan'*
doctor врач *VRACH*
dollar доллар *DOlar*
door дверь (f) *DVYER'*
down вниз *VNIS*
downhill skis горные лыжи *GORniye LYzhi*
downtown центр *TSENTR*
drama (tragedy) трагедия *traGYEdiya*
dress платье *PLAt'ye*
dress (oneself) одеваться (i) *adiVAtsa*
drink пить (i) *PIT'*, выпить (p) *VYpit'*
drive by заехать (p) *zaYEkhat'*
driver водитель (m) *vaDItil'*
driver's license водительские права *vaDItil'skiye praVA*
drop (n) капля *KAplya*
drop уронить (p) *uraNIT'*

drugstore аптека *apTYEka*
dry сухой *suKHOY*
dry cleaner's химчистка *khimCHISTka*
dry cleaning чистка *CHISTka*
duck утка *UTka*
during во время *va VRYEmya*
duty (customs) пошлина *POSHlina*

E

each каждый *KAZHdy*
ear ухо *Ukha*
ear drops ушные капли *ushNIye KApli*
early рано *RAna*
earring серьга *sir'GA*
east восток *vaSTOK*
easy лёгкий *LYOki*
edition издание *iZDAniye*
egg яйцо *yayTSO;* **hard-boiled egg** яйцо вкрутую *yayTSO fkruTUyu;* **soft-boiled egg** яйцо всмятку *yayTSO FSMYATku*
eggplant баклажан *baklaZHAN*
eight восемь *VOsim'*
eight hundred восемьсот *vasim'SOT*
eighteen восемнадцать *vasimNAtsat'*
eighth восьмой *vaS'MOY*
eighty восемьдесят *VOsim'disit*
elbow локоть (m) *LOkat'*
elderly пожилой *pashiLOY*
electrical электрический *elikTRIchiski*
electronic электронный *elikTROni*
elevator лифт *LIFT*
eleven одиннадцать *aDInatsat'*
embassy посольство *paSOL'stva*

e-mail электронная почта *elikTROnaya POCHta*

emerald изумруд *izumRUT*

emergency exit запасный выход *zaPASny VYkhat*

end конец *kaNETS*

end кончать(ся) (i) *kanCHAtsa*

engagement/wedding ring обручальное кольцо *abruCHAL'naye kal'TSO*

England Англия *ANgliya*

English английский *anGLIYski*

enlarge (be) увеличить (p) *uviLIchit'*

enough (be) хватить (p) *KHVAtit'*

enter, come in входить (i) *fkhaDIT*

enter text вводить текст *vaDIT' TYEKST*

enterprise предприятие *pridpriYAtiye*

entirely совсем *saFSYEM*

entrance вход *FKHOT*

entrance ticket, cover charge входной билет *fkhadNOY biLYET*

entry въезд *VYEST*

envelope конверт *kanVYERT*

eraser ластик *LAStik*

err ошибиться (p) *ashiBItsa*

escort проводить (i) *pravaDIT*

etc., et cetera и т. д., и так далее *I TAK DAliye*

even out подравнять (p) *padravNYAT*

evening вечер *VYEchir*; **in the evening** вечером *VYEchiram*; **good evening!** добрый вечер! *DObry VYEchir*

everyone все *FSYE*

everything всё *FSYO*

except кроме *KROmye*

exchange обменять (i) *abmiNYAT*

exchange rate обменный курс *abMYEny KURS*

excursion экскурсия *ekSKURsiya*

excuse извинить (p) *izviNIT*; **excuse me!** извините! *izviNItye*

exhaust pipe выхлопная трубка *vykhlapNAya TRUPka*

exhibition выставка *VYstafka*

exit выход *VYKhat*

exit выходить (i) *vykhaDIT*, выйти (p) *VYti*

expenses затраты *zaTRAty*, расходы *rasKHOdy*

expensive дорогой *daraGOY*; **more expensive** подороже *padaROzhe*

exposure кадр *KADR*

extension cord удлинитель (m) *udliNItil'*

extra лишний *LISHni*

extra (spare) запасный *zaPASny*

eye глаз *GLAS*

eye drops глазные капли *glazNIye KApli*

eyebrow бровь (f) *BROF'*

F

fabric ткань (f) *TKAN'*

face лицо *liTSO*

fall осень (f) *Osin'*; **in the fall** осенью *Osin'yu*

fall упасть (p) *uPAST'*

false tooth вставной зуб *fstavNOY ZUP*

family семья *siM'YA*

family name фамилия *faMIliya*

fan вентилятор *vintiLYAtar*

fan belt ремень вентилятора *riMYEN' vintiLYAtara*

far далеко *daliKO*

farewell! прощайте! *praSHAYtye*

fast быстрый *BYStry*

father отец *aTYETS*

faucet смеситель (m) *smiSItil'*

fax телефакс *tiliFAKS*

February февраль (m) *fiVRAL'*

fee плата *PLAta*

feed кормить (i) *karMIT"*

feel чувствовать себя (i) *CHUSTvavat' siBYA*

felt войлок *VOYlak*

fender решётка *riSHOTka*

fever жар *ZHAR*; **I have a fever** у меня температура *u miNYA timpiraTUra*

few несколько *NYEskal'ka*

field поле *POlye*

fifteen пятнадцать *pitNAtsat'*

fifth пятый *PYAty*

fifty пятьдесят *pidiSYAT*

fig фига *FIga*

figure skates фигурные коньки *fiGURniye kan'KI*

file файл *FAIL*

filet of sturgeon балык *baLYK*

filling (dental) пломба *PLOMba*

film (photographic) плёнка *PLYONka*

filter фильтр *FIL'TR*

find найти (p) *nayTI*

finger палец *PAlits*

fingernail ноготь (m) *NOgat'*

fire пожар *paZHAR*

first первый *PYERvy*

fish рыба *RYba*

five пять *PYAT"*

five hundred пятьсот *pit'SOT*

fix чинить (i) *chiNIT",* починить (p) *pachiNIT"*

flannel фланель (f) *flaNYEL'*

flash вспышка *FSPYSHka*

flashlight фонарь (m) *faNAR'*

flight полёт *paLYOT*

flints кремни *krimNI*

floor этаж *eTASH*

flowers цветы *tsviTY*

folder папка *PAPka*

folk народ *naROT*

folk music народная музыка *naRODnaya MUzyka*

food блюдо *BLYUda*

fool дурак *duRAK*

foot ступня *stupNYA*

for для *DLYA*

foreign иностранный *inaSTRAny*

forest лес *LYES*

fork вилка *VILka*

forty сорок *SOrak*

four четыре *chiTYrye*

four hundred четыреста *chiTYrista*

foursome четверо *CHETvira*

fourteen четырнадцать *chiTYRnatsat'*

fourth четвёртый *chitVYORty*

fox лиса *liSA*

frame (for glasses) оправа *aPRAva*

free (vacant) свободный *svaBODny*

fresh свежий *SVYEzhi*

Friday пятница *PYATnitsa*

fried жареный *ZHAriny*

friend друг *DRUK*

from из *IS,* от *OT,* с *S*

front (in front) перед *PYErit,* спереди *SPYEridi*

fruits фрукты *FRUKty*

fuel pump бензонасос *binzanaSOS*

fund фонд *FONT*

fur (n) мех *MYEKH*

fur (adj) меховой *mikhaVOY*

future будущий *BUdushi*

G

gabardine габардин *gabarDIN*

gallery галерея *galiRYEya*

gallon галлон *gaLON*

garden сад *SAT*

garlic чеснок *chiSNOK*

gas (butane) газ *GAS*

gasoline бензин *binZIN*

gas tank бензобак *binzaBAK*

gauze (sanitary) napkin марлевая салфетка *MARlivaya salFYETka*

gear скорость (f) *SKOrast'*

gear shift сцепление *tsiPLYEniye*

general delivery до востребования *da vasTRYEbavaniya*

get off выйти (p) *VYti*

get to проехать (p) *praYEkhat'*

gift подарок *paDArak*

give дать (p) *DAT*

glass стакан *staKAN*

glasses очки *achKI*

gloss гланц *GLANTS*

glove перчатка *pirCHATka*

glue клей *KLYEY*

go by foot идти (i) *iTI*

go by vehicle ехать (i) *YEkhat'*

gold золото *ZOlata*

gold(en) золотой *zalaTOY*

gold-plated позолоченый *pazaLOchiny*

good хороший *khaROshi*

good-bye! до свидания! *da sviDAniya*

goodness: my goodness! боже мой! *BOzhe MOY*

goods, items товары *taVAry*

goose гусь (m) *GUS'*

gram грамм *GRAM*

grape виноград *vinaGRAT*

grapefruit грейпфрут *GRYEYPfrut*

gray серый *SYEry*

grease смазать (p) *SMAzat'*

great великий *viLIki*

grill гриль (m) *GRIL'*

grilled обжаренный *abZHAriny*

group группа *GRUpa*

guest (m) гость *GOST'*

guest card карта гостя *KARta gaSTYA*

guidebook путеводитель (m) *putivaDItil'*

GUM ГУМ *GUM*

gum десна *diSNA*

Н

hair волос *vaLOS*

haircut стрижка *STRISHka;* **have a haircut** постричься (p) *paSTRICHtsa*

hairdo причёска *priCHOSka*

hair dryer фен *FYEN*

hair spray лак для волос *LAK dlya vaLOS*

half половина *palaVIna*

hall зал *ZAL*

ham ветчина *vichiNA*

hammer молоток *malaTOK*

hand кисть (f) *KIST'*

hand brake ручной тормоз *ruchNOY TORmas*

handicapped инвалид *invaLIT*

handkerchief носовой платок *nasaVOY plaTOK*

handle ручка *RUCHka*

hanger вешалка *VYEshalka*

happen случиться (p) *sluCHItsa*

hard disk жесткий диск *ZHOski DISK*

hat шапка *SHAPka*

have/there is есть *YEST'*

hay fever сенная лихорадка *SYEnaya likhaRATka*

he он *ON*

head голова *galaVA*

headache головная боль *galavNAya BOL'*

headlight фара *FAra*

health здоровье *zdaROv'ye*

hearing aid слуховой аппарат *slukhaVOY apaRAT*

heart сердце *SYERtse*

heart attack сердечный приступ *sirDYECHny PRIstup*

hearts (cards) черви *CHERvi*
hectare гектар *gikTAR*
heel каблук *kaBLUK*
height рост *ROST*
hello! здраствуйте!
   ZDRASTvuytye
help помочь (р) *paMOCH*
here здесь *ZDYES'*
here it is вот оно *VOT aNO*
herring селёдка *siLYOTka*
herringbone ёлочка
   YOlachka
high высокий *vySOki*
hill холм *KHOLM*
hip бедро *biDRO*
history история *iSTOriya*
hockey хоккей *khaKYEY*
hockey skates хоккейные
   коньки *khaKYEYniye kan'KI*
holiday праздник *PRAZnik*
home / house дом *DOM*
at home дома *DOma*
(to) home домой *daMOY*
hood капот *kaPOT*
horn гудок *guDOK*
hospital больница *bal'NItsa*
hospitality гостеприимство
   gastipriIMstva
hot (temperature) жаркий
   ZHARki
hot (object) горячий
   gaRYAchi
hotel гостиница *gaSTInitsa*
hour час *CHAS*
household хозяйственный
   khaZYAYSTviny
how как *KAK*
how many, how much
   сколько *SKOL'ka*
humor юмор *YUmar*
hundred сто *STO*
hungry (m) голоден *GOladin*
hungry (f) голодна *galaDNA*
hurry спешить (i) *spiSHYT'*
hurt болеть (i) *baLYET'*; it
  hurts болит *baLIT*; that
  hurts больно *BOL'na*
husband муж *MUSH*

I

I я *YA*
ice лёд *LYOT*
ice skates коньки *kan'KI*
if если *YEsli*
ignition зажигание
   zazhiGAniye
in в *V*
inch дюйм *DYUYM*
(be) included входить (i)
   fkhaDIT'
inexpensive дешёвый
   diSHOvy
infection инфекция
   inFYEKtsiya
information информация
   infarMAtsiya
initial первоначальный
   pirvanaCHAL'ny
inside внутри *vnuTRI*
insole стелька *STYEL'ka*
insomnia бессоница
   biSOnitsa
inspection инспекция
   inSPYEKtsiya
institute институт *instiTUT*
instrument инструмент
   instruMYENT
insurance страхование
   strakhaVAniye
intermission антракт
   anTRAKT
international международный
   mizhdunaRODny
internet интернет *intirNET*
interpreter переводчик
   piriVOTchik
into в *V*
Intourist Интурист
   intuRIST
introduce (oneself)
   представить(ся) (р)
   pritSTAvit'/pritSTAvitsa
invite пригласить (р)
   priglaSIT'
iodine йод *YOT*
ironing глажка *GLASHka*

item штука *SHTUka*
ivory слоновая кость *slaNOvaya KOST"*

J

jack (car) домкрат *damKRAT*
jack (cards) валет *vaLYET*
jacket пиджак *pidZHAK*
jade нефрит *niFRIT*
January январь (m) *yinVAR'*
jasper яшма *YASHma*
jeans джинсы *DZHYNsy*
jelly варенье *vaRYEn'ye*
jewelry store ювелирный магазин *yuviLIRny magaZIN*
juice сок *SOK*
julienne жульен *zhuL'YEN*
July июль (m) *iYUL'*
June июнь (m) *iYUN'*
junior младший *MLADshi*
just in case (string bag) авоська *aVOS'ka*

K

key ключ *KLYUCH*
keyboard клавиатура *klaviaTUra*
key card (pass) пропуск *PROpusk*
"key lady" дежурная *diZHURnaya*
kidney soup рассольник *raSOL'nik*
kilo(gram) кило (грамм) *kiLO / kilaGRAM*
kilometer километр *kilaMYETR*
king король (m) *kaROL'*
kiosk киоск *kiOSK*
knee колено *kaLYEna*
knife нож *NOSH*
knight (chess) офицер *afiTSER*
knock over сбить (p) *ZBIT"*

know знать (i) *ZNAT"*
know how уметь (i) *uMYET"*
kopeck копейка *kaPYEYka*
Kremlin Кремль (m) *KRYEML'*
kvass квас *KVAS*

L

lace кружева *kruzhiVA*
ladies' женский *ZHENski*
lake озеро *Ozira*
lamb баранина *baRAnina*
lame (f) хромая *khraMAya*
lame (m) хромой *khraMOY*
lamp лампа *LAMpa*
land приплывать (i) *priplyVAT'*
language язык *yiZYK*
lapel pin значок *znaCHOK*
laptop computer ноутбук *NOTbuk*
large крупный *KRUPny*
larger больше *BOL'she*
last длиться (i) *DLIItsa*
late поздно *POZna*
(be) late опаздывать (i) *aPAZdyvat'*
later позже *POzhe*
laundromat прачечная самообслуживания *PRAchichnaya samaapSLUzhivaniya*
laundry прачечная *PRAchichnaya*
lawyer адвокат *advaKAT*
laxative слабительное *slaBItil'naye*
leak протекать (i) *pratiKAT"*
lean прислоняться (i) *prislaNYAtsa*
leather кожа *KOzha*
leave, depart отправляться (i) *atpraVLYAtsa*
leave (something) оставить (p) *aSTAvit'*
left левый *LYEvy*; **to the left** налево *naLYEva*; **on the left** слева *SLYEva*

leg нога *naGA*
lemon лимон *liMON*
lend одолжить (p) *adalZHYT'*
length длинна *dliNA*
Lenin Ленин *LYEnin*
Leningrad Ленинград *lininGRAT*
lens (eyeglass) стекло *stiKLO*
lens (contact) контактная линза *kanTAKTnaya LINza*
less меньше *MYEN'she*
let (allow) пусть *PUST'*
let in пускать (i) *puSKAT'*
letter письмо *piS'MO*
lettuce салат *saLAT*
library библиотека *bibliaTYEka*
lie (in bed) лежать (i) *liZHAT'*
lie down ложиться (i) *laZHYtsa*, лечь (p) *LYECH*
lifeguard спасатель (m) *spaSAtil'*
light светлый *SVYETly*
lighter зажигалка *zazhiGALka*
like, be pleasing to нравиться *NRAvitsa*
like, love любить (i) *lyuBIT'*
I'd like мне хочется *MNYE KHOchitsa*
lined paper бумага в линейку *buMAga v liNYEYku*
linen полотно *palatNO*
linen towel, sheet простыня *praSTYnya*
lip губа *GUba*
lipstick губная помада *gubNAya paMAda*
liqueur ликёр *liKYOR*
list список *SPIsak*
listen слушать (i) *SLUshat'*
liter литр *LITR*
little немного *niMNOga*, мало *MAla*
liver печень (f) *PYEchin'*
loaf батон *baTON*

long длинный *DLIny*
(a) long time долго *DOLga*
long-distance call междугородный разговор *mizhdugaRODny razgaVOR*
look смотреть (i) *smaTRYET*
look at взглянуть (p) *vzgliNUT'*
lose потерять(ся) (p) *patiRYAtsa*
lose a game проиграть (p) *praiGRAT'*
lotion крем *KRYEM*, лосьон *laS'YON*
loud громко *GROMka*
lousy плохо *PLOkha*
love любить (i) *lyuBIT'*
lunch обед *aBYET*

M

magazine журнал *zhurNAL*
magnesia магнезия *magNYEziya*
mail почта *POCHta*
mailbox почтовый ящик *pachTOvy YAshik*
main главный *GLAVny*
maitre d'hotel метрдотель (m) *mitradaTYEL'*
make сделать (p) *ZDYElat'*
make-up мэйк-ап *meyk-AP*
malachite малахит *malaKHIT*
Maly Theater Малый театр *MAly tiATR*
man мужчина *mushCHIna*; **young man** молодой человек *malaDOY chilaVYEK*
manager заведующий *zaVYEduyushi*
manicure маникюр *maniKYUR*
many, much много *MNOga*, **how many?** сколько? *SKOL'ka*
map план *PLAN*

March март *MART*

market рынок *RYnak*

marmot сурок *suROK*

married: are you married? (of a man) вы женаты? *VY zhiNAty;* **are you married? (of a woman)** вы замужем? *VY ZAmuzhim*

mascara тушь для ресниц *TUSH dlya risNITS*

massage массаж *maSASH*

matches спички *SPICHki*

material, fabric ткань (f) *TKAN*

matte матовый *MAtavy*

matter дело *DYEla*

mattress матрац *maTRATS*

mausoleum мавзолей *mavzaLYEY*

maximum максимальный *maksiMAL'ny*

may (one) можно *MOZHna*

maybe может быть *MOzhit BYT'*

mayonnaise майонез *mayaNYES*

mead медовуха *midaVUkha*

mean значить (i) *ZNAchit'*

meat мясо *MYAsa*

medicine лекарство *liKARSTva*

medium средний *SRYEDni*

meeting встреча *FSTRYEcha*

melon дыня *DYnya*

memory память (f) *PAmit'*

men's мужской *mushSKOY*

menthol ментол *minTOL*

menu меню *miNYU*

meter метр *MYETR*

Metro метро *miTRO*

mezzanine бельэтаж *bileTASH*

midnight полночь (f) *POLnach*

mild слабый *SLAby*

milk молоко *malaKO*

millimeter миллиметр *miliMYETR*

million миллион *miliON*

mind ум *UM*

mine, my мой, моя, мое, мои *MOY, maYA, maYO, maI*

mineral water минеральная вода *miniRAL'naya vaDA*

minimal минимальный *miniMAL'ny*

minister пастор *PAStar*

mink норка *NORka*

Mint Монетный двор *maNYETny DVOR*

minute минута *miNUta;* **just a minute!** минуточку! *miNUtachku*

mirror зеркало *ZYERkala*

Miss, Mrs. госпожа *gaspaZHA*

Miss! девушка! *DYEvushka*

Mister господин *gaspaDIN*

mitten рукавица *rukaVItsa*

mixture микстура *mikSTUra*

modem модем *MOdem*

modern современный *savriMYEny*

monastery монастырь (m) *manaSTYR'*

Monday понедельник *paniDYEL'nik*

money деньги *DYEN'gi*

money order денежный перевод *DYEnizhny piriVOT*

monitor монитор *MOnitar*

month месяц *MYEsits*

monument памятник *PAmitnik*

more больше *BOL'she*

morning утро *Utra;* **in the morning** утром *Utram;* **good morning** доброе утро *DObraye Utra*

Moscow Москва *maskVA*

mosque мечеть (f) *miCHET'*

mother мать (f) *MAT'*

mountain гора *gaRA*

mouse мышь *MYSH*

mouth рот *ROT*

mouthwash зубной эликсир *zubNOY elikSIR*

movie фильм *FIL'M*
much много *MNOga*
muffin кекс *KYEKS*
museum музей *muZYEY*
mushroom гриб *GRIP*
music музыка *MUzyka*
musical музыкальный *muzyKAL'ny*
must надо *NAda*
mustache усы *uSY*
mustard горчица *garCHItsa*
mustard plaster горчичник *garCHICHnik*
myself (m) сам *SAM*
myself (f) сама *saMA*
mystery (film, novel) детектив *ditikTIF*

N

nail clippers кусачки *kuSACHki*
nail file пилка *PILka*
nail polish remover ацетон *atsiTON*
name: first name имя (n) *Imya*; **patronymic** отчество *Ochistva*; **family name** фамилия *faMIliya*; **my name is** меня зовут *miNYA zaVUT*; **what is your name?** как вас зовут? *KAK VAS zaVUT*
napkin салфетка *salFYETka*
narrow (too tight) тесны *tiSNY*
nationality национальность (f) *natsiaNAL'nast'*
nausea тошнота *tashnaTA*
near близко *BLISka*
nearby поблизости *paBLIzasti*
nearest ближайший *bliZHAYshi*
necessary нужно *NUZHna*
neck шея *SHEya*
necklace ожерелье *azhiRYEl'ye*

need: I need мне нужен *MNYE NUzhin*; мне нужна *MNYE nuzhNA*; мне нужно *MNYE NUZHna*; мне нужны *MNYE nuzhNY*
needle иголка *iGOLka*
nested doll матрёшка *maTRYOSHka*
never никогда *nikagDA*
new новый *NOvy*
newspaper газета *gaZYEta*
newsstand разетный киоск *gaZYETny kiOSK*
next следующий *SLYEduyushi*
night ночь (f) *NOCH*; **good night!** спокойной ночи! *spaKOYnay NOchi*
nightclub ночной клуб *nachNOY KLUP*
nine девять *DYEvit'*
nine hundred девятьсот *divit'SOT*
nineteen девятнадцать *divitNAtsat'*
ninety девяносто *diviNOSta*
ninth девятый *diVYAty*
no нет *NYET*
nonprescription безрецептный *bizriTSEPTny*
non-smoking некуряший *nikuRYAshi*
nonsense ерунда *yirunDA*
noodles лапша *lapSHA*
noodle soup суп-лапша *SUP-lapSHA*
noon полдень (m) *POLdin'*
no one никто *niKTO*
normal нормальный *narMAL'ny*
north север *SYEvir*
nose нос *NOS*
not не *NYE*
notebook тетрадь (f) *tiTRAT'*
nothing ничего *nichiVO*
novel роман *raMAN*
November ноябрь (m) *naYABR'*

now сейчас *siCHAS*
number номер *NOmir*, число *chiSLO*
nurse медсестра *midsiSTRA*
nut гайка *GAYka*
nut (food) орех *aRYEKH*
nylon нейлон *niyLON*

O

oatmeal овсянный *aFSYAny*
obligation обязательство *abiZAtil'stva*
occupied занято *ZAnita*
o'clock (hour) час *CHAS*
October октябрь (m) *akTYABR'*
of course конечно *kaNYESHna*
office канцелярский *kantsiLYARski*
often часто *CHASta*
oil масло *MAsla*
ointment мазь (f) *MAS'*
on на *NA*
once раз *RAS*
oncoming встречный *FSTRYECHny*
one (m) один *aDIN*
one (f) одна *aDNA*
oneself себе, себя *siBYE, siBYA*
onion лук *LUK*
only только *TOL'ka*
on time вовремя *VOvrimya*
onto на *NA*
onyx оникс *Oniks*
open открывать(ся) (i) *atkryVAtsa*, открыть(ся) (p) *atKRYtsa*
opened открыто *atKRYta*
opera опера *Opira*
opera glasses бинокль (m) *biNOKL'*
operetta оперетта *apiRYEta*
opposite напротив *naPROtif*
optician оптика *OPtika*
or или *Ili*

orange (n) апельсин *apil'SIN*
orange (adj) апельсиновый *apil'SInavy*
orchestra seat партер *parTYER*
order порядок *paRYAdak*
order заказывать (i) *zaKAzyvat'*, заказать (p) *zakaZAT'*
Orthodox православный *pravaSLAVny*
ouch! ой! *OY*
our наш, наша, наше, наши *NASH, NAsha, NAshe, NAshi*
outside вне *VNYE*
overheat перегреваться (i) *pirigriVAtsa*
owe: I owe (m) я должен *YA DOLzhin;* **I owe (f)** я должна *YA dalzhNA;* **You owe** Вы должны *VY dalzhNY*

P

pack пачка *PACHka*
package посылка *paSYLka*
packet пакет *paKYET*
page страница *straNItsa*
pair пара *PAra*
pajamas пижама *piZHAma*
palace дворец *dvaRYETS*
Palace of Congresses Дворец съездов *dvaRYETS SYEZdaf*
pancake house блинная *BLInaya*
panties трусики *TRUsiki*
pants брюки *BRYUki*
pantyhose колготки *kalGOTki*
paper (n) бумага *buMAga*
paper (adj) бумажный *buMAZHny*
paper clip скрепка *SKRYEPka*
pardon простить (i) *praSTIT'*
pardon me! простите! *praSTItye*

park парк *PARK*
parking стоянка *staYANka*
part часть (f) *CHAST'*
part (in the hair) пробор *praBOR*
partial частичный *chaSTICHny*
partner партнёр *partNYOR*
party (political) партия *PARtiya*
pass by проходить (i) *prakhaDIT'*
passenger пассажир *pasaZHYR*
passing обгон *abGON*
passport паспорт *PASpart*
past прошлый *PROshly*
paste паста *PASta*
paste (v) вставить *FSTAvit'*
pastry пирожное *piROZHnaye*
path дорожка *daROSHka*, путь (m) *PUT'*, тропинка *traPINka*
patronymic отчество *Ochistva*
pawn (chess) пешка *PYESHka*
pay платить (i) *plaTIT'*
pay telephone телефон-афтомат *tiliFON-aftaMAT*
payment оплата *aPLAta*, плата *PLАta*, платёж *plaTYOSH*
peach персик *PYERsik*
pear груша *GRUsha*
pearl жемчуг *ZHEMchuk*
pedestrian пешеходный *pishiKHODny*
pelmeni (Siberian dumplings) пельмени *pil'MYEni*
pen ручка *RUCHka*
pencil карандаш *karanDASH*
penicillin пенициллин *pinitsiLIN*
people's народный *naRODny*
pepper перец *PYErits*
performance спектакль (m) *spikTAKL'*

perfume духи *duKHI*
permanent химическая завивка *khiMIchiskaya zaVIFka*
person to person на человека *na chilaVYEka*
personal личный *LICHny*
personal computer персональный компьютер *persaNAL'ni kamPYUter*
Petersburg Петербург *pitirBURK*
pharmacy аптека *apTYEka*
pheasant фасан *faSAN*
phone посвонить (p) *pazvaNIT'*
photograph фотографировать (i) *fatagraFIravat'*
phrasebook разговорник *razgaVORnik*
pick up (drive by) заехать (p) *zaYEkhat'*
picture картина *karTIna*
picture (photo) фотография *fataGRAfiya*
pie пирог *piROK*
piece (chess) фигура *fiGUra*
pike/perch судак *suDAK*
pillow подушка *paDUSHka*
pin булавка *buLAFka*
pinch жать (i) *ZHAT'*
pineapple ананас *anaNAS*
pink розовый *ROzavy*
pipe трубка *TRUPka*
pipe tobacco трубочный табак *TRUbachny taBAK*
place место *MYESta*
plaid в клетку *f KLYETku*
plans планы *PLАny*
plant растение *raSTYEniye*
plate тарелка *taRYELka*
platform платформа *platFORma*
platinum платина *PLАtina*
play играть (i) *iGRAT'*
please пожалуйста *paZHАlusta*
pleasing приятно *priYATna*

pleasure удовольствие *udaVOL'stviye;* **with pleasure** с удовольствием *s udaVOL'stviyim*

pliers плоскогубцы *plaskaGUPtsy*

plug розетка *raZYETka*

plum слива *SLIva*

pocket (adj) карманный *karMAny*

pocketbook сумка *SUMka*

poetry стихотворение *stikhatvaRYEniye*

point пункт *PUNKT*

pole палка *PALka*

police милиция *miLItsiya*

polka dot горошек *gaROshik*

polyclinic поликлиника *paliKLInika*

polyester полиэфир *palieFIR*

pomegranate гранат *graNAT*

pond пруд *PRUT*

pony tail хвост *KHVOST*

poplin поплин *paPLIN*

popular популярный *papuLYARny*

porcelain фарфоровый *farFOravy*

pork свиной *sviNOY*

portable computer переносный компьютер *piriNOSny kamPYUter*

porter носильщик *naSIL'shik*

post office почта *POCHta*

postcard открытка *atKRYTka*

poster плакат *plaKAT*

potatoes картофель (m) *karTOfil'*

pound фунт *FUNT*

powder пудра *PUdra*

practically практически *prakTIchiski*

prefer предпочитать (i) *pritpachiTAT'*

prescription рецепт *riTSEPT*

press гладить (i) *GLAdit'*

price цена *tsiNA*

priest священник *sviSHEnik*

print напечатать *napiCHAtat'*

printed matter бандероль (f) *bandiROL'*

printer принтер *PRINter*

private taxi частник *CHASnik*

problem проблема *praBLYEma*

process процесс *praTSES*

profession профессия *praFYEsiya*

profit прибыль (f) *PRIbyl'*

program программка *praGRAMka*

prohibited запрещено *zaprishiNO*

Protestant протестантский *pratiSTANTski*

provider провайдер *praVAIdyer*

pull! (toward oneself) к себе *k siBYE*

pull (a tooth) удалить (р) *udaLIT'*

pump насос *naSOS*

pumpkin тыква *TYKva*

punch (a ticket) пробить (р) *praBIT'*

purchase покупка *paKUPka*

push! (away from oneself) от себя *at siBYA*

put, place положить (р) *palaZHYT'*, поставить (р) *paSTAvit'*

Q

quality качество *KAchistva*

quart кварта *KVARta*

quarter четверть (f) *CHETvirt'*

quartz кварцовый *KVARtsavy*

queen королева *karaLYEva*

queen (cards) дама *DAma*

quiet! тише! *TIshe*

R

rabbi раввин *raVIN*

rabbit кролик *KROlik*

radiator радиатор *radiAtar*

radio радио *RAdio*

radish редиска *riDISka*

ragout рагу *raGU*

railroad железнодорожный *zhiliznadaROZHny*

raincoat плащ *PLASH*

rain дождь (m) *DOSH*

raisin изюм *iZYUM*

raspberries малина *maLIna*

rayon вискоза *viSKOza*

razor бритва *BRITva*

razor blade лезвие *LYEZviye*

reach (get to) попасть (p) *paPAST'*

ready готово *gaTOva*

rear задний *ZADni*

rear orchestra амфитеатр *amfitiATR*

receipt квитанция *kviTANtsiya*

receive, pick up получить (p) *paluCHIT'*

reception room приёмная *priYOMnaya*

recommend рекомендовать (i) *rikamindaVAT'*

record пластинка *plaSTINka*

record player проигрыватель (m) *praIgryvatil'*

red красный *KRASny*

Red Square Красная площадь *KRASnaya PLOshat'*

refrigerator холодильник *khalaDIL'nik*

regards! привет! *priVYET*

registered letter заказное письмо *zakazNOye piS'MO*

registration (check-in counter) регистрация *rigiSTRAtsiya*

remembrance на память *na PAmit'*

rent взять на прокат *VZYAT' na praKAT*

rental прокат *praKAT*

repair чинить (i) *chiNIT'*, починить (p) *pachiNIT'*

repairs ремонт *riMONT*; **auto repair shop** автосервис *aftaSYERvis*

repeat повторить (p) *paftaRIT'*

replace заменить (p) *zamiNIT'*

republic республика *riSPUblika*

reservation бронирование *braNIravaniye*

reserve забронировать (p) *zabraNIravat'*

reserved заказано *zaKAzana*

restaurant ресторан *ristaRAN*

restriction ограничение *agraniCHEniye*

restroom (men's) мужской туалет *mushSKOY tuaLYET*; **(ladies')** женский туалет *ZHENsky tuaLYET*

retail price розничная цена *ROZnichnaya tsiNA*

return обратный *aBRATny*; **there and back** туда и обратно *tuDA I aBRATna*

return восвращать(ся) (i) *vazvraSHAtsa*, вернуть(ся) (p) *virNUtsa*

revolution революция *rivaLYUtsiya*

rib ребро *riBRO*

rice рис *RIS*

ride проезд *praYEST*

right правый *PRAvy*; **to the right** направо *naPRAva*; **on the right** справа *SPRAva*

right of way преимущество *priiMUshistva*

ring кольцо *kal'TSO*

ring (theater) ярус *YArus*

river река *riKA*
road дорога *daROga*
road map автодорожная карта *aftadaROZHnaya KARta*
roast beef ростбиф *rastBIF*
robe халат *khaLAT*
roll булочка *BUlachka*
roll (of something) рулон *ruLON*
rook (chess) ладья *laD'YA*
room (hotel) номер *NOmir*
rouge румяна *ruMYAna*
row ряд *RYAT*
rubber band резинка *riZINka*
ruble рубль (m) *RUBL'*
ruby рубин *ruBIN*
ruler линейка *liNYEka*
Russia Россия *raSIya*
Russian российский *raSIski*
Russian (m) русский *RUski*
Russian (f) русская *RUskaya*
Russian citizen (f) россиянка *rasiYANka*
Russian citizen (m) россиянин *rasiYAnin*
Russian Federation Российская Федерация *raSIskaya fidiRAtsiya*
rye ржаной *rzhaNOY*

sable соболь (m) *SObal'*
saccharin сахарин *sakhaRIN*
sail away отплывать (i) *atplyVAT'*
salad салат *saLAT*
salami колбаса *kalbaSA*
sale продажа *praDAzha*
sale items товары по сниженным ценам *taVAry pa SNIzhinym tsiNAM*
salmon сёмга *SYOMga*
salt соль (f) *SOL'*
sample попробовать (p) *paPRObavat'*
sandwich бутерброд *butirBROT*

sanitary napkins гигиенические салфетки *gigiiNIchiskiye salFYETki*
sapphire сапфир *sapFIR*
sateen сатин *saTIN*
satin атлас *atLAS*
Saturday суббота *suBOta*
sauce соуса *SOUsa*
sauerkraut квашеная капуста *KVAshinaya kaPUSta*
sauna сауна *SAUna*
save сохранить *sakhraNIT'*
say сказать (p) *skaZAT'*
scanner сканер *SKAner*
scarf шарф *SHARF*
schedule расписание *raspiSAniye*
schnitzel шницель (m) *SHNItsil'*
science наука *naUka*
science fiction научно-популярный *naUCHna-papuLYARny*
scissors ножницы *NOZHnitsy*
score счёт *SHOT*
Scotch tape скотч *SKOTCH*
scrambled eggs яичница-болтунья *yaICHnitsa-balTUn'ya*
screw винтик *VINtik*
screwdriver отвёртка *atVYORTka*
sea море *MOrye*
seasickness морская болезнь *marSKAya baLYEZN'*
seasoning приправа *priPRAva*
seat место *MYESta*
second (sixtieth part of a minute) секунда *siKUNda*
second второй *ftaROY*
section отдел *aDYEL*
security безопасность (f) *bizaPASnast'*
sedative успокаивающее *uspaKAivayushiye*

see смотреть (i) *smaTRYET'*
seem казаться (i) *kaZAtsa*
self сам *SAM*
sell продавать (i) *pradaVAT'*
semi-dry полусухое *palusuKHOye*
send послать (p) *paSLAT'*
senior старший *STARshi*
separately отдельно *aDYEL'na*
September сентябрь (m) *sinTYABR'*
seriously серьёзно *siR'YOZna*
service обслуживание *apSLUzhivaniye*
service bureau бюро обслуживания *byuRO apSLUzhivaniya*
service (religious) служба *SLUZHba*
service station бензоколонка *binzakaLONka*
set (hairdo) укладка *uKLATka*
seven семь *SYEM'*
seven hundred семьсот *sim'SOT*
seventeen семнадцать *simNAtsat'*
seventh седьмой *sid'MOY*
seventy семьдесят *SYEM'disit*
sew пришить (p) *priSHYT'*
shadow тень (f) *TYEN'*
shame: what a shame! как жаль! *KAK ZHAL'*
shampoo шампунь (m) *shamPUN'*
sharpener точилка *taCHILka*
shave побриться (p) *paBRItsa*
she она *aNA*
sheepskin овчина *afCHIna*
shift (gear) сцепление *tsiPLYEniye*
shine светить (i) *SVYEtit'*
shipment отправка *atPRAFka*

shirt рубашка *ruBASHka*, сорочка *saROCHka*
shoelace шнурок *shnuROK*
shoes обувь (f) *Obuf'*; **men's shoes** ботинки *baTINki*; **women's shoes** туфли *TUfli*
shop, store магазин *magaZIN*
short короткий *kaROTki*
shoulder плечо *pliCHO*
show варьете *var'yiTE*
shower душ *DUSH*
shuffle перетасовать (p) *piriTAsavat'*
shut up (keep silent) молчать (i) *malCHAT'*
sick: I feel sick я заболел *YA zabaLYEL*
sickness болезнь (f) *baLYEZN'*
side сторона *staraNA*
side бок *BOK*
sideburn височка *viSOCHka*
sign расписаться (p) *raspiSAtsa*
signal сигнальный *sigNAL'ny*
sign language немая азбука *neMAya AZbuka*
silk шёлк *SHOLK*
silver (n) серебро *siriBRO*
silver (adj) серебряный *siRYEbriny*
sing петь (i) *PYET'*
single ticket единый билет *yiDIny biLYET*
sink умывальник *umyVAL'nik*
sister сестра *siSTRA*
sit сидеть (i) *siDYET'*, посидеть (p) *pasiDYET'*
six шесть *SHEST'*
six hundred шестьсот *shist'SOT*
sixteen шестнадцать *shistNAtsat'*
sixth шестой *shiSTOY*
sixty шестьдесят *shizdiSYAT*
size размер *razMYER*

skate кататься на коньках *kaTAtsa na kan'KAKH*
skates коньки *kan'KI*
ski кататься на лыжах *kaTAtsa na LYzhakh*
skin кожа *KOzha*
skirt юбка *YUPka*
skis лыжи *LYzhi*
slacks штаны *shtaNY*
sled санки *SANki*
sleeping pills снотворное *snaTVORnaye*
sleeve рукав *ruKAF*
slide слайд *SLAYT*
slip (ladies') комбинация *kambiNAtsiya*
slipper тапочка *TApachka*
slippery скользкий *SKOL'ski*
slow медленный *MYEdliny*
small мелький *MYEL'ki*
smaller меньше *MYEN'she*
smile улыбаться (i) *ulyBAtsa*
smoke курить (i) *kuRIT'*, закурить (p) *zakuRIT'*
smoking курящий *kuRYAshi*
smorgasbord шведский стол *SHVYETski STOL*
snack bar закусочная *zaKUsachnaya*
snow снег *SNYEK*
so так *TAK*
soap мыло *MYla*
soccer футбол *fudBOL*
socialist социалистический *satsialiSTIchiski*
sock носок *naSOK*
soft мягкий *MYAki*
soft drink лимонад *limaNAT*
sole (shoe) подмётка *padMYOTka*
solid-color однотонное *adnaTOnaye*
solyanka (fish or meat soup) солянка *saLYANka*
someone кто-нибудь *KTO-nibut'*
something что-нибудь *SHTO-nibut'*

son сын *SYN*
soon скоро *SKOra*
sore throat ангина *anGIna*
soup суп *SUP*
sour cream сметана *smiTAna*
south юг *YUK*
souvenir сувенир *suviNIR*
Soviet советский *saVYETski*
space космос *KOSmas*
spades (cards) пики *PIki*
spare part запчасть (f) *zapCHAST'*
spark plug свеча *sviCHA*
speak говорить (i) *gavaRIT'*, поговорить (p) *pagavaRIT'*
special особый *aSOby*
special delivery письмо с доставкой *piS'MO z daSTAFkay*
specialty (of the house) фирменное блюдо *FIRminaye BLYUda*
speed скорость (f) *SKOrast'*
spin кружиться (i) *kruZHYtsa*
spinach шпинат *shpiNAT*
splendid прекрасный *priKRASny*
sponge мочалка *maCHALka*
spoon ложка *LOSHka*
sporting goods спорттовары *sparttaVAry*
spot пятно *pitNO*
spring весна *viSNA*; **in the spring** весной *viSNOY*
square площадь (f) *PLOshat'*; **Red Square** Красная площадь *KRASnaya PLOshat'*
St. Petersburg Санкт Петербург *SANKT pitirBURK*
stadium стадион *stadiON*
stage сцена *TSEna*
stainless steel нержавейка *nirzhaVYEYka*
stamp марка *MARka*

stand стоять (i) *staYAT'*; **taxi stand** стоянка такси *staYANka taKSI*

stand up вставать (i) *fstaVAT'*

starting time начало *naCHAla*

state (one of the United States) штат *SHTAT*

state государственный *gasuDARSTviny*

station станция *STANtsiya*

station (railroad) вокзал *vagZAL*

station-to-station на номер *na NOmir*

steak бифштекс *bifSHTYEKS*

steal украсть (p) *uKRAST'*

steam room парильня *paRIL'nya*

steering wheel руль (m) *RUL'*, рулевое колесо *ruliVOye kaliSO*

stem (of a watch) головка *gaLOFka*

stewed тушёный *tuSHOny*

stewed fruit компот *kamPOT*

stocking чулок *chuLOK*

stomach желудок *zhiLUdak*; **upset stomach** желудочное расстройство *zhiLUdachnaye raSTROYSTva*

stone камень (f) *KAmin'*

stop! стоп! *STOP*

stop (bus, trolley) остановка *astaNOFka*

stop (restrain) задержать (p) *zadirZHAT'*

stop (halt) остановиться (p) *astanaVItsa*

store магазин *magaZIN*

story (tale) рассказ *raSKAS*

straight прямой *priMOY*; **straight ahead** прямо *PRYAma*

strawberries клубника *klubNIka*

street улица *Ulitsa*

striking (extravagant) экстравагантное *ekstravaGANTnaye*

string шпагат *shpaGAT*

string beans стручковая фасоль *struchKOvaya faSOL'*

stripe полоска *paLOSka*

strong крепкий *KRYEPki*

student студент *stuDYENT*

stuffed cabbage голубцы *galupTSY*

sturgeon осетрина *asiTRIna*

sturgeon soup солянка *saLYANka*

stylish модный *MODny*

subway метро *miTRO*

such такой *taKOY*

suede замша *zamSHA*

sugar сахар *SAkhar*

suit костюм *kaSTYUM*

suitcase чемодан *chimaDAN*

summer лето *LYEta*; **in the summer** летом *LYEtam*

sun солнце *SONtse*

sunburn солнечный ожог *SOLnichny aZHOK*

Sunday воскресенье *vaskriSYEn'ye*

sunglasses солнечные очки *SOLnichniye achKI*

suntan загар *zaGAR*

suntan lotion крем от загара *KRYEM at zaGAra*

super: you're super! молодец! *malaDYETS*

supermarket гастроном *gastraNOM*

supplies товары *taVАry*

suppository свеча *sviCHA*

sweater свитер *SVItir*

sweet сладкий *SLATki*

swelling опухоль (f) *Opukhal'*

swim купаться (i) *kuPAtsa*, плавать (i) *PLAvat'*

swimming pool бассейн *baSYEYN*

switch выключатель (m) *vyklyuCHAtil'*

swollen вздут *VZDUT*

synagogue синагога *sinaGOga*

system система *siSTYEma*

T

table стол *STOL*, столик *STOlik*

taillight задняя фара *ZADniya FAra*

tailor ателье мод *atiL'YE MOT*

take, get взять (p) *VZYAT'*

take (escort) проводить (i) *pravaDIT'*

take (medicine) принимать (i) *priniMAT'*

take (transport by vehicle) отвезти (p) *atviSTI*

talcum тальк *TAL'K*

tall высокий *vySOki*

tampon тампон *tamPON*

tangerine мандарин *mandaRIN*

tape лента *LYENta*, плёнка *PLYONka*

tax налог *naLOK*

taxi такси (n) *taKSI*

taxi stand стоянка такси *staYANka taKSI*

tea чай *CHAY*

teacher преподаватель (m) *pripadaVAtil'*

telegram телеграмма *tiliGRAma*

telephone телефон *tiliFON*

telephone booth телефонная кабина *tiliFOnaya kaBIna*; **pay telephone** телефон-автомат *tiliFON-aftaMAT*

telephone call разговор *razgaVOR*

telephone card телефонная карта *tiliFOnaya KARta*

telephone receiver трубка *TRUPka*

television телевизор *tiliVIzar*

telex телекс *TYEliks*

temperature температура *timpiraTUra*

temporary временный *VRYEminy*

ten десять *DYEsit'*

tenth десятый *diSYAty*

terrible страшный *STRASHny*

terrycloth махровая ткань *maKHROvaya TKAN'*

thank you спасибо *spaSIba*

that one то *TO*

theater театр *tiATR*

their их *IKH*

there там *TAM*, туда *tuDA*

thermometer термометр *tirMOmitr*

they они *aNI*

thing вещь (f) *VYESH*

think думать (i) *DUmat'*

third третий *TRYEti*

thirsty: I'm thirsty мне хочется пить *MNYE KHOchitsa PIT*

thirteen тринадцать *triNATsat'*

thirty тридцать *TRItsat'*

this это *Eta*

thousand тысяча *TYsicha*

three три *TRI*

three hundred триста *TRISta*

threesome трое *TROye*

throat горло *GORla*

through через *CHEris*

thumbtack кнопка *KNOPka*

Thursday четверг *chitVYERK*

thus так *TAK*

ticket билет *biLYET*

ticket punch компостер *kamPOStir*

tie галстук *GALstuk*

tighten подвернуть (p) *padvirNUT'*

time время (n) *VRYEmya;*
how long (how much time)
сколько времени *SKOL'ka*
VRYEmini

tint тон *TON*

tire шина *SHYna;* **the tire is**
flat спустила шина
SPUStila SHYna

tired (m) устал *uSTAL*

tired (f) устала *uSTAla*

tissue салфетка *salFYETka*

title название *naZVAniye*

to в *V,* на *NA*

toaster тостер *TOStir*

tobacco табак *taBAK*

today сегодня *siVODnya*

toenail ноготь (m) *NOgat'*

together вместе *VMYEStye*

toilet унитаз *uniTAS*

toilet paper туалетная
бумажка *tuaLYETnaya*
buMAZHka

toiletries shop парфюмерия
parfyuMYEriya

token жетон *zhiTON*

tomato помидор *pamiDOR*

tomorrow завтра *ZAFtra*

tongue язык *yiZYK*

tonight сегодня вечером
siVODnya VYEchiram

too (excessively) слишком
SLISHkam

tooth зуб *ZUP*

toothache зубная боль
zubNAya BOL'

toothbrush зубная щётка
zubNAya SHOTka

toothpaste зубная паста
zubNAya PASta

top: from the top сверху
SVYERkhu; **on top** над
NAT

topaz топаз *taPAS*

touch-up поправка
paPRAFka

tourist (n) турист *tuRIST*

tourist (adj) туристический
turiSTIchiski

tourmaline турмалин
turmaLIN

toward к *K*

towel полотенце
palaTYENtse

tower башня *BASHnya*

toy игрушка *iGRUSHka*

trade торговля *targOvlya*

traffic движение *dviZHEniye*

train поезд *POyist*

train car вагон *vaGON*

tram/trolleycar трамвай
tramVAY

transfer перевод *piriVOT,*
переход *piriKHOT*

transfer передать (p)
piriDAT', пересесть (p)
piriSYEST'

transformer трансформатор
transfarMAtar

translation перевод
piriVOT

transmission (auto)
переключение скоростей
piriklyuCHEniye
skaraSTYEY

transportation перевозка
piriVOSka, транспорт
TRANSpart

traveler's check дорожный
чек *daROZHny CHEK*

tree дерево *DYEriva*

trim подстричь (p)
padSTRICH'

trip проезд *praYEST*

trolleybus троллейбус
traLYEYbus

trout форель (m) *faRYEL'*

trunk (of a car) багажник
baGAZHnik

try on примерить (p)
priMYErit'

tsar царь (m) *TSAR'*

Tuesday вторник *FTORnik*

turkey индейка *inDYEYka*

turn (in a line) очередь (f)
Ochirit'

turn оборот *abaROT*

turn повернуть (p) *pavirNUT'*
turnip репька *RYEP'ka*
turquoise бирюза *biRYUza*
tweezers щипчики *SHIPchiki*
twelve двенадцать *dviNAtsat'*
twenty двадцать *DVAtsat'*
twigs веник *VYEnik*
twisted растянут *raSTYAnut*
two два *DVA*
twosome двое *DVOye*
two hundred двести *DVYESti*
typewriter пишущая машина *PIshushaya maSHYna*

U

ugh! фу! *FU*
umbrella зонт *ZONT*
under под *POT*
underpants (men's) трусы *truSY*
undershirt майка *MAYka*
understand понимать (i) *paniMAT'*
undress раздеться (p) *razDYEtsa*
union союз *saYUS*
United States Соединённые Штаты *sayidiNYOniye SHTAty*
until до *DO*
until later! пока! *paKA*
up вверх *VVYERKH*
upset stomach желудочное расстройство *zhiLUdachnaye raSTROYSTva*
urgently срочно *SROCHna*
USA США *SA SHA A*
USSR СССР *ES ES ES ER*
U-turn разворот *razvaROT*

V

vacancy: no vacancy мест нет *MYEST NYET*
valley долина *daLIna*

valuable ценный *TSEny*
valuables ценные вещи *TSEniye VYEshi*
value (market) рыночная цена *RYnachnaya tsiNA*
van микроавтобус *mikraaFTObus*
vanilla сливочное *SLIvachnaye*
VCR видео-магнитофон *VIdiomagnitaFON*
veal телятина *tiLYAtina*
vegetables овощи *Ovashi*
velvet бархат *BARkhat*
velveteen вельвет *vil'VYET*
very очень *Ochin'*
(the) very самый *SAmy*
victory победа *paBYEda*
village село *siLO*
vinegar уксус *UKsus*
visa виза *VIza*
vitamin витамин *vitaMIN*
vodka вотка *VOTka*
vodka glass рюмка *RYUMka*
voice голос *GOlas*
voucher ваучер *VAUchir*
voyage: Bon voyage! Счастливого пути! *shastLIvava puTI*

W

waist талия *TAliya*
wait ждать (i) *ZHDAT'*, подождать (p) *padaZHDAT'*
waiter официант *afitsiANT*
waiter! молодой человек! *malaDOY chilaVYEK*
waitress официантка *afitsiANTka*
waitress! девушка! *DYEvushka*
wake разбудить (p) *razbuDIT'*
walk ходить (i) *khaDIT'*
walker ходунки *khadunKI*
wallet бумажник *buMAZHnik*

want хотеть (i) *khaTYET'*;
I want я хочу *YA khaCHU*; **you want** ты хочешь *TY KHOchish*; **he/she wants** он/она хочет *ON/aNA KHOchit*; **we want** мы хотим *MY khaTIM*; **you want** вы хотите *VY khaTItye*; **they want** они хотят *aNI khaTYAT*

war война *vayNA*

warm тёплый *TYOply*

warmth тепло *tiPLO*

wash, washing (of clothes) стирка *STIRka*

wash (clothes) стирать (i) *stiRAT'*

wash (shampoo) мытьё *myT"YO*

wash (give a shampoo) помыть голову *paMYT' GOlavu*

washbasin тазик *TAzik*

wash and wear немнущаяся ткань *niMNUshayasya TKAN'*

watch часы *chiSY*

water вода *vaDA*

watermelon арбуз *arBUS*

wave волна *valNA*

we мы *MY*

weak слабый *SLAby*

weakness слабость (f) *SLAbast'*

weather погода *paGOda*

web page Web страница *WEB straNItsa*

wedding ring обручальное кольцо *abruCHAL'naye kal'TSO*

Wednesday среда *sriDA*

week неделя *niDYElya*

well! ну! *NU*

west запад *ZApat*

what что *SHTO*

wheel колесо *kaliSO*

wheelchair инвалидное кресло *invaLIDnaye KRESla*

when когда *kagDA*

where где *GDYE*

where from откуда *atKUda*

where to, which way куда *kuDA*

which какой *kaKOY*, который *kaTOry*

whipped взбитый *VZBIty*

whipped cream взбитые сливки *VZBItiye SLIFki*

white белый *BYEly*

who кто *KTO*

whose чей, чья, чьё, чьи *CHEY, CHYA, CHYO, CHI*

why почему *pachiMU*

wide широкий *shiROki*

wife жена *zhiNA*

will be быть (i) *BYT'*; **I will be** я буду *YA BUdu*; **you will be** ты будешь *TY BUdish*; **he/she will be** он/она будет *ON/aNA BUdit*; **we will be** мы будем *MY BUdim*; **you will be** вы будете *VY BUditye*; **they will be** они будут *aNI BUdut*

win выиграть (p) *VYigrat'*

wind ветер *VYEtir*

wind (a watch) заводить (i) *zavaDIT'*

window окно *akNO*

windshield ветровое стекло *vitraVOye stiKLO*

windshield wiper стеклочиститель (m) *stiklachiSTItil'*

wine вино *viNO*

winter зима *ziMA*; **in the winter** зимой *ziMOY*

wish желать (i) *zhiLAT'*

with с *S*

withdrawal slip расходный ордер *rasKHODny ORdir*; **make a withdrawal** принять вклад *priNYAT' FKLAT*

without без *BYES*

wolf волк *VOLK*

woman женщина *ZHENshina*

women's женский *ZHENski*

wonderful замечательно *zamiCHAtil'na*

wool шерсть (f) *SHERST'*

word слово *SLOva*

work работать (f) *raBOtat'*

worker, working рабочий *raBOchi*

worse хуже *KHUzhe*

would бы *BY*

wound рана *RAna*

wrap завернуть (p) *zavirNUT'*

wraparound накидка *naKITka*

wrench гаечный ключ *GAyichny KLYUCH*

wrist запястье *zaPYASt'ye*

wristwatch наручные часы *naRUCHniye chiSY*

write писать (i) *piSAT'*, написать (p) *napiSAT'*; **write down** записать (p) *zapiSAT'*; **write out** выписать (p) *VYpisat'*

writer писатель *piSAtil'*

writing pad блокнот *blakNOT*

writing paper бумага для писем *buMAga dlya PIsim*

wrong: you've reached a wrong number вы не туда попали *VY NYE tuDA paPAli*; **something wrong** проблема *praBLYEma*

yard ярд *YART*

year год *GOT*

yellow жёлтый *ZHOLty*

yes да *DA*

yesterday вчера *fchiRA*

yet уже *uZHE*

yield уступить (p) *ustuPIT'*

yogurt кефир *kiFIR*

you ты, вы *TY, VY*

young молодой *malaDOY*

young man! молодой человек! *malaDOY chilaVYEK*

your твой, твоя, твое, твои *TVOY, tvaYA, tvaYO, tvaI*, ваш, ваша, ваше, ваши *VASH, VAsha, VAshe, VAshi*

Z

zero нуль (m) *NUL'*

zoo зоопарк *zaaPARK*

RUSSIAN-ENGLISH DICTIONARY

А

а   and, but
абонементная книжка   book of tickets
абрикос   apricot
август   August
авиаписьмо   airmail letter
авоська   "just in case" (string bag)
австралиец (m)   Australian
австралийка (f)   Australian
Австралия   Australia
автобус   bus
автодорожная карта   road map
автоматически   automatically
автоматический   automatic
автомобиль (m)   car
автор   author
авторизованный   authorized
автосервис   auto repair shop
адаптер   adapter
адвокат   lawyer
администратор   administrator
адрес   address
Азия   Asia
аквамарин   aquamarine
аккумулятор   car battery
аллергия   allergy
амальгама   amalgam filling
Америка   America
американец (m)   American
американка (f)   American
американский   American
аметист   amethyst
амфитеатр   rear orchestra
ананас   pineapple
ангина   sore throat
английский   English
англичанин (m)   British (Englishman)

англичанка (f)   British (Englishwoman)
Англия   England
антисептик   antiseptic
антракт   intermission
апельсин (n)   orange
апельсиновый (adj)   orange
апрель (m)   April
аптека   pharmacy, drugstore
арбуз   watermelon
аспирин   aspirin
ассорти (n)   assortment
ателье мод   tailor
атлас   satin
Африка   Africa
ацетон   nail polish remover
аэропорт   airport

Б

багаж   baggage
багажная бирка   baggage claim check
багажник   trunk (of a car)
баклажан   eggplant
балет   ballet
балкон   balcony
балык   filet of sturgeon
бампер   bumper
банан   banana
бандероль (f)   printed matter
банк   bank
банка   can, jar
банкомат   ATM (automatic teller machine)
баня   bathhouse
бар   bar
баранина   lamb
бархат   velvet
бассейн   swimming pool
батерейка, батерея   battery
батон   loaf

башня tower
беговые лыжи cross-country skis
бедро hip
без without
безопасность (f) security
безрецептный nonprescription
белокурый blond
белый white
бельэтаж mezzanine
бензин gasoline
бензобак gas tank
бензоколонка service station
бензонасос fuel pump
бессоница insomnia
беф-строганов beef Stroganoff
библиотека library
бизнес business
бизнесмен businessman
билет ticket
бинокль (m) opera glasses
бинт bandage
бирка claim check
бирюза turquoise
бифштекс steak
бланк blank form
ближайший nearest
близко near
блинная pancake house
блокнот writing pad
блузка blouse
блюдо dish, food
бог god
Боже мой! My goodness!
бок side
более more
болезнь (f) sickness
болеть (i) ache; **болит** it hurts
болт bolt (fastener)
боль (f) pain, ache
больница hospital
больно painful, it hurts
больше more, larger
большой large
Большой театр Bolshoi Theater
борода beard

борщ beet soup
ботинки men's shoes
браслет bracelet
брат brother
брелок charm
бриллиант diamond
бритва razor
бритьё a shave
бровь (f) eyebrow
бронирование reservation
бронхит chest cold
брошь (f) brooch
брюки pants
брюнетка brunette
бубны diamonds (cards)
будильник alarm clock
будущий future; **в будущем году** next year
булавка pin
булочка roll
булочная bakery
бульон bouillon
бумага (n) paper
бумажник wallet
бумажный (adj) paper
бусы beads
бутерброд sandwich
бутылка bottle
буфет buffet, snack bar
бы would
бывать (i) to be
быстрый fast
быть (i) to be, will be; **я буду** I will be; **ты будешь** you will be; **он/она будет** he/she will be; **мы будем** we will be; **вы будете** you will be; **они будут** they will be
бюро bureau
бюро обслуживания service bureau
бюстгальтер bra

В

в in, into, to
вагон train car

валет jack (cards)
валюта foreign currency
варёный boiled
варенье jelly
варьете show
вата cotton
ваучер voucher
ваш, ваша, ваше, ваши your
вверх up
веер fan
век century
великий great (too big)
вельвет velveteen
веник bunch of twigs
вентилятор auto fan
вернуть(ся) (p) return
весна spring; **весной** in the spring
ветер wind
ветровое стекло windshield
ветчина ham
вечер evening; **вечером** in the evening
вешалка hanger
вещь (f) thing
взбитый whipped
взглянуть (p) look at
вздут swollen
взять (p) take, get
видео-магнитофон VCR
виза visa
вилка fork
вино wine
виноград grape(s)
виноградный (adj) grape
винтик screw
вискоза rayon
височка sideburn
витамин vitamin
вишня cherry
вклад deposit
вместе together
вне outside
вниз down
внутри inside
во время during
вовремя on time

вода water
водитель (m) driver
водительские права driver's license
водка vodka
возвращать(ся) (i) return
возраст age
войлок felt
война war
вокзал (railroad) station
вокруг around
волк wolf
волна wave
волос hair
восемнадцать eighteen
восемь eight
восемьдесят eighty
восемьсот eight hundred
воскресенье Sunday
восток east
востребование demand; **до востребования** general delivery
восьмой eighth
вот here is
врач doctor
временный temporary
время (n) time
сколько времени how long, how much time
все everyone
всё everything
вспышка flash
вставать (i) stand up
вставить (p) paste, put in
вставной зуб false tooth
встреча meeting
встречный oncoming
вторник Tuesday
второй second
вход entrance
входить (i) enter; **входить в стоимость** included in the price
восдной билет entrance ticket, cover charge
вчера yesterday
въезд entry

вы you (plural and polite singular)
вывыхнут dislocated
выдать вклад make a deposit
вызвать (p) call for, summon
выиграть (p) win
выйти (p) exit, get out
выключатель (m) switch
вылетать (i) fly away
выписать (p) write out
выпить (p) drink
вырезать cut
высокий high, tall
выставка exhibition
выхлопная трубка exhaust pipe
выход exit
выходить (i) exit, get out
выходной день day off

Г

габардин gabardine
гаечный ключ wrench
газ butane gas
газета newspaper
газетный киоск newsstand
гайка nut
галерея gallery
галлон gallon
галстук tie
гардероб coatroom
гастроном supermarket
где where
гектар hectare
гигиенические салфетки sanitary napkins
главный main
гладить (i) press
глаз eye
гланц gloss
глажка ironing
глубоко deeply
глухая (f) deaf
глухой (m) deaf
говорить (i) speak
год year
годовщина anniversary

гол goal
голландский Dutch
голова head
головка stem of a watch
головной head; **головная боль** headache
голоден (m), голодна (f) hungry
голубой light blue
голубцы stuffed cabbage
горло throat
гора mountain
горные лыжи downhill skis
город city
горошек polka dot
горчица mustard
горчичник mustard plaster
горячий hot
господин Mister
госпожа Miss, Mrs.
ГОСТ ASA (film speed)
гостеприимство hospitality
гостиница hotel
гость (m) guest
государственный state
готово ready
градус degree (of temperature)
гражданин (m), гражданка (f) citizen
грамм gram
гранат pomegranate
грейпфрут grapefruit
гриб mushroom
гриль (m) grill
громко loudly
громче louder
грудь (f) breast
груша pear
губа lip
губка sponge
губная помада lipstick
гудок horn
гусь (m) goose

Д

да yes
далее farther

далеко far
дама queen (cards)
дать (p) give
дача dacha (country house)
два (m), две (f) two
двадцать twenty
двенадцать twelve
дверь (f) door
двести two hundred
движение traffic
двое twosome
дворец palace
Дворец съездов Palace of
  Congresses
двушка two-kopeck coin
девушка young girl, miss (to
  waitress)
девяносто ninety
девятнадцать nineteen
девятый ninth
девять nine
девятьсот nine hundred
дежурная "key lady"
дезодорант deodorant
действующий active
декабрь (m) December
декларация customs
  declaration
декларировать (i) declare
дело matter, business
денежный fiscal, money;
  денежный перевод money
  order
день (m) day; днём in the
  afternoon
деньги money
деревня countryside
деревья trees
десна gum
десятый tenth
десять ten
детектив mystery (film,
  novel)
дети children
детский children's
дешёвый cheap, inexpensive
джинсы jeans
диета diet

дипломат diplomat
директор director
дирижёр musical conductor
диск disc, disk
дискотека discotheque
длина length
длинный long
длиться (i) last
для for
до before, until
добрый good; доброе утро
  good morning; добрый вечер
  good evening; добрый день
  good afternoon
дождь (m) rain; идёт дождь
  it's raining
долго a long time
должен (m), должна (f) I
  must, I owe
долина valley
доллар dollar
дом home; дома at home;
  домой (to) home
домкрат auto jack
доплатно collect (telegram)
дорога road, path, way
дорогой dear, expensive
дорожка path
дорожный чек traveler's
  check
доска board
доставка delivery; письмо с
  доставкой special delivery
  letter
достижение achievement
достопримечательность (f)
  attraction
дочка daughter
дочь (f) daughter
друг friend
дуть (i) blow
думать (i) think
дурак fool
духи perfume
душ shower
дыня melon
дышать (i) breathe
дюйм inch

Е–Ё

Европа Europe
единый билет single ticket
ёлочка herringbone
ерунда nonsense
если if
есть (i) there is
ехать (i) go (by vehicle)
ещё another, more

Ж

жаль it's a pity; **как жаль** what a shame
жар fever
жареный fried
жаркий hot (temperature)
жать (i) pinch; **они жмут** they pinch
ждать (i) wait
жевать (i) chew
желать (i) wish
железнодорожный переезд railroad crossing
жёлтый yellow
желудок stomach
желудочное расстройство upset stomach
жемчуг pearl
жена wife
женат married (of a man)
женский ladies', women's
женский салон beauty parlor
женщина woman
жёсткий диск hard disk
жетон token
живот abdomen
жульен julienne
журнал magazine

З

за behind
заболеть (p) fall ill
забронировать (p) reserve
заведующий manager

завернуть (p) wrap
завивка a permanent
заводить (i) wind (a watch)
заводиться (i) turn over (car)
завтра tomorrow
завтрак breakfast
загар sunburn
задержать (p) stop, restrain
задний rear, tail
заехать (p) pick up, drive by
зажигалка lighter
зажигание ignition
заказано reserved
заказать (p) order
заказное письмо registered letter
заказывать (i) order
заколка bobby pin
закрывать(ся) (i) close
закрыто closed
закрыть(ся) (p) close
закурить (p) smoke
закуска appetizer
закусочная snack bar
зал hall
залог security deposit
заменить (p) replace
замечательно wonderful
замужем married (of a woman)
замша suede
занято occupied
запад west
запасный emergency, spare
запасный выход emergency exit
записать(ся) (p) write down, register
запор constipation
запрещено prohibited
запчасть (f) spare part
запястье wrist
заранее in advance
зарядить (p) charge (the car battery)
затраты expenses
заушник eyeglass arm
зачёсывать (i) comb

звать (i)   call; меня зовут
   my name is; как вас зовут?
   what is your name?
здание   building
здесь   here
здоровье   health; На здоровье!
   Cheers! (to your health).
Здравствуйте!   Hello!
зелёный   green
зеркало   mirror
зернистая икра   black caviar
зима   winter; зимой   in the
   winter
знать (i)   know
значить (i)   mean
значок   lapel pin
золото   gold
золотой   gold(en)
зонт   umbrella
зоопарк   zoo
зуб   tooth
зубной   dental
зубная боль   toothache
зубной врач   dentist
зубной протез   denture
зубной эликсир   mouthwash

И

и   and
иголка   needle
играть (i)   play
игрушка   toy
идти (i)   go (by foot); идите!
   go!
из   from
извинить (p)   excuse;
   извините!   excuse me!
издание   edition
изделия   goods
изумруд   emerald
изюм   raisin
икра   caviar; зернистая икра
   black caviar; кетовая икра
   red caviar
или   or
имущество   property
имя (n)   first name

инвалид   handicapped
инвалидное кресло
   wheelchair
индейка   turkey
индостранный   foreign
инспекция   inspection
институт   institute
инструмент   instrument
интернет   internet
Интурист   Intourist
инфекция   infection
информация   information
искусство   art
история   history
июль (m)   July
июнь (m)   June

Й

йод   iodine

К

к   toward
кабина   cabin
каблук   heel
кадр   exposure (film)
каждый   each, every
казаться (i)   seem
казино   casino
как   how
какой   which
камень (f)   stone
камера хранения   checkroom
Канада   Canada
канадец (m)   Canadian
канадка (f)   Canadian
канадский   Canadian
канцелярский   office,
   stationery
капля   drop; ушные капли
   ear drops; глазные капли
   eye drops
капот   hood
капуста   cabbage
карандаш   pencil
карат   carat

карбюратор   carburetor
карманный   pocket
карп   carp
карта   card, map
карта гостя   guest card
картина   picture
картофель (m)   potatoes
касса   cashier
кассета   cassette
кататься (i)   ride; кататься
   на коньках   go ice skating;
   кататься на лыжах   go
   skiing; кататься на санках
   go sledding
католический   Catholic
кафе   cafe
качество   quality
каша   warm cereal
кашель (m)   cough
каштан   chestnut
каштановый   auburn
каюта   cabin
кварта   quart
кварцовый   quartz
квас   kvass
крашенная капуста
   sauerkraut
квитанция   receipt
кекс   cupcake, muffin
керамика   ceramics
кефир   yogurt-like beverage
кило, килограмм   kilo(gram)
километр   kilometer
киоск   kiosk; газетный киоск
   newspaper stand
кипяток   boiling water
кисть (f)   hand
клавиатура   keyboard
кладбище   cemetery
класс   class
классический   classical
класть (i)   put down; не
   кладите трубку!   don't
   hang up!
клей   glue
клетка   plaid
клеющая лента   Scotch tape
клубника   strawberries

ключ   key
книга   book
книжный магазин   bookstore
кнопка   thumbtack
когда   when
код города   area code
кожа   skin, leather
колбаса   salami
колготки   pantyhose
колено   knee
колесо   wheel, tire
коллега (m & f)   colleague
коллекционный   collector's
колода   deck of cards
кольцо   ring, circle
комбинация   ladies' slip
комедия   comedy
комиссионый магазин
   antique store
комитет   committee
компактный диск   CD
   (compact disc)
компостер   ticket punch
компот   stewed fruit
компьютер (n)   computer
компьютерный (adj)
   computer
конверт   envelope
кондитерская   pastry shop
конец   end
конечно   of course
конкуренция   competition
конституция   constitution
контактная линза   contact
   lens
контракт   contract
контроль (m)   control
конфета   candy
концерт   concert
кончать(ся) (i)   end
коньки   ice skates
коньяк   cognac
копейка   kopeck
коридор   corridor, lane
коричневый   brown
кормить (i)   feed, serve food
коробка   box
королева   queen

король (m) king
коронка dental crown
короткий short
корреспондент correspondent
космонавт cosmonaut
космос cosmos, space
костёл Catholic church
костыли crutches
кость (f) bone
костюм suit
котлета cutlet
который who, what, which
кофе (m) coffee
краб crab
красивый beautiful
Красная площадь Red
  Square
красный red
кредитная карточка credit
  card
крем cream, lotion
Кремль (m) Kremlin
кремни flints
крепкий strong
крепления bindings
кровотечение bleeding
кровь (f) blood
кролик rabbit
кроме except
кружева lace
кружиться (i) spin; **голова
  кружится** I'm dizzy
крупа cold cereal
крупный large
кто who
кто-нибудь anyone
куда where to, which way
кудри curls
купальник bathing suit
купаться (i) swim
купе compartment
купить (p) buy
купюра bill (paper currency)
курить (i) smoke; **не курить**
  no smoking
курица chicken
курс course (currency
  exchange rate)

курящий smoking, smoker;
  для курящих smoking
  section
кусачки nail clippers
кусок piece, bar (of soap, etc.)
кухня cuisine

Л

ладья rook (chess)
лак для волос hair spray
лампа lamp
лампочка bulb
лапша noodles
ластик eraser
левый left
лёгкий easy, light
лёковой автомобиль
  passenger car
лежать (i) lie (in bed)
лезвие razor blade
лекарство medicine;
  рецептное лекарство
  prescription medicine;
  безрецептное лекарство
  nonprescription medicine
Ленин Lenin
Ленинград Leningrad
лента tape, film
лес forest
лето summer; **летом** in the
  summer
лечь (p) lie down; **лечь в
  больницу** go to the hospital
ли if, whether
ликёр liqueur
лимон lemon
лимонад soft drink
линейка ruler; **бумага в
  линейку** lined paper
линза lens
линия line
лиса fox
литр liter
лифт elevator
лихорадка fever; **сенная
  лихорадка** hay fever
лицо face

личный   personal
лишний   extra
лодка   boat
лодышка   ankle
ложа   box, loge
ложиться (i)   lie down
ложка   spoon
локоть (m)   elbow
лосьон   face lotion
лук   onion
лучше   better
лучший   best
лыжи   skis
любить (i)   like, love
люкс   deluxe

M

мавзолей   mausoleum
магазин   store, shop
магнезия   magnesia
магнитофон   cassette recorder
мазь (f)   ointment
май   May
майка   undershirt
майонез   mayonnaise
максимальный   maximum
мал, мала, малы   too small
малахит   malachite
маленький   little, small
малина   raspberries
мало   a little
мандарин   tangerine
маникюр   manicure
маникюрные ножницы
   cuticle scissors
марка   stamp, brand
марлевый   gauze; марлевая
   салфетка   gauze (sanitary)
   napkin
март   March
масло   butter, oil
массаж   massage
мат!   checkmate!
матовый   matte
матрац   mattress
матрёшка   nested doll
мать (f)   mother

махорка   chewing tobacco
махровая ткань   terrycloth
машина   car
медленный   slow
медовуха   mead
медсестра   nurse
между   between
междугородный   intercity;
   междугородный разговор
   long-distance call
международный   international
мелький   small
менее   less
ментол   menthol
меньше   less, smaller
меню (n)   menu
место   seat, place; мест нет
   no vacancies
месяц   month
метр   meter
метрдотель (m)   maitre d'hotel
метро   subway (metro)
мех (n)   fur
меховой (adj)   fur
мечеть (f)   mosque
микроавтобус   van
микстура   mixture; микстура
   от кашля   cough syrup
милиционер   cop
милиция   police
миллиард   billion
миллиметр   millimeter
миллион   million
миндаль (m)   almonds
минеральная вода   mineral
   water
минимальный   minimal
минута   minute; минуточку!
   just a minute!
младший   younger, junior
много   many, much
модем   modem
модный   stylish, fashionable
может быть   maybe, perhaps
можно   may (one)
мой, моя, моё, мои   mine
молодец!   you're super!
молодой   young

молодой человек! young man!
waiter!
молоко milk
молоток hammer
молчать (i) shut up (silent)
монастырь (m) monastery
Монетный двор Russia's Mint
монитор monitor
море sea
морковь (f) carrot
мороженое ice cream
морская болезнь seasickness
Москва Moscow
мост bridge
мочалка sponge
мочь (i) can, be able to;
я могу I can; ты можешь
you can; он/она может
he/she can; мы можем we
can; вы можете you can;
они могут they can
муж husband
мужской male, men's
мужчина man
музей museum
музыка music
музыкальный musical
мундштук cigarette holder
мы we
мыло soap
мытьё (n) wash (shampoo)
мышь mouse
мэйк-ап make-up
мягкий soft
мясо (m) meat
мяч ball

Н

на on, onto, to
набирать (i) dial
набор set, collection
набраться (p) accumulate
над on top of
надо must (one)
надувной inflatable, pneumatic
назад ago, backwards
название title

найти (p) find
накидка wraparound
налево to the left
наличные (деньги) cash
налог tax
напечатать print
написать (p) write
напиток beverage
направление direction
направо to the right
напротив opposite
народный folk (adj), people's
наручные часы wristwatch
нарушение violation
нарыв abscess
насморк cold (in the head)
насос pump
настольный компьютер
desktop computer
наука science
научно-популярный science
fiction
начало beginning, starting time
нанинать(ся) (i) begin
наш, наша, наше, наши our
не no
неделя week
нейлон nylon
некурящий non-smoking; для
некурящих non-smoking
section
немая азбука sign language
немного a little
немнущаяся ткань wash and
wear
нержавейка stainless steel
несколько few
нет no
нефрит jade
нечего nothing
нижний lower; нижняя юбка
half slip
никто no one
ничего nothing, never mind
но but
новый new
нога leg
ноготь (m) fingernail, toenail

нож knife

ножницы scissors

номер number, hotel room; **на номер** station-to-station call

норка mink

нормальный normal

нос nose

носильщик porter

носок sock

носовой платок handkerchief

ноутбук laptop computer

ночной клуб nightclub

ночь (f) night

ноябрь (m) November

нравиться like, be pleasing to

ну! well!

нужен, нужна, нужно, нужны necessary, I need

нуль (m) zero

O

о/об about

обвариться (p) burn oneself

обгон passing

обед lunch

обжаренный grilled

обмен балюты currency exchange

обменный курс exchange rate

обменять (i) exchange

оборот curve, turn

обратный return

обручальное кольцо engagement/wedding ring

обслуживаться (i) be waited on

обслуживание service

обувь (f) shoes

обхват circumference

объезд detour

объявляться (i) announce

обязательство obligation

овощи vegetables

овсянный oatmeal

овчина sheepskin

огонь (m) fire

ограничение restriction

огурец cucumber

одеваться (i) dress (oneself)

одежда clothing

одеколон cologne

одеяло blanket

один (m), одна (f) one

одиннадцать eleven

однотонный solid color

одолжить (p) lend

ожерелье necklace

ожог a burn

озеро lake

озноб chills

ой! ouch!

окно window

около near

октябрь (m) October

он he

она she

они they

оникс onyx

оно it

опаздывать (i) be late

опасность (f) caution

опасный dangerous

опера opera

оперетта operetta

оплата payment

оправа frame for eyeglasses

оптика optician

опухоль (f) swelling

орех nut

освобождённый exempt, free from

осень (f) fall; **осенью** in the fall

осетрина sturgeon

особый special

оставить (p) leave (something)

остановиться (p) stop (halt)

остановка (bus, trolley) stop

осторожно carefully

от from

отбивная котлета chop/cutlet

отвезти (p) take (by vehicle)

отвёртка screwdriver

отдел section

отдельно separately
отец father
открывать(ся) (i) open
открытка postcard
открыто open
открыть(ся) (p) open
откуда from where
отойти (p) go away
отплывать (i) sail away
отправка shipment
отправлять(ся) (i) leave,
  depart, send
отставать (i) lag behind; **они
  отстают** my watch is slow
отчество patronymic
офицер knight (chess)
официант waiter
официантка waitress
оценивать (i) appraise
очень very
очередь (f) turn in a line
очки eyeglasses
ошибиться (p) err

П

пакет box, packet
палец finger
палка cane, pole
пальто coat
памятник monument
память (f) memory; **на
  память** in remembrance
папка folder
пара pair
парикмахерская barber shop
парильня steam room
парк park
партер orchestra (in the
  theater)
партия (political) party
партнёр partner
парфюмерия toiletry shop
паспорт passport
пассажир passenger
паста paste
пастор minister (pastor)
пачка pack, package

пелёнка diaper
пельмени pelmeni, Siberian
  dumplings
пельменная pelmeni cafe
пеницилин penicillin
пепельница ashtray
первоначальный initial
первый first
перевод translation, transfer
переводчик interpreter
перевозка transportation
перегреваться (i) overheat
перед before, in front of
передать (p) transfer
переезд (vehicular) crossing
перезвонить (p) call back
переключение скоростей
  transmission;
  **автоматическое
  переключение скоростей**
  automatic transmission
перелом broken bone
переносный компьютер
  portable computer
перерыв break (recess)
пересесть (p) transfer
перетасовать (p) shuffle
переход transfer, (pedestrian)
  crossing
перец pepper
персик peach
персональный компьютер
  personal computer
перчатка glove
Петербург Petersburg
петь (i) sing
печёный baked
печень (f) liver
печенье cookie
пешеходный pedestrian
пешка pawn (chess)
пиво beer
пиджак jacket
пижама pajamas
пики spades (cards)
пилка nail file
пирог pie
пирожное pastry

писатель (m) writer
письмо letter
питательный nourishing, moisturizing
пить (i) drink; мне хочется пить I'm thirsty
пишущая машинка typewriter
плавать (i) swim
плавки bathing trunks
плакат poster
план map
планы plans
пластинка musical record
пластырь (m) adhesive tape
плата charge, fee, payment
платёж payment
платина platinum
платить (i) pay
платок kerchief; носовой платок handkerchief
платформа platform
платье dress
плащ raincoat
плёнка photographic film, tape
плечо shoulder
плиссированная ткань permanent press
пломба dental filling
плоскогубцы pliers
плохой bad, poor
площадь (f) square
пляж beach
по according to
победа victory
поближе nearer
поблизости nearby
побольше more
побриться (p) have a shave
повернуть (p) turn
поворот curve, turn
повторить (p) repeat
повторять (i) repeat
поговорить (p) speak (with)
погода weather
под under
подарок gift
подвернуть (p) tighten

подешевле less expensive
подключиться (p) connect
подлиннее longer
подмётка sole of a shoe
подобный similar; и тому подобное and so forth
подождать (p) wait
подойти (p) approach
подороже more expensive
подравнять (p) even out
подстричь (p) trim
подтвердить (p) confirm
подушка pillow
поезд train
поехать (p) go (by vehicle); поедем! let's go!
пожалуйста please, you're welcome
пожар fire
Пожарная охрана Fire Department
поживать (i): как вы поживаете? how are you?
пожилой elderly
позавчера day before yesterday
позвать (p) call, summon
позвонить (p) call on the telephone
поздно late
позже later
познакомиться (p) get acquainted
позолоченый gold-plated
пойти (p) go (by foot)
пока! until later!
показать (p) show
покашлять (p) cough
покой peace (of mind)
покороче shorter
покупка purchase
пол floor
полдень (m) noon
поле field
полёт flight
поликлиника clinic
полиэфир polyester
полночь (f) midnight

половина half
положить (p) put, place
полоска stripe
полотенце towel
полотно linen
полусухое semi-dry
получить (p) receve, pick up
помада: губная помада
  lipstick
помидор tomato
помочь (p) help; **помогите!**
  help!
помощь (f) help; **скорая**
  помощь first aid,
  ambulance
помыть (p) wash
понедельник Monday
понести (p) carry
понимать (i) understand
понос diarrhea
попасть (p) get to; **вы не**
  туда попали you've
  reached a wrong number
поплин poplin
поправка touch-up
попробовать (p) sample
популярный popular
порез a cut
порезаться (p) cut oneself
портфель (m) briefcase
порядок order; **всё в порядке**
  everything is in order
посадка boarding, landing of
  an airplane
посадочный билет boarding
  pass
посветлее lighter
посидеть (p) sit
послать (p) send
после after
послезавтра day after
  tomorrow
посмотреть (p) look
посольство embassy
поставить (p) put in
поставка delivery
постричься (p) have a haircut
посчитать (p) count, add up

посылка package
потемнее darker
потерять (p) lose
почему why
починить (p) repair
почистить (p) clean
почта post office; **Главный**
  Почтамт General Post
  Office
почтовый postal
почтовый ящик mailbox
пошлина (customs) duty
пояс belt
правый right (direction)
правильный right, correct
православный Orthodox
праздник holiday
практически practically
прачечная laundry
прачечная самообслуживания
  laundromat
предпочитать (i) prefer
предприятие enterprise
представить(ся) (p) introduce
  (oneself)
преимущество advantage,
  right of way
прекрасный splendid
преподаватель (m) teacher
прибывать (i) arrive
прибыль (f) profit
привет! regards!
пригласить (p) invite
приёмная reception room,
  waiting room
прийти (p) arrive, come
примерить (p) try on
примерочная кабина
  changing room
принести (p) bring
принимать (i) accept, take
  (medicine)
приносить (i) bring
принтер printer
принято accepted, acceptable
принять вклад make a
  withdrawal
приплывать (i) land

приправа seasoning
прислоняться (i) lean on
пристань (f) dock
приступ attack; **сердечный приступ** heart attack
приходный ордер deposit slip
причёска hairdo
пришить (p) sew on
приятно pleasing
пробить (p) punch a ticket
проблема problem, something wrong
пробор part (in the hair)
провайдер provider
проверить (p) check
проводить (i) take, escort
программка program
продавать (i) sell
продажа sale
проезд ride, trip
проездной билет trip ticket
проехать (p) get to
проиграть (p) lose a game
проигрыватель (m) record player
прокат rental; **на прокат** for rent
пропуск key card (pass)
просветить (p) X-ray
простить pardon; **простите!** pardon me!
простыня linen towel, sheet
протез (зубной) denture
протекать (i) leak
протестантский Protestant
профессия profession
прохладный cool
проход aisle
проходить (i) pass by
процесс process
прошлый past, previous; **в прошлом году** last year
прощайте! farewell!
проявлять (i) develop film
пруд pond
прямо straight ahead
прямой straight
птица bird

пуговица button
пудра powder
пункт point
пускать (i) let in
пусть let, allow
путеводитель (m) guidebook
путешествие trip
путь (m) way, path
пучок bun (hairdo)
пятнадцать fifteen
пятница Friday
пятно spot
пятый fifth
пять five
пятьдесят fifty
пятьсот five hundred

Р

работать (i) work
рабочий worker, working
рабочий стол desktop
раввин rabbi
рагу ragout
радиатор car radiator
радио radio
раз one time, once
разбить(ся) (p) break, shatter
разбудить (p) wake
разворот U-turn
разговор conversation, telephone call
разговорник phrasebook
раздеться (p) undress (oneself)
размен change (money)
разменять (i) change
размер size
разрешить (p) allow
разъединить (p) disconnect
рана wound
рано early
раскладушка cot
расписаться (p) sign
расписание schedule
рассказ short story
рассольник kidney soup

расстройство disorder;
   желудочное расстройство
   upset stomach
растение plant
растительное масло vegetable
   oil
растянут twisted
расходный ордер withdrawal
   slip
расходы expenses
расчёска comb
расчётный час check-out time
ребро rib
революция revolution
регистрация registration,
   check-in
редиска radish
резинка rubber band
резьба carved object
рейс flight
река river
рекомендовать (i) recommend
ремень (m) belt
ремень вентилятора (m) fan
   belt
ремонт repairs
репька turnip
ресница eyelash
республика republic
ресторан restaurant
рецепт prescription
рецептный отдел prescription
   section (pharmacy)
решётка fender
ржаной rye
рис rice
рисование drawing
рождение birth; **с днём
   рождения!** happy birthday!
розетка plug
розничная цена retail price
розовый rose, pink
роман novel
Российская Федерация
   Russian Federation
российский Russian
Россия Russia
россиянин (m) Russian citizen

россиянка (f) Russian citizen
рост height
ростбиф roast beef
рот mouth
рубашка shirt
рубин ruby
рубль (m) ruble
рубчатый вельвет corduroy
рука arm
рукав sleeve
рукавица mitten
рулевое колесо steering
   wheel
руль (m) steering wheel
рулон roll (of something)
румяна rouge
русский (m) Russian, Russian
   man
русская (f) Russian woman
ручей brook
ручка pen, door handle
ручной hand
ручной тормоз hand brake
ручные часы wristwatch
рыба (n) fish
рыбный (adj) fish
рынок market
рыночная цена market value
   (price)
рычаг lever; **рычаг
   переключения** gear shift
рюмка vodka glass
ряд row

C

с from, with
сад garden
салат salad, lettuce
салон section on an airplane
салфетка napkin, tissue
сам self
самолёт aircraft
самообслуживание self-service
самый the very (best, least)
Санкт Петербург St.
   Petersburg
сантиметр centimeter

санки   sled
сапог   boot
сапфир   sapphire
сатин   sateen
сауна   sauna
сахар   sugar
сахарин   saccharin
сбить (p)   knock over
сборник   collection
свежий   fresh
свёкла   beets
сверху   from the top
светить (i)   shine
светлый   light
свеча   suppository, spark plug
свидание   appointment; **до свидания**   good-bye
свиной   pork
свитер   sweater
свободный   free
священник   priest
сдавать (i)   deal the cards, give over
сделать (p)   do, make
себе, себя   oneself
север   north
сегодня   today
седьмой   seventh
сейчас   now
секунда   second (sixtieth part of a minute)
секундная стрелка   second hand
селёдка   herring
село   village
сёмга   salmon
семнадцать   seventeen
семь   seven
семьдесят   seventy
семьсот   seven hundred
семья   family
сенная лихорадка   hay fever
сентябрь (m)   September
сердце   heart
серебро (n)   silver
серебряный (adj)   silver
середина   center
серый   gray

серьга   earring
серьёзно   seriously
сестра   sister
сзади   in the back
сигарета   cigarette
сигар   cigar
сигнальный огонь   directional signal
сидеть (i)   sit
синагога   synagogue
синий   dark blue
система   system
системный блок   CPU
сказать (p)   say
сканер   scanner
скольский   slippery
сколько   how much, how many
скопировать   copy
скорая помощь   first aid, ambulance
скоро   soon
скорость (f)   speed, gear
скотч   Scotch tape
скрепка   paper clip
слабительное   laxative
слабость (f)   weakness
слабый   weak, mild
сладкий   sweet
сладкое   dessert
слайд   slide
слева   on the left
следующий   next
слепая (f)   blind
слепой (m)   blind
слива   plum
сливки   cream
сливочное   creamy (vanilla)
слишком   too (excessively)
словарь (m)   dictionary
слово   word
сломать (p)   break
слон   bishop (chess)
слоновая кость   ivory
служба   service
слуховой аппарат   hearing aid
случиться (p)   happen
слушать (i)   listen
слышно   audible

смазать (p)   grease
сменить (p)   change, replace;
   сменить масло   change the
   oil
смеситель   faucet
сметана   sour cream
смородина   currants
смотреть (i)   look, see, watch
СНГ   CIS
снег   snow; идёт снег   it's
   snowing
сниженный   reduced; товары
   по сниженным ценам   sale
   items
снимите!   cut the deck!
снотворное   sleeping pills
соболь (m)   sable
собор   cathedral
советский   Soviet
современный   modern
совсем   completely, entirely
Содружество Независимых
   Государтсв   Confederation
   of Independent States
Соединённые Штаты   United
   States
сойти (p)   go out; вы с ума
   сошли?   are you crazy?
сокавыжиматель (m)   blender
солнечные очки   sunglasses
солнечный ожог   sunburn
солнце   sun
соль (f)   salt
солянка   solyanka (fish or meat
   soup)
сорок   forty
сорочка   shirt
сосиска   hot dog
сотовый телефон   cellular
   phone
соуса   sauce
сохранить   save
социалистический   socialist
союз   union
спаржа   asparagus
спасатель (m)   lifeguard
спасибо   thank you
спектакль (m)   performance

спереди   in the front
спешить (i)   hurry; они
   спешат   my watch is fast
спина   back
спирт   alcohol
список   list
спичка   match
спокойной ночи!   good night!
спорттовары   sporting goods
справа   on the right
спрашивать (i)   ask
спустить (p)   descend;
   спустила шина   the tire is
   flat
среда   Wednesday
среди   among
средний   medium
срочно   urgently
СССР   USSR
стадион   stadium
стакан   glass
станция   station
стартер   starter
старший   elder, senior
стекло   glass, eyeglass lens
стеклочиститель (m)
   windshield wiper
стелька   insole
стирать (i)   wash clothes
стирка   wash, washing
   (clothes)
стихотворение   poetry
сто   hundred
стоимость (f)   cost, price
стоить (i)   cost
стол   desk, table
столик   table
столовая   cafeteria
стоп   stop
сторона   side
стоянка   parking; стоянка
   такси   taxi stand
стоять (i)   stand; стойте!
   wait!
страна   country
страница   page
страхование   insurance
страшный   terrible

стрелка   hand of a watch
стрижка   haircut
стричь (i)   cut hair
строитель (m)   builder
стручковая фасоль   string
  beans
студент   student
ступня   foot
суббота   Saturday
сувенир   souvenir
судак   pike/perch
судорога   cramp
сумка   pocketbook
сумма   amount
суп   soup
сурок   marmot
сухой   dry
сцена   stage
сцепление   gear shift, clutch
  pedal
счастливого пути!   bon voyage!
счёт   account, score
США   USA
сын   son
сыр   cheese
сюда   here

Т

табак   tobacco
таблетка   tablet
тазик   washbasin
так   so, thus, this way
такой   such
также   also
такси (n)   taxi
талия   waist
талон   ticket, coupon
тальк   talcum powder
там   there
тампон   tampon
танцевать (i)   dance
тапочка   slipper
тарелка   plate
твой, твоя, твоё, твои   your
творог   cream cheese
театр   theater
театральный   theatrical

телевизор   television
телеграмма   telegram
тележка   (baggage) cart
телекс   telex
телефакс   fax
телефон   telephone
телефон-автомат   pay
  telephone
телефонная кабина   telephone
  booth
телефонная карта   telephone
  card
тело   body
телятина   veal
темно (adv)   darkly
тёмный (adj)   dark
температура   temperature
тень (f)   shadow
тепло   warmth
тёплый   warm
теплоход   boat
термометр   thermometer
тесны   too narrow
тетрадь (f)   notebook
тётя   aunt
тише   quieter
ткань (f)   material, fabric
то   that one
товарищ   comrade
товары   goods, items, supplies
только   only
томатный   tomato
тон   tint
топаз   topaz
торговля (n)   trade
торговый (adj)   trade
тормоз   brake
торт   cake
тостер   toaster
точилка   sharpener
тошнота   nausea
трагедия   tragedy (drama)
трамвай   tram, trolleycar
транспорт   transportation
трансформатор   transformer
треска   cod
третий   third
трефы   clubs (cards)

три three
тридцать thirty
тринадцать thirteen
триста three hundred
трогать (i) touch; **не трогать** don't touch
трое threesome
троллейбус trolleybus
тропинка path
трубка pipe, telephone receiver
трубочный табак pipe tobacco
трусики ladies' panties
трусы men's underpants
туалет bathroom, restroom
туалетная бумажка toilet paper
туда there
туз ace (cards)
тупик dead end
турист (n) tourist
туристический (adj) tourist; **туристический класс** economy class
турмалин tourmaline
туфли women's shoes
тушёный stewed
тушь (f) mascara
ты you (singular)
тыква pumpkin
тысяча thousand

У

у at, near
убран cleaned, picked up
убыток a loss
увеличить (p) enlarge
удалить (p) delete, pull (a tooth)
удлинитель (m) extension cord
удовольствие pleasure; **с удовольствием** with pleasure
у.е. conventional units
уезжать (i) depart

ужасно awful
уже already
ужин dinner
укладка set (hairdo)
украсть (p) steal
украска color rinse
уксус vinegar
улыбаться (i) smile
ум mind
уметь (i) know how
умывальник sink
универмаг (универсальный магазин) department store
университет university
унитаз toilet
упасть (p) fall
уронить (p) drop
успокаивающее sedative
устал (m), устала (f) tired
уступить (p) yield
усы mustache
утка duck
утро morning; **утром** in the morning
ухо ear
ушиб bruise
ушные капли ear drops

Ф

файл file
фамилия family name
фара headlight
фарфоровый porcelain
фасан pheasant
фасоль (f) beans
февраль (m) February
фен hair dryer
фига fig
фигура chess piece
фигурные коньки figure skates
фильм movie
фильтр filter
финик date (fruit)
фирма business firm
фирменное блюдо house specialty

фланель (f) flannel
фонарь (m) flashlight
фонд fund
форель (m) trout
фотоаппарат camera
фотографировать (i) photograph
фотография picture
фототовары photographic supplies
фрукты fruits
фу! ugh!
фунт pound
фут foot (measurement)
футбол soccer

Х

халат robe
хватить (p) be enough
хвост (pony) tail
химический chemical
химчистка dry cleaner's
хлеб bread
хлопчатобумажная ткань cotton fabric
ходить (i) go, walk
ходунки walker
хозяйство economy
хозяйственный household
хоккей hockey
хоккейные коньки hockey skates
холодильник refrigerator
холодный cold
холм hill
хороший good
хорошо! that's good/okay!
хотеть(ся) (i) want, like; **я хочу** I want; **ты хочешь** you want; **он/она хочет** he/she wants; **мы хотим** we want; **вы хотите** you want; **они хотят** they want
хрен horseradish
хромая (f) lame
хромой (m) lame
хрусталь (m) crystal

Ц

царь (m) tsar
цвет color
цветная капуста cauliflower
цветы flowers
цена price
ценный valuable
ценное письмо certified letter
центральный central
центр downtown
цепочка chain
церковь (f) church
цирк circus
цыплёнок chicken

Ч

чай tea
час hour, o'clock; **в котором часу?** at what time?
часовая стрелка hour hand
частичный partial
частник private taxi driver
часто often
часть (f) part
часы watch, clock
чей, чья, чьё, чьи whose
чек check, bill
чёлка bangs
человек person; **на человека** person-to-person call; **молодой человек!** young man! waiter!
чемодан suitcase
черви hearts (cards)
через across, through
чёрный black
чёрт devil; **чёрт возьми!** darn it!
чеснок garlic
четверг Thursday
четверо foursome

четвёртый   fourth
четверть (f)   quarter
четыре   four
четыреста   four hundred
четырнадцать   fourteen
чинить (i)   repair
число   number, date; какое
    сегодня число?   what's
    today's date?
чистка   dry cleaning
читать (i)   read
что   what
что-нибудь   something
чувствовать себя (i)   feel
чулок   stocking
чуть   almost

Ш

шампанское   champagne
шампунь (m)   shampoo
шапка   hat
шапочка   cap
шарф   scarf
шасси (n)   chassis
шах!   check! (in chess)
шахматы   chess
шашечка   check; в шашешку
    checked
шашки   checkers
шашлык   shish kebab
шашлычная   shish kebab cafe
шведский стол   smorgasbord
швейцар   bellboy
шезлонг   chaise longue
шёлк   silk
шерсть (f)   wool
шестнадцать   sixteen
шестой   sixth
шесть   six
шестьдесят   sixty
шестьсот   six hundred
шея   neck
шина   car tire
широкий   wide
шифон   chiffon
шницель (m)   schnitzel
шнур   cord

шнурок   shoelace
шоколадный   chocolate
шпагат   string
шпилька   bobby pin
шпинат   spinach
штаны   slacks
штат   state
штука   item
шуба   fur coat

Щ

щека   cheek
щёлочь (f)   antacid
щётка   brush
щи   cabbage soup
щипчики   tweezers

Ъ

ъ   the hard sign

Ы

Ь

ь   the soft sign

Э

экскурсионный (adj)
    excursion
экскурсия (n)   excursion
экскурсия по городу   city tour
экстравагантный   extravagant,
    striking
электрический   electrical
электронная почта   e-mail
электронный   electronic
электронные часы   digital
    watch
электронный билет   electronic
    ticket
электротовары   electrical
    supplies
эликсир; зубной эликсир
    mouthwash

Эрмитаж Hermitage
этаж floor
это this, that
эхо echo

Ю

юбка skirt
ювелирный jewelry
юг south
юмор humor

Я

я I
яблоко (n) apple

яблочный (adj) apple
язык tongue, language
яичница omelet; **яичница-болтунья** scrambled eggs; **яичница-глазунья** fried eggs
яйцо egg; **яйцо вкрутую** hard-boiled egg; **яйцо всмятку** soft-boiled egg
январь (m) January
янтарь (m) amber
ярд yard (measurement)
ярус (theater) circle, ring
яшма jasper
ящик box; **почтовый ящик** mailbox

INDEX

Митино
Волоколамская
Строгино
Крылатское
Молодежная
Кунцевская
Пионерская
Филевский Парк
Багратионовская
Фили
Кутузовская
Студенческая
Улица 1905 Года
Баррикадная
Краснопресненская

Планерная
Сходненская
Тушинская
Щукинская
Октябрьское Поле
Полежаевская
Беговая

Речной Вокзал
Водный Стадион
Войковская
Сокол
Аэропорт
Динамо

Алтуфьево
Бибирево
Отрадное
Владыкино
Петровско-Разумовская

Медведково
Бабушкинская
Свиблово
Ботанический Сад
ВДНХ
Алексеевская
Рижская

Улица Подбельского
Черкизовская
Преображенская Площадь
Сокольники
Красносельская

Тимирязевская
Дмитровская
Савеловская

Марьина Роща

Щелковская
Первомайская
Измайловская
Измайловский Парк
Семеновская
Электрозаводская
Бауманская

Менделеевская
Новослободская
Белорусская
Цветной Бульвар
Маяковская

Достоевская
Площадь Суворова
Сухаревская
Трубная
Тургеневская
Чистые Пруды
Кузнецкий Мост
Лубянка

Проспект Мира
Комсомольская
Красные Ворота
Сретенский Бульвар
Курская
Чкаловская

Новогиреево
Перово
Шоссе Энтузиастов
Авиамоторная

Парк Победы
Пушкинская
Чеховская
Смоленская
Арбатская
Смоленская
Александровский Сад
Боровицкая
Арбатская
Библиотека Имени Ленина

Тверская

Охотный Ряд
Театральная
Площадь Революции

Китай-город

Площадь Ильича
Римская
Марксистская
Таганская

Киевская

Третьяковская
Новокузнецкая

Парк Культуры
Кропоткинская

Октябрьская

Полянка
Добрынинская

Крестьянская Застава
Павелецкая
Автозаводская
Коломенская
Каширская

Дубровка
Пролетарскаяа
Кожуховская
Печатники
Волжская
Люблино
Братиславская
Марьино
Борисово
Шипиловская
Зябликово

Серпуховская
Тульская
Нагатинская
Нагорная
Нахимовский Проспект
Севастопольская

Шаболовская
Ленинский проспект
Академическая
Профсоюзная
Новые Черемушки
Калужская
Беляево
Коньково
Теплый Стан
Ясенево
Битцевский Парк

Фрунзенская
Спортивная
Ленинские Горы
Университет
Проспект Вернадского
Юго-Западная

Варшавская
Кантемировская
Каховская
Чертановская
Южная
Пражская
Россошанская
Анино
Качалово

Царицыно
Орехово
Домодедовская
Красногвардейская
Братеево

Волгоградский Проспект
Текстильщики
Кузьминки
Рязанский Проспект
Выхино

■ Сокольническая Линия
■ Замоскворецкая Линия
■ Арбатско-Покровская Линия
■ Филевская Линия
■ Кольцевая Линия
■ Калужско-Рижская Линия
■ Таганско-Краснопресненская Линия

■ Калининская Линия
■ Серпуховско-Тимирязевская Линия
■ Люблинская Линия
■ Каховская Линия
□ Строящиеся Линии
◉ Станции Пересадок